THE ULTIMATE POWER

How Love Will Revolutionize Our Lives and Our World

MARK KRECEK

First Edition: November 2015

ISBN-10: 1492717118
ISBN-13: 978-1492717119

DEDICATION

This book is dedicated to my family and friends. It is also dedicated to you. Let's make the revolution happen.

CONTENTS

INTRODUCTION

THE MISSION

Imagine what your life would be like if you lived in a world where people did not judge you by your failures or successes, how much money you have, or how you looked. They simply loved you for yourself. Imagine a world where you really understood and connected with your children, your parents, and your friends, and were even able to relate to people who seem completely opposite of you.

In this world, people learn to see beyond the superficial images and stereotypes that we use to define each other. This is a world where people learn to work well as a community, not just with those close to them, but with everyone. They develop deep social connections that go beyond shared experiences, interests, and similarities. As idealistic as this may sound, it is not only possible, but I believe it is the future of society, and it is closer to becoming reality than you may imagine.

Since I was young, I dreamt about what the ultimate society would be like. I was so fascinated with this vision, that I made it my mission to revolutionize society. I read books like *1984* and saw movies like *THX-1138*, which were stories that presented a nightmarish vision of the future. I pictured myself in those worlds and thought about how I would go about changing such an oppressive society. Feeling a strong sense of connection to life and having an extremely high level of empathy towards others are the underlying reasons for this mission.

With this feeling of connection, I always felt there was much more to life than just survival: that we were all a part of a shared experience. I would look up at the night sky, seeing the moon and the stars, and think about how the sun was lighting up the other side of the planet as people were having lunch. At that very moment, war was taking place somewhere. The moon I was looking at is the same moon people across the nation, as well as people in other countries, were looking at, at that very moment. It is the same moon that people thousands of years ago, and even dinosaurs over a hundred million years ago saw with wonder and curiosity.

I realized that the best and the worst experiences that I ever felt in my life are similar to what someone else is feeling at this very moment. All of our experiences, our emotions, and even our problems are interconnected. We are all in this together and it is all happening right now! It's like a world symphony! At this moment as a plane is taking off in Paris, another plane is landing in Bangalore. A car just crashed in Perth. Someone at this moment is recovering from surgery. Another person is celebrating at the bar with friends. Someone is being raped right now. A child was just hit by his or her parents who are only trying to do the right thing. At this very moment a baby is just taking her first breath of life in this world and another person just took his last.

As the sun is rising in Los Angeles, it is setting in New Delhi. As you read this right now, the sun has just dipped below the horizon line somewhere in the world, and is rising somewhere else. These two events are constant, as they have been for billions of years. When you watch the sunrise or set, there is something absolutely amazing about it, as if it is a celebration of the day to come, or knowing that you just experienced another day here on Earth.

On this day…you will be born, you will experience love…you will experience loss… hate…laughter, …and you will die. Just realize that this is your day…you will only get so many. Would you rather spend it making things more difficult for others, and in return, for yourself, or would you rather spend it doing meaningful stuff that helps make society and our world a better place? Love this day. You can change your life and the world. You are a part of a revolution, which is changing the world forever.

So how do you even go about building a better world? For me, it was learning from my experiences in life, and writing down my thoughts and observations over the years.

I thought about going into education, but realized that my focus would be on teaching and not on the mission. I thought about religion, but realized that if I were speaking from one religion, only some people would listen. I thought about going into politics but even the president, is mired in political disputes.

If the president of the United States is not effective enough, then who is? So I imagined what I would do if I were God. I realized that if I were God, I would not just tell people to love, I would teach people what it means to love…and this is something we are all capable of doing.

My attitude has been if one person had the power to convince a nation to hate and even kill millions of people, then why couldn't another person have the power to convince the world to love? If this is possible, imagine harnessing the full power of all people towards this common goal. This is Ultimate Power!

I realized that if I wanted to help society, I needed to study society. I earned a Bachelors and Masters degree in Sociology and a minor in Peace & Justice. In my undergraduate program, I noticed that a lack of connection, i.e. alienation, was a common theme in personal problems and social issues. In my Masters program, I examined alienation in the family and school environment – two major pillars of society. Not only did I find that alienation was a leading cause of problems in these environments, it was a foundation for most personal and social problems.

I enjoyed observing how people interacted in conversations and conducted numerous on camera interviews with people about their experiences in life. In these interviews, many people opened up about whom they were deep down.

I learned that much of what we think we know about a person is mostly superficial information that does not even scratch the surface. In order to survive in this world, it is important to be able to judge a situation and respond accordingly. Unfortunately, because we know so little about each other, the judgments we make are based on our limited, and often, inaccurate perception, which can have devastating consequences.

Naturally, when the various components of something, be it connectors in a pipe, parts in a computer, or neurons in the body, are not connecting or communicating properly, leaks, errors, and glitches happen. Similarly, when people are not connecting solidly with each other, problems arise.

When you go beyond these perceptions, you will see that the categories we place people in, say very little about them deep down. None of this helps us understand a person's feelings.

So much of the problem boils down to how we deal with each other. People who are socially well developed and can relate to others do better than people who have poor social skills and don't connect with others. So much of this comes down to learning social skills and learning how to connect with each other. These connections are a major part of your life.

If you were able to learn about a person deep down, even someone you may consider your enemy, you would be able to understand why they are the way they are, and your empathy would increase. When you think about it, the bond between a mother and her baby is as strong as a bond can get, yet it has nothing to do with any of the information that we learn about each other. When you look into each other's eyes, you see a soul, just like yours.

So who are you when you take away all the experiences you have in life and when you take away all the physical and chemical influences on your personality? I am essentially asking what or who is your core soul? Is it an illusion that we are different deep down? When you think about it, regardless of the minerals or pollutants in water, water is still water. Is life simply life?

The Ultimate Power is not just a "self-help" book, it is also a "society-help" book. While self-help plays an important role in building a better life, accomplishing this can be difficult if you live in an abusive environment. You would be far better off living in a world where people built you up instead of tore you down. This book will not only change how you see yourself, but it will also change how you see others, which is an important step in changing how we operate as a whole society.

Many of the studies referenced in this book have been replicated many times, and have been backed up by similar studies. A lot of this research has been published in reputable journals that have evaluated the accuracy of the research. Volumes of books have been written on some of the topics I present here. *The Ultimate Power* shows how all of this is connected.

The Ultimate Power is divided into five parts:

- Part I looks at our perceptions of reality – how we perceive our world, each other, ourselves, and how we perceive <u>and deal with</u> personal problems and public issues. Because some of these perceptions are false, how we go about trying to solve these problems can have devastating consequences.

- Part II goes beyond these false perceptions and the consequential problems that bog down our lives. Things such as success, failure, and intelligence, do not define who you are. In order to understand people, you need to understand their feelings. Our emotions are a major part of our life, affecting everything we do. These emotions are also interconnected with other people's emotions. Our emotions are greatly affected by how we perceive each other. Because we understand each other less than we think we do, we don't understand how we affect each other. Society is essentially the sum of it's social connections, so when these connections fail, society fails.

- Part III looks at ways in which people are disconnected/alienated, and how alienation is an underlying cause of many personal problems and public issues. Alienation is essentially a lack of connection and is therefore the direct opposite of society.

- Part IV will give you a better understanding of what deep social connection is and how we can learn to build better connections in marriage and in the school environment – two major pillars of society. Improving how we connect with each other should be the number one priority of society.

- In the final part of the book, you will see the tremendous impact social connections will have on your life and society overall. In understanding each other, and ourselves, we will get to that question of who we are deep down. When we connect with each other deeply, we learn empathy, and we learn to love. By learning to love, we will revolutionize our lives and our world.

What I experienced in my life was critical in developing my understanding of how we can build a better world. A major reason my research focused on alienation was because I felt alienated for much of my life. Feeling extremely isolated and distanced from others for as long as I have while having a very high level of empathy, helped me understand how others may feel when they are alienated.

I have seen too many people suffer through too much pain, to just go about my life as if nothing happened. As much as I wanted to have a "normal" life: having a real job, a family and kids, I felt that this mission was not so much a choice as it was an obligation that I needed to pursue.

So, I am doing this for Tim Morsman, who was like a younger brother from long ago. I wish I could have been there for him, and I regret that I wasn't. I am doing this for Michael Kramer, who overdosed on drugs, because he felt like he did not amount to anything. I am doing this for all the people who were victims of bullying, and all the people who felt like they never fit in. I am doing this for everyone who is experiencing the toughest time in his or her life at this very moment, knowing we will all face extremely difficult times in our lives. I am doing this for all the people who have been sacrificed in the name of war and all the people who have had loved ones who died in war.

I am doing this for all the people who have committed atrocities in the past...because they themselves were tortured souls. We can blame others and we can label people as evil, but when people commit such horrible acts, it does not mean that they are horrible people, it means that we have failed as a society.

Finally, I am doing this for you. I am doing this, not to inspire you, but to convince you. I am doing this because we have the power to change this world in a revolutionary way. This is your life and it is your chance to make a difference. So get ready, because we are about to start a revolution...

A revolution of unimaginable scope!

PART I:

PERCEPTIONS OF REALITY

We go through life accepting reality for what it appears to be. For some people, it appears that society is on the decline and that there is nothing they can do to change it. This mindset can justify selfish and reckless behavior. But for as obvious as some things appear to be, this is not always the reality. The reality is that things have been improving ever since the beginning of society.

In trying to understand how to make this world a better place, I learned more about people, but what I learned was that people were not who they appeared to be. Some people may appear to have it all, but when you peel back the layers, you realize these people can be the complete opposite of what you think. In reality, a lot of people face problems that can seem unsolvable. Part of the reason for this is due to the fact that greater social forces beyond your control can influence these problems.

In order to fix these problems we seek whom to blame. But if we do not fully understand these problems, we will not be able to solve them. We react on false perceptions, causing more harm than good.

All of this blaming leads to anger, violence, and even war, which only deepen the problem. Innocent lives are lost, and the victims seek revenge. We think we know who's responsible for these problems, but we don't. We think we know who is the enemy, but we don't. We don't even know those who are close to us.

CHAPTER 1

MY PERCEPTION OF REALITY

Years ago, I was watching *Rudolph, The Red-Nosed Reindeer* with my friend, his wife, and kids. I had seen the special many times over the years but for some reason, this time it hit me like a ton of bricks. I had to leave the room so I could breathe. I was also hiding my true emotions. I realized that I was Rudolph!

Being different from the other reindeer, Rudolph ventured out on his own, feeling that his family, his girlfriend Clarisse, and the greater society would be better off without him. All of the other reindeer that laughed and called him names were a part of this social pecking order. If they were to associate with him, they may be seen as a loser too, so they want to set themselves as far away from him as they can. Even Clarisse would have felt pressured from her friends to be with the "normal" reindeer.

What's interesting is that not one child or adult watching this show would have cheered on Rudolph's demise, not even those we consider evil. We all cheered for Rudolph. We all wanted to see Rudolph make it big. Why? It gives us hope. But sadly, this is rarely the case in real life. Many people are so concerned about where they stand socially, that they would rather reject Rudolph, or other misfits, to show that they are not misfits themself. When people do this, they lack confidence and are afraid to show who they really are – different.

Watching the show, you can see that Rudolph engages in reckless, dangerous behavior. He runs across an unstable log over a chasm, and when he gets to the other side, he either kicks the log (or maybe it fell on its own) into the chasm. Either way, it was a clear indication that he was saying good riddance to society. He ventures off into the wild with at least some knowledge that it is cold and dangerous.

Later, Rudolph leaves the island of misfit toys on his own, even though his friends warned him that he would freeze to death. Once again, thinking that he was a detriment to others with his glowing nose, Rudolph essentially sacrificed himself for the greater good.

If Rudolph's nose did not glow as bright as it did, Christmas would have been cancelled and Rudolph would have never been the hero. If Rudolph were never accepted, he would have likely remained a loner the rest of his life. Maybe he would have committed suicide. Inward, Rudolph felt defeated and was self-destructive. Over time, he may have become so hardened that he may have expressed these emotions outward by going on a shooting spree. Or if he guided the sleigh that night, maybe he would choose a revenge more subtle, such as eating a few cans of beans just before the flight.

Like Rudolph, I am different. As a child, I was described, not as someone who marched to the beat of his own drum, but as someone who marched to the beat of his own symphony.

I grew up in Omaha, Nebraska in a middle class family. There was nothing really wrong with me or my upbringing. I appeared to have a lot going for me. I wasn't suffering from extreme physical pain, nor was I really ever teased or bullied. But it did not take long for classmates or co-workers to realize that I was different. I was different enough where others could tell that I was different, but nothing specific where they could use something against me; such as the color of my skin, having a stutter, or having a glowing red nose. I was considered learning disabled, yet even after numerous tests, I was never diagnosed as having any specific learning disability. I felt inferior and worthless because it appeared to me that I was not intelligent.

The fact was that I felt severely alienated and showed few signs of it. I had hardly any friends and I wanted to die. Many people were surprised when I told them I felt alienated for much of my life. It did not even make sense to them. Some of my friends thought I was extroverted and were baffled when I told them that I had social anxiety. Most or even all of my closest friends had no clue how much pain I was really in. In many ways I felt like an extrovert trapped in an introvert's body…kind of like a dog that wanted to go out and play with the kids, but was confined in a cage. While some people held it against me for being different, I now realize it was much less than I thought.

It is difficult revealing what I felt, because people form opinions and make judgments based on the little information they have. It would be easy to think that I was simply depressed. But what I felt was based on the fact that I was missing out on social interactions that everybody else was having, and the older I got, the more I was missing out. This was very painful, because I am a person who does not like to miss out on anything.

If you went through what I went through, and your mind was designed like my mind, you would have felt the same way. If you were to see my life in full, you would be able to see where I started falling through the cracks.

Ponies and Black Cats

When I entered the first grade, I was excited, but a little nervous going to the big kids' school. I had a fun time and made friends. If I had nothing for show and tell, I would tell the class about a dream I had the night before. But it did not take long for me to realize that there was something wrong with me.

Compared to the other kids, not only was I different, I also did not perform as well as they did. I was in the slowest reading group with only a small handful other students. Our group was called the 'Ponies', which as I saw it, were the slow little babies who where just coming into the world. I felt so embarrassed when the teacher called my group back to the reading center. The middle reading group was called the 'Stars', which had an obvious positive connotation to it.

The cool kids' reading group was the 'Black Cats', which was also the top reading group. They didn't need to be told they were 'stars' because they were smarter than everyone else and they knew it. I thought they were cool, not just because they had a cool name, but also because Jenny, a girl I liked, was in that group.

Struggling academically, physically, or socially, is not necessarily alienating in and of itself. It is the feeling of being negatively judged by others. In order to fit in, many students learn to hide their weaknesses from others so they won't be rejected. It can feel very alienating when a student appears to be less than his or her peers.

On a daily basis, for almost my entire grade school education, it was pretty obvious that I was less than other students. It was not just about being in the lowest reading group. It was having to read out loud where everybody in class could tell that you were struggling. It was being the last student to finish a test. It was saying the wrong answer in class, or giving a different answer, where everyone else looked at you strangely. It was being the last to be picked for a team. It was about leaving the classroom to go off to a "special" room to get extra help. The other students knew why you left the classroom. Working as a substitute teacher, I noticed that when a student would leave the regular classroom to get extra help, the other kids would tell me that the student who left was slow.

What was embarrassing was that even though I tried my best, I was still a failure. Sometimes teachers would track students' progress on a chart on the wall. The really smart kids would usually have a long line of gold stars or checks by their name showing that they read the most books, completed the most math packets or whatever. Since I 'knew' that I was slower than the other kids, I would pretend that I just did not care. I would much rather have my peers think of me as a rebel who did not care about the rules, than appear as a slow, stupid dimwit. If nobody else saw my score, I would have worked much faster. I've seen this attitude countless times when substitute teaching. As a teacher, the reality appears to be that these students don't care because they don't try. I suspect that many of these cases are students who are just playing a role to hide their real feelings.

When I first learned about the concept of flunking and how a student could be made to repeat a grade, I thought about how it would feel to go back to the same teacher you had the prior year, while all your peers advanced to the next grade level. The idea of this scared me so much, that I was sure that I would have made some sort of attempt at suicide.

One thing I started realizing about myself was that there were times where I would feel completely paralyzed. This became apparent one day after school when I was walking with a friend to his house. My friend told me that Jenny lived right down the street we were walking by. Like a puppy who does not seem to notice the tugging of the leash, despite my friend's protest, I made my way down to her house. My friend waited in the neighbor's yard as I went and knocked on her door. Her older brother answered and I asked him if Jenny was home. When he called out her name and she came to the door, my heart started pounding. Not having a clue what to say, I told her I was going to wear a different shirt the next day. Realizing how strange this sounded, I followed it by telling her that I was going to everybody's house to tell them the same thing. After I left, I could not figure out why my mind turned to jelly like that.

In second grade, the problem was becoming more apparent. One day when we were all getting on the bus to go home, the bus driver being upset with our constant talking, decided to make us sit boy-girl-boy-girl and everybody complained. The bus driver had all the boys sit down, then he made the girls sit down. He sat the girl whom I had a crush on, Cindy, next to me. For a brief moment, this turned into the best day ever. Unfortunately, that brief moment was followed by me pulling down my winter hat over my face and sitting as close to the window as I possibly could. For the entire trip, I did not move a muscle. As we made our way across town, I tried to relax so I could say something to her. Then when we got to our neighborhood, one-by-one, the students were getting off at their designated stops. I had to make my move. But then her stop came, and she got off the bus. I was never so disappointed and frustrated with myself in all my life. When I got home, I kept saying "Shit! Shit!

Shit!" The babysitter told me that if I kept saying that word, I would go to hell. So I went up to my room and kept saying it, hoping and praying that I would go to hell.

The one thing I did have was hope. I was always excited about what was in store for the future. A new school year would soon approach as it did in past years. I was nervous that it would be like years prior, yet excited because I was sure that it would be a better year. This was going to be the year I was going to make friends and have fun. But each new school year ended up being like the last.

In junior high everybody had different class schedules, so there was an element of anonymity, allowing you to disappear into the crowd. For me, the damage was already done. The couple of friends I had, had other friends who they did fun things with, like going to co-ed parties and making out with girls. I did not even realize that my friends had these other social lives until well into my thirties. I had no clue that there were even parties.

Missing out on these experiences only alienated me further, and over time, the few friends I had, disappeared. I simply did not know how to interact with people because I missed out on the subtle rules of social interaction, making everyday conversations with people that much more difficult and awkward for me. Not only that, but people saw me as awkward. The older I got, the more social norms I missed out on, and the more alienated I became. There were many times in junior high that I wish I were dead.

High School

High school was a relief for me. I was known as "John's little brother", so I had some instant acquaintances. I say "acquaintances" because we really didn't do things together outside of school. Actually, I hardly hung out with anybody. I still felt like a pony while everybody else was a black cat. In this socially stratified world of black cats and ponies, ponies were never allowed to take the initiative and invite themselves or invite others – ponies could only be invited. THOSE WERE THE RULES! And no standard invitation would do. When people invite a pony, they are only teasing. They are just playing nice – a formality. But this does not mean that you are to accept. Like trying to tame a wild stallion, you would have had to work really hard to convince me that you liked me. (Just a heads up…there are a lot of people out there who feel like this.)

If I lived in a very inclusive environment, I would have soared. I just needed that invitation to come hang out. I needed to know that I was liked. Otherwise, I was paralyzed in my own world.

I did not know any of these games like Spin the Bottle or Truth or Dare, and to this day, I never played any of these games. At one 'party', we were playing some card games where I had to kiss the girl to my left. Not having any understanding of the rules, social norms, or if one of the guys was her boyfriend, I licked my lips and gently kissed her…on the hand.

Out at Memorial Park, just as the sun was setting, a girl I was out on a date with asked to kiss me. Suffering from the same problem I had all these years, I froze up and was completely paralyzed – I could not even move if I tried. While kissing me, she obviously took this as a sign that I was not interested, and told me "Never mind!" It took me about a second or two to snap out of my stupor, but it was too late. The date ended right there, and there was no recovery. Being so removed from the social norms and over thinking made it even more difficult to make a move on a date.

In my senior year, one of the most beautiful girls in school sat by me in two classes. I remember in homeroom one morning at the beginning of the school year, I turned around and saw that she was staring at me. This was no fluke as it happened several times. Every day was a new day to say something to her and I had two chances a day to do it. One day she was telling those around me that she had two tickets to a concert and was wondering if someone wanted to go with her. I managed to tell her that I wanted to go to the concert with her, but by that time it was too late – being that it was at our twentieth-year reunion.

Was I Really a Black Cat?

For eleven years of school, I faced these daily reminders that I was less than other students. As I saw it, I was still the slow, stupid Pony who had a difficult time in remedial classes. What I found frustrating was when my parents and teachers would tell me that I was smart, but that I just was not trying hard enough. What was embarrassing was that even when I tried as hard as I could, I still was a failure.

My senior year started off like all the other years. In my history class, I would get an 'F' on my weekly chapter test, despite the huge effort I put into studying for it. When taking notes on the chapter, I did as we were all taught. I even made nice detailed outlines, but none of this helped. Again, based on my perception of reality, I presumed it was a fact that I was stupid, and nothing changed…that is until I tried a very different approach to learning.

I finally decided to try this different note taking strategy I learned over the summer. Instead of taking the typical notes, I learned to draw pictures for my notes, even though my drawing skills were embarrassingly horrible. My teacher saw the chapter notes that I turned in with many pages of poorly drawn pictures, and did not know what to think at first. I remember the first test I took using this new method of learning. For the first time in my life, taking a test was so easy that I almost started laughing while taking it. I did not just ace that test, I also aced every test after that. My perception of reality completely changed.

If I did not learn how to learn, based on how I think, I might not have ever gone to college. I would have remained in my own world feeling rejected by society, thinking that it was a fact that I was stupid. Understanding that I learned in a different way changed my life forever.

Thinking back on this, I sit here and wonder how many others simply had a different style of learning, like me. Are we really all black cats?

College

Since I was young, my family would fly out to Los Angeles and drive up to Ojai, California to see my grandparents. For many of these years, I would study the map of the Los Angeles area and look at the seemingly endless names of the various places in the area; Beverly Hills, Watts, Hollywood, Sunset Beach, Thousand Oaks, and so on. So it should probably be no shock that I decided to move out to the LA area for college.

As much as I loved college, after spending most of my life believing that I was less than others, deep down, it was still very much etched in my mind that academically and socially, I was still less than others. I missed out on so many opportunities because I had no clue how to interact with people. After many years of the same thing, you start to believe that nothing will ever change, because nothing has ever changed.

I wanted to have a girlfriend, but I did not know how to connect with anyone. It was especially frustrating when I would freeze up. There were plenty of missed opportunities I had with women. One woman even told me she would sleep with "anyone" who bought her lingerie. The next thing I remembered was that I was back in my dorm room, and as my brain started functioning again, I started to wonder if I was included as "anyone". It wasn't until my fourth year in college that I had sex or even kissed a girl, other than that failed effort in high school.

What was most frustrating about these moments of feeling paralyzed, was that once I snapped out of my state, I felt that if I had that option again, I would have no problem acting on it. Yet every time a new situation would come up, the same thing would happen.

These moments of paralyzation were not so much based on low self-esteem, but more of a mild cataplectic feeling, due to a rush of emotions. I jokingly refer to this as Homer Simpson Syndrome. If you are familiar with Homer on the TV show *The Simpsons*, when he thinks of beer or donuts, he becomes momentarily paralyzed, makes a groaning sound and starts to drool. I think that when it comes to beautiful women, many men seem to go into this state briefly. Women, who I never thought of as shy, have described to me this momentarily feeling of paralyzation too.

After College

When I graduated from college, I realized that my best years were probably behind me. The years where I should have been meeting women left and right were now over. I only had a few friends and I was not connecting with people. It was still difficult to understand where I stood with others, because many people knew I was different. Were people rejecting me because I was different, were they just not inviting me, was I just excluding myself, or was it the likely combination of all of these? All it took was an infrequent rude comment from someone about my intelligence to perpetuate my belief.

Thinking different in the workplace was a major handicap because people frequently held it against me. Some people treated me as if I did not know what I was talking about. There were plenty of times I've heard people say rude things behind my back and even directly at me, as if I were somehow less than them.

However thinking differently had major advantages too. I often noticed obvious things that other people did not see. This was what I was good at. I could see the big picture and understand what the underlying problem was.

Having an unbreakable determination to follow through with my mission, I knew I was going to face some rough times. After working for a few years, I stopped and focused on developing my theories and getting my masters degree.

Back in college, I had a vision where just when I thought I would be unstoppable, I would lose everything. Among several other things, I predicted I would go $30,000 in debt, have no one to turn to, and be living in a small apartment in a not too good part of Los

Angeles. In the end, it would not come down to if I would blow my brains out, but how hard I squeezed the trigger.

Sure enough, years later, every detail of this nightmare was coming together just as I had envisioned. I lost all my savings and was approaching $30,000 in debt, not because I had a spending problem, but because of my focus on the mission. I made a decision to get aggressive seeking jobs in the movie industry with plans to move up to L.A., from Orange County. As it turned out, due to time constraints and my budget, the only place I could afford was in a not too good part of town.

As difficult as this was, I was staying strong. I would not let any of this get me down. Losing everything hurt, but it did not stop me. Living a life of failure, I had nothing, so therefore I had nothing to lose. I felt unstoppable! I have long had the attitude that if someone put a gun to my head and told me to stop my mission or they would shoot, I would have told them that they better shoot to kill, because I was not going to stop.

This was also the time when I re-met up with the woman of my dreams. When I first met her back in college, I could tell just seeing how she interacted with people that she had a very good heart. Even though I had such a hard time talking to women, nothing would have stopped me from talking to her. As far as I was concerned, I could have married her a hundred times over. As it turns out, she was in a serious relationship at the time, but that did not bother me. Just meeting her was like how other people get excited meeting their favorite celebrity.

When I re-met up with her eight years later on a trip with some friends, she was everything and more of what I imagined. It was clear that she liked me. Unlike other women who, after the first date, told me "good luck", knowing they did not want to see me again, she instead called me to get together. Never having a serious girlfriend in my life, I was finally with the woman of my dreams. This was the best thing that could ever happen to me.

But this is when it all sank in. Just when I felt unstoppable, the one thing that mattered more to me than anything else, it was as if all of a sudden, I had everything to lose. Just as all these problems I faced were unimportant, they suddenly mattered. It felt like all these problems were shackled to me like cement blocks and I was pushed into the ocean. Even though I explained to her about my dire situation and the massive debt I accumulated, due to my focus on the mission, she did not seem to mind...but it sure bothered me. I was in a deep hole and there was no way I would be able to turn this around anytime soon. To have a life with her, I tried to walk away from my project and get a real job, but no matter how hard I tried, I could not get any job. Being jobless, deep in debt, and in the middle of moving from a fun apartment with a great roommate, to a place in a questionable neighborhood far away was hard enough. But there were also many other factors that were bringing my life to a grinding halt.

Just like how Rudolph left Clarisse, I felt that it was better that I not bring this woman down with me. All I could think about was how this had to come to an end. I had to let go, yet I could not let go. As painful as it was, it was actually a bit of a relief when she let me go.

The Mariana Trench

There will be a time in your life when you thought you hit rock bottom, like you are at the bottom of the ocean. Then there may be times where after you hit rock bottom, everything gets much worse. This is when you sink to the bottom of the Mariana Trench – the deepest, darkest part of the ocean. After a lifetime of failure and learning to be OK with it, it seems like things could not get worse, but they did. It all came crashing down on me and I was sinking quickly into the deep, dark abyss. As much as I tried to turn things around, even if I could have worked around the clock without sleep, there was no way to recover from this for many years to come.

My life was a complete failure and I was losing all hope. My vision of building a better world, which I still had a hard time describing to people, was a complete embarrassment. I felt defective and did not want to try anymore. I felt separated and foreign from everybody else. There was no escape. Even when I slept, I had nightmares about it, and when I woke up, nothing changed…my life was the real nightmare.

I felt so powerless with my financial situation and all, it seemed that my only option was to move up to Seattle, stay at a friend's house, and work at his company, doing warehouse work that not even warehouse workers wanted to do. As the months and years went by, I was holding on by a thread. I was an empty shell going through the motions.

When you get this far, you not only wish you would die, you wish you were never born. I wanted to dissolve – to completely disappear. No after life, nothing. I wanted to be gone from people's memories. I wanted to execute my soul. All I had to do was go out, buy the gun, pull that trigger, and blow my worthless head off. But I felt like a coward for not having the guts too follow through with this.

So one evening after work on my way home in the dark, in a very emotionless state I stopped by the gun shop to buy a gun. Unfortunately, the gun shop was closed. When I arrived home, I had a notice from my credit card company, which was acquired by another bank. Because I was over my credit limit, the new bank said I had no more credit to use, and they were reigning in the amount that I was over. I could not even buy a gun if I chose to.

People asked me why I never told them how I felt. I didn't tell anyone because I did not want to be alive or be encouraged to stay alive. I did not want people telling me how things were not that bad, how others had it worse than me, or how our problems are all relative.

Think about it. Imagine that you are staring down the barrel of a loaded gun. You can pull the trigger, or you can wait a few hours. What is one more day? If you are about to die, it no longer matters what others think of you, how much wealth you have, or how successful you are. None of that is important. It is just about survival. When tragedy strikes someone close to you, or with major events that affect the entire society, like on September 11th, 2001, you sort of forget about your personal problems for a while, because people need your help.

When you feel worthless, or when it feels like everybody else sees you as worthless, it is easy to become self-destructive. To help relieve extreme mental pain, people (and even animals) may resort to self-harm, in order to take the focus off the mental pain, or they may even act out aggressively towards others. Feeling excluded or completely defective can be more painful than breaking an arm.

Imagine feeling so worthless that you want to destroy yourself. Imagine giving yourself a black eye or sticking a knife in your leg. Have you wanted to take a hammer and smash your skull in or take a large butcher knife and cut off your fingers or your whole hand? I even remember reading about how a person took a chainsaw and intentionally cut off his own arm.

Even after moving back to Los Angeles, things did not improve for many years to come. In almost every job I ever had, including temp jobs, there was always someone who made it clear to me that I was "stupid", "creepy", or just weird. To this day, it is almost as if it is hardwired into me on a semi-subconscious level that I am less than others. When you deal with the same issues for so many years, it is only understandable that you will lose hope from time to time. While it is important to love yourself, when you feel that you are responsible for your own failings, it can be difficult at times.

It was frustrating when people told me that I just had a low self-esteem, that it was all in my head, or that I was just depressed. It was painful seeing how romantic relationships were a normal part of everyday life, even for teenagers, something that I never really experienced. It felt like everybody else was having fun except me.

After years of failure of having dates that did not go past the first one, I just stopped dating. I even stopped going out, because it reminded me of what I was missing. I've been through the routine many times. I would psych myself up, go out to a bar and despite how confident I was, I was not able to engage in small talk. Failing miserably, I would come home and beat myself up mentally and physically. By avoiding it all, I could live a somewhat stable life. But by doing this, life would continue to pass me by, and one day I would put my life to an immediate halt. I was a ticking time bomb that was bound to go off.

The one thing that kept me going was that while I was right about the nightmare that I predicted, I was also right about the woman I liked, so I was probably also right about the mission. So, no matter how painful it would get, I would have to just keep going, and maybe…just maybe, one day I would rescue the princess and revolutionize the world. Even though I felt like I was still at the bottom of the Mariana Trench, I worked as much as I could, and in my spare time I focused on my mission. My hope was no longer on a day-to-day basis, but more on the distant future.

The Rise of The Ultimate Power

I spent many painstaking years, rising back up. I eventually got out of debt, and while I was working on my mission I took whatever job I could get. I had no life because I could not afford a life. Even though I was still dealing with the same issues for much of this time, I was getting used to it. With all of this, there is a numbness that sets in. I'm not really sure to what degree that this is a bad thing or a good thing. As long as I had food, shelter, and power for my computer, I could continue to work. It was really important having supportive friends and family who all seemed to accept that I was not just going to give up this mission.

It is often said that what does not kill you, only makes you stronger. After being knocked down so many times…and just when you think you can't be taken down any further, something comes along and completely destroys you…almost. But you get back up and dust yourself off. You will get knocked down again, and again, and again. But let me tell you something! You keep getting back up! Why? Because this is your life!

While chaos ensued around me, I realized that I could have a choice in my reaction. Despite barely getting by in my real life, I was actually doing pretty well. I was no longer afraid of failure, what people thought of me, or of taking risks – I was no longer afraid of life and I was no longer afraid of death. I was experiencing life.

I learned that I was intelligent like the Black Cats, but just in different ways. I learned that as much as I wanted to be "normal" like everybody else, I would always be a Pony... after all these years, I finally learned to embrace being a Pony! I am not slower. I just think differently. I learn differently. I see things in different ways. I struggled a lot to get to where I am and I've learned so much.

I also learned something else. Everybody will face difficult times in their life...Even Black Cats. Some people going through times that are seriously challenging them. Some people will face divorce, or cancer. A person may have a typical day like any other, and just like that, find out that a son or daughter died unexpectedly, or have a small accident that leaves them paralyzed from the neck down. Life is short and it can end – just like that.

So like I said before; if someone put a gun to my head and told me to stop my mission or they would shoot, I would have told them they better shoot to kill, because I was not going to stop. Do you want to know what I would have said next? "You should have shot me when you had the chance, because I am not going down."

CHAPTER 2

HOW WE SEE THE WORLD

Several years ago when I was substitute teaching, I asked a class of seventh graders where they saw the world one hundred years from now. One student, apparently making a joke of the situation, told me that she didn't care because she would be dead by then. I then asked her if she was planning on having kids. Realizing this, her attitude quickly changed. The smile on her face disappeared as she sat up and became more interested in the discussion.

One person I interviewed, Chris, said that the world would be "…gone, non-existent! Something's happening…it's going to be Armageddon, like it says in the Bible…people are going to destroy mankind. I think we are going to kill ourselves…you can already tell, because it's already heading in that direction." I asked him what he was going to do to change this. He laughed and said "…not a goddamn thing!" But towards the end of the interview, he said he wanted to help people. "For a better world, no drugs, no chemical weapons, no nuclear weapons…no more hatred…I think that's one of society's big issues…A lot of people hate too much. If there was a lot more love…then I think we would be better off…a lot better off."

Unfortunately, there are a lot of people who believe we live in dangerous times, that humanity is worse off than it ever was, and that there is nothing they can do about it to change it. If you are convinced that your actions do not make a difference, then as you see it, regardless of what you do, good or bad, it will not matter. This kind of thinking can justify apathetic, and even negative behavior, where people are more likely to focus on doing what ever it takes to get ahead, even if it is at the expense of others.

In the interviews I conducted, many respondents said that they thought the world would be worse off one hundred years from now, and clearly indicated that they had no desire to try to change this. However, in the course of these interviews, I noticed that as they became more conscious of other people's lives, they showed a stronger desire to change things for the better. When people become aware of a problem, and are convinced that change needs to take place and that their effort can make a difference, they will act. In the movie *Gandhi*, Gandhi said, "When you are fighting in a just cause, people seem to pop up…right out of the pavement. Even when it is dangerous…" The reality is that people want to make a difference. In some cases, they are even willing to risk their lives for the greater good.

Understanding Different Perspectives

We go through life seeing what we think is real. In many ways, it can seem that society has never really changed, and sometimes, it can seem like society is on the verge of collapse. But what if I were to tell you that this common perception of reality is simply that – a perception.

If you saw a brick wall in front of you, you likely would not try to run through it, because you know it is a brick wall. The brick wall is a reality and so it is also a reality that you would likely hurt yourself trying to run through it. But in your life, there are walls that you will come across that seem just as real as a brick wall that you can see and feel, but they are not real.

Seeing a wall up close, you may feel like there would be no way to get past it. But if you step back and look at the bigger picture, it may be quite obvious that you can walk around it. We know that when we see things up close such as a puzzle piece, we are only looking at the little picture. In order to understand how all the pieces come together, we need to see the bigger picture on the box.

If you have ever looked up directions using mapping software, you may have noticed that the directions show the big picture layout of the entire route as well as the turn-by-turn directions along with close-up images of those locations. If you were only to look at the little picture, you may wind up in Hollywood, Florida, instead of Hollywood, California. When you only see the little picture, there is a danger that you will see this as reality and miss the context of seeing it as it fits into the whole.

In the little picture, we think we know and understand people. These become our walls of reality. But when we see the bigger picture, we realize that people have a lot more going on in their lives and therefore are much more complex.

While it is natural for people to judge other people's behavior, it is also important to realize that what you see is not necessarily what someone else sees. Just because two people may have two completely opposite opinions, does not make them wrong. It is said that the brilliant mind can see two direct opposites, yet see how they are both right.

Every single one of us is wrong sometimes; even when we are absolutely sure we are right. One day while substitute teaching at an elementary school, I said something to the class that got these kids onto a religious debate, and it was getting out of control. Thinking quickly, I grabbed a calculator off the desk and showed it to the class. I then asked the students to describe what they saw. In unison, they all screamed out "A calculator!" I responded; "Ok, it's a calculator, but now describe to me what it looks like." They tell me that it was grey and that there were buttons on it. With an exaggerated attitude, I told them that they did not know what they were talking about, because what I saw was smooth and black. They all seemed to unanimously yell out to me that I was looking at the other side. I told them, "Oh wow, we are looking at the same thing, and we are both right, but we are just looking at it from two different perspectives."

There are different points of view to every issue, but we think we need to form an opinion and stick to it. But if you only understand the little picture, how in the world are you to form an opinion based on this small amount of information, and then stick to it? People can get so focused on being "right" about a political issue that they are unable to see a different perspective. They may be so focused on getting their point across that they really don't take the time to understand what the other person is saying.

Inattentional Blindness

If you see something or someone as bad, then the only things you will focus on are the bad traits. With this limited focus, there are often things that we miss in the bigger picture. This is what is known as inattentional blindness. One example of inattentional blindness can be seen in a commonly replicated experiment that shows a video of men passing a basketball to each other. A group of people watching the video are told to count how many times the men in yellow jerseys pass the ball to each other. The video is played and afterwards they talk about how many times the ball was passed. They are then asked if anyone noticed anything unusual about the video and only a few of the fifteen or so people raised their hand. What was unusual was that while everybody was busy counting how many times the ball was being passed, a person dressed in a gorilla outfit walked out in front of the camera and banged his chest several times, then walked off screen.[1]

On July 6, 2013, Asiana Flight 214 was on its final approach from Seoul, South Korea to San Francisco. The plane narrowly missed the runway and crashed. Several days after the crash, a local news station in Oakland, California, reported the names of the pilots on that flight. On air, they mentioned the following names in order: Captain Sum Ting Wong, Wi Tu Lo, Ho Lee Fuk, and Bang Ding Ow. When I first heard about this story, I thought it was some childish joke. But the sad truth was that it was real. How in the world could they make such a blatant mistake? While probably very embarrassed, I hope this news crew was not so hard on themselves. As obvious as this mistake may seem to most people, this is an example of inattentional blindness. When people are so focused on making sure names are spelled and pronounced correctly, they might just overlook something as obvious as this. But as blatant as this may seem to you, would you have missed the man in the gorilla suit, like most people? In case you are wondering how obvious the gorilla was; if you watched the video and were not focused on counting the number of times the ball was passed, the gorilla would have been as obvious as Ho Lee Fuk!

It should also be noted that the news station even verified the names with an intern at the National Transportation Safety Board (NTSB). Unfortunately, the intern was blamed for what he or she probably thought was an obvious prank call made by some juveniles.

People Who Have Been Disproved

If you are convinced that you are stupid, then you will be discouraged from learning. If you are convinced that the next one hundred years are only going to get worse and that there is nothing you can do, then you will not do anything about it. If you are convinced that you really don't make a difference, then you will not try to make a difference. It is you who accepts these walls of 'reality', and it is you who can shatter them.

For me, it seemed pretty obvious that I was slow and stupid. My thinking was reinforced by my performance on a daily basis for eleven plus years. And then, just like that, my perception of reality was turned on its head. Instead of accepting what was thought to be a wall of reality; not just by me, but also by the standards of society, I learned that this was just a commonly held perception. As much as we want to convince ourselves that these walls exist, they don't. Just because society as a whole believes something to be true, does not make it true. While we have all these ways of measuring intelligence, that, in no way means that we have every way of measuring intelligence. Doing poorly on a test does not define you as unintelligent. Getting the highest score on a test does not define you as smarter than everybody else. It only means that you did well on this test. It was quite apparent that these measurements did not define my intelligence.

There have been plenty of "experts" who were wrong. Sometimes these mistakes have cost us hundreds of billions of dollars, as with the Y2K scare. Charles Duell, the Commissioner of the U.S. Office of Patents (1899), said (supposedly misquoted) that everything that could be invented has been invented. This was said just before we experienced a technological revolution. There are many examples of people who have been disproved.

> "Louis Pasteur's theory of germs is ridiculous fiction." PIERRE PACHET (Professor of Physiology at Toulouse, 1872)

> This 'telephone' has too many shortcomings to be seriously considered as a means of communication. The device is inherently of no value to us." WESTERN UNION (Internal memo, 1876)

> "Stocks have reached what looks like a permanently high plateau." IRVING FISHER (Professor of Economics, Yale University, 1929)

> "I think there is a world market for maybe five computers." THOMAS WATSON (Chairman of IBM, 1943)

> "While theoretically and technically television may be feasible, commercially and financially it is an impossibility." LEE DEFOREST (Inventor)

"I have traveled the length and breadth of this country and talked with the best people, and I can assure you that data processing is a fad that won't last out the year." (The Editor in Charge of Business Books for Prentice Hall, 1957)

"There is no reason anyone would want a computer in their home." KEN OLSON (President, Chairman, and Founder of Digital Equipment Corp., 1977)

In 1984, John Dvorak's review of the Macintosh: "There is no evidence that people want to use [a mouse] these things."

It was thought that you can't put living cells in magnetic fields without killing them. The MRI proved that was wrong

"Airplanes are interesting toys but of no military value." MARECHAL FERDINAND FOCH (Professor of Strategy, Ecole Superieure de Guerre)

It was assumed by most people that we would never reach the moon even a year before we went to the moon.

As much as it may seem that nothing ever changes, things are changing all the time. What could not be done one day, may be possible the next. And individuals who refuse to accept these "walls", instead change the world.

CHAPTER 3

ARE WE REALLY WORSE OFF TODAY THAN IN THE PAST?

Society is simply the coming together of individuals to form a better life. The success of society as a whole is based on how good the social connections within the society are.

Societies can be in the form of families, communities, towns, states, and nations. With global commerce and technological advances, we are also becoming a global society.

You, yourself are also a society – made up of trillions of cells. The cells in an organism communicate with each other in super efficient ways, far beyond what we humans are capable of. If the lines of connection are blocked, the organism along with the cells that make up that organism will suffer. Similarly, if the lines of connection in society are weak, the whole societal organism, as well as each of us, will suffer.

Societies are not just limited to humans. Societies can be in the form of whale pods, wolf packs, and even ant colonies. Ants cultivated their own food and even had coordinated labor forces, millions of years before humans did. Some ants even developed their own hybrid pesticides. While there is a queen ant, nobody is really in charge, yet as a whole, they operate efficiently and know what to do.[1]

Let's now go back to a time long before there were any towns or villages and see how communication and our connection to each other evolved over thousands of years. We can see that society has become less violent and more civilized over time, but I was shocked by how many people believe that society is worse off and more violent today than it was in the past.

By forming into towns and villages, we were able to provide better means of protecting ourselves more than what could be provided in a tribe of hunter-gatherers. Being able to cultivate the land and grow food means that more food can be provided which means that more people can live together. But it also means an end to a nomadic life where people were constantly on the search for food.

With more people living together, we were able to collaborate on new ideas. We were able to build new things that we could never have done in small separate tribes. When we work together, we can create amazing things – we can build a better world. However, when we work against each other, we end up with so many of the problems we see today.

For thousands of years, the progress we made was so slow that there wasn't much of anything to show for it, but this gradual evolution of society can be shown both technologically and socially.

Technological advancements are more tangible than social advancements, and are therefore easier to measure. We can more clearly see when things have been created or invented. What we often don't see with technological advancements are all the failures that are made before a product comes out.

Social advancement is much more difficult to assess than technological advancement and can take place over years, decades, and even centuries. There can also be many setbacks. Some people have seen societies go from better to worse and even crumble into non-existence over the course of their lives.

The Evolution of Humanity

So how did we get to where we are today? Just the design of the human body has many small advantages over other animals. Imagine where we would be today if we did not have thumbs.

Humans also have an extensive vocal range to help in communication. Our ability to speak is due to the development of the hyoid bone. While other animals have this bone, only humans have this bone in just the right spot to work with the tongue and larynx.

One may think that if dogs were more intelligent, they would learn to walk upright. But if you look at the design of a dog's back leg and the way the joints move, it makes more sense for a dog to keep walking on all four legs and carry stuff in its mouth, than to try to walk upright. Within minutes to hours after being born, a deer or a horse has already learned to walk. Babies learn to crawl using their arms and legs long before they learn to walk. Learning to walk upright takes a lot of coordination and skill and is learned over several months.

Evidence of humans using basic primitive tools goes back a few million years. It appears that the most common references show that the discovery and ability to make fire date as far back as 1.5 million years ago. Being able to do things like figuring out how to make fire by rubbing two sticks together or striking stones together to make a spark is difficult enough. Being able to use this energy source was an extremely difficult process that took place over hundreds of thousands of years.

Before society, people lived in tribes and their focus was on survival. After being around for a few million years, it wasn't until just roughly 35,000 years ago, that people developed primitive forms of communication composed of language and drawings. As communication slowly developed, allowing people to think in more complex ways, we were able to begin to wonder about things like that great big bright thing that brings the day, and those pinpoints of light that appear during the night, along with that other thing that we call the moon. Was this some sort of message to us? Why are we able to make things like fire…why me?

Language allowed us to think in more complex ways, which led to the development of a more advanced belief system 3,000 years later [or about 32,000 years ago]. While looking over the entire scope of humanity, it is easy to think that spiritual beliefs "soon" followed communication, but that was three thousand years later! Three thousand years is a very long period of time in the scope of our own lives. As it is, we have a hard time imagining three thousand years ago, or much less, even one thousand or one hundred years into the future!

Dr. Paul Apodaca[2], a professor at Chapman University who specializes in American Indian studies, explains that Emile Durkheim speculated that spirituality first started off as animistic, where there is a soul to everything. The way in which people were spiritual was affected by where they lived. In the Americas long before Europeans came, some Indian tribes were probably animistic in their belief systems. They lived in an environment that teemed with wildlife. It has been said that there were buffalo herds so large that you would be able to see these herds from outer space as dark patches on the North American continent. In such an environment, one had to blend in, in order to survive. People were an equal part of this ecosystem just like every other animal.

In areas where there was not as much wildlife, such as the Middle East, over tens of thousands of years, people slowly were able to advance and become the dominant species. Religions naturally became more theistic, where there was a belief in a god or gods. People saw themselves above animals and therefore something must be above humans. Peoples' perceptions of God changed over the centuries. This change in spirituality from an animistic to a theistic and even a monotheistic (meaning one god) view, took place around the neo-lithic revolution; a period of time which set us further apart from other animals.

The Beginnings of Structured Society
And A New Level of Consciousness

Around 10,000 years ago the Neolithic age (or New Stone era) was a period of time where people started developing stone tools. This brought about an agricultural revolution within the next 3,000 years, allowing people to move from a nomadic life of hunting and gathering in tribes to a life where they could grow their own food. By cultivating the land, developing methods of irrigation for crops and techniques for storing food, people were able to settle in larger groups with this greater food supply. Moving from a tribal existence into a more social environment of villages, people were able to better communicate, which further developed language and thinking skills. As people came together, they were able to socialize and share ideas. This formed a basic collective conscious, a higher level of conscious, a gathering of some (but not all) minds.

When we have a gathering of some minds, but not all, society becomes more stratified. Later, as written communication developed, there were a very small number of people who knew how to read and write. This was in part due to the fact that many people had to focus on manual labor in order for society to function, while only a few could be a part of this intellectual society. This is also due to the fact that there were no tools for mass communication such as the printing press, radio, television, or the Internet. Everything that was learned was from a build up of knowledge gained over thousands and thousands of years.

It is interesting that, in general, the first small societies began popping up between 6,000 and 10,000 years ago. These first forms of organized societies formed a collective conscious. This collective conscious was a revolution in thinking, where ideas were shared and built upon. What makes this so interesting is that this is also when people of various religions believe that the world was created – 6,000 to 10,000 years ago!

The Evolution of Technology

As humans improved upon basic communication skills, and were able to create tools that led to agriculture and the formation of societies, people were able to collaborate more and more on their thoughts and ideas.

It took thousands of years to invent some of the most basic technologies. The wheel and axle, along with the lever, pulley, inclined plane, wedge, and screw, were six basic machines that led to even more technological advances. Rolling technology came into use roughly 10,000 years ago, about the same time as the Neolithic age. It wasn't until 4,000 years later (6,000 years ago) that we saw the first evidence of wheeled technology. It took another 2,000 years (about 4,000 years ago) to design the spoked wheel, which could hold more weight. That is a period of about 6,000 years to invent something as basic as a wheel!

The use of bronze came about 5,300 years ago, iron about 3,500 years ago, and glass about 2,500 years ago. Paper was created about 1,800 years ago in China, and then was brought to the Middle East 600 years later. The first paper mill came about 800 years ago.

The first evidence of a written language was about 5,500 years ago, before this, people drew pictures of what they did. The language was made up of numerals, pictures and symbols for words. As it is, we have a hard enough time keeping an accurate history with a written language. Even with the past few hundred years, written history has been greatly distorted, depending on who the writers were. Other than personal writings such as journals, it wasn't that long ago that almost all historical information was written by a very small number of men and their point of view. Very little could be described from a woman's or a slave's point of view.

The Technological Revolution

Technology has increased at an exponential rate. The more technology advances, the more it can be used to build even greater and more complex technology. In the days of the Roman Empire, I am sure many people thought they were at the pinnacle of technology. But as we look back two thousand years later, we see how much further we have come.

The past one hundred years have changed so much in terms of technology that it was completely unimaginable just prior to that. Even though Charles Duell may have been misquoted when he said that everything that could be invented has been invented in 1899, a lot of other people were thinking this, just as people thought this way in the days of the Roman Empire. If you went back a few hundred years and tried to explain a computer to someone, they would have absolutely no understanding of what you were talking about. Even in more recent times, when motion pictures came out, people were frightened at first, thinking that the objects on the screen were really coming straight at them. Before the invention of the iPhone, "smart" phones had a screen and buttons. But most people, including myself, could not even conceive of phones like we now have along with the many useful applications they have.

Why We Perceive Society in Decline

While we have advanced technologically, have we really advanced socially? In a junior high history class, one of the students read about how Alexander Hamilton, who was one of the co-authors of the *Federalist Papers* and was America's first secretary of treasury, had a duel with Aaron Burr, the vice president of the United States of America. I asked the students if they really thought that we were living in more violent times than in the past. Since Hamilton already lost a son to a duel, you would think he was intelligent enough not to engage in duels, but this did not stop him. Sure enough, Hamilton died the next day. There were others like Henry Clay and Andrew Jackson, who had several duels. Jackson, who was shot several times, even claimed to "rattle like a bag of marbles" when he walked from all the bullets that were in him.[3] James Monroe was going to challenge John Adams to a duel, but thought twice about it since Adams was the current president.

This violent behavior was just part of the culture back then. If something like this happened today, we would be in total crisis mode with news teams from all over the world reporting on unfolding events 24/7. Today, not even kids who are in gangs would challenge each other to a dual. They are smart enough to shoot and run.

In a survey on perceptions of violence, respondents were asked which period of time they thought had higher rates of violent death. People guessed that 20th-century England was about 14 percent more violent than 14th-century England, when in fact, 20th-century England is actually 95 percent less violent than in the 14th century.[4] Respondents were also asked this question in regards to: prehistoric hunter-gatherer tribes or when the first states of the United States formed; modern hunter-gatherer tribes or modern western society; warfare in the 1950's or the 2000's; and homicide rates in the United States in the 1970's or the 2000's. In each of these questions, respondents thought that the later culture was more violent by a factor of 1.1 to 4.6. In reality, the earlier culture was more violent by a factor of 1.6 to more than 30.[5]

Our greater access to constant information can make it seem like society is falling apart. Even though many of us go about our daily lives without experiencing or seeing any acts of violence, when we see or read about acts of violence in the news, these major events stick in our minds.

The crime rate is more accurately recorded these days than it ever has been, and when we hear about crime in the news, it may be something that happened in our own town or on the other side of our country that has over 300 million people, or even on the other side of the planet.

When we see these news clips, we are looking at clips of the little picture, and not the bigger picture that surrounds it. On January 1, 2011 in Beebe, Arkansas, it was reported that 5,000 blackbirds fell from the sky. We saw the instant news, which included photos and video. Then soon after, there were other similar stories that were coming out. In Labarre, Louisiana, 500 birds fell from the sky, 80,000 fish died along the Arkansas River, a million plus fish washed up on shore of the Chesapeake Bay, and we even heard about dead birds in Italy and Sweden, along with dead crabs washing ashore in England. On January 4, 2011, a news headline read "Apocalypse now? Mystery bird deaths hit Louisiana".[6] It was quite chilling to read about all this at once. Was this the beginning of Armageddon? Well it sure could have seemed that way. The reality is that while these things happen more often around the world than what's reported, it is much more rare that it would happen where you live. If a story were to make national headlines, other similar stories would be sure to follow.

Even stories that are not true, or are an isolated incident, fuel our misperception about our safety. We hear rumors of people who stuck razor blades in apples and gave them out as Halloween treats, yet there is no account of this ever happening. We hear about how people can drug you to steal your kidneys, yet there are no police reports of this happening in the Unites States.[7] Nonetheless, these things stick with us. The rumors that are spread can sometimes have very dangerous consequences. There are plenty of historical accounts of "ethnic cleansing" where millions of people have been murdered, all based on rumors or fear of "the other."

Regardless of how safe things are, people react on their fears. Some people have a fear of flying, yet don't think twice about driving a car or even a motorcycle. As of April 2013, the last major commercial US airline crash with fatalities was on November 12, 2001. Since then, one Southwest Airlines flight skidded off the runway, hit two cars and killed a six-year old boy on the ground. There were also three commuter airline crashes killing a total of 119 people and one person on the ground, bringing the total to 121 people killed. With an average of over 28,000 commercial flights per day in the United States and an average of about two million passengers per day, with over 7.8 billion passengers on US carriers alone, 121 fatalities is enough to make conspiracy theorists believe that there is a cover up. In the same time frame, there were 418,000 people who died in car accidents, averaging out to 104.19 deaths per day over the eleven years.[8]

With major events such as mass genocide or wars, it can seem that it is in our nature to destroy ourselves. These events are essentially a black eye on humanity, but they are only low points in a spectrum moving upward. Compare this to the stock market. Major "black eyes" occurred on Black Monday in 1929 and again in 2008. Like the stock market, there will be many dips, and even major depressions, however, in the big picture, we have continued to advance socially. If you look at the stock market on a day-to-day basis – in the little picture, you will see a stock go up and down constantly. When looking at the whole day, some days are good, and some days are bad. If we were trying to make a judgment based on a snapshot of a single day, we would be looking at too small of a picture. A snapshot of a bigger picture showing months or even years could even show a constant decline. In some cases, a person or even whole generations of people have lived in times of social decline. But a lot of this depends on what period of time you look at. After the 1929 stock market crash, a time known as the Great Depression, it would have appeared that the stock market would never recover, but we all know now that we eventually recovered and continued to grow stronger than ever. Similarly, tragic events such as World War I and World War II, and even much smaller events such as 9/11 do not doom humanity to failure.

Advances in Social Skills

As societies formed, it was a very long and gradual process for people to become more civilized and more socialized in how they relate to each other. Because social skills are learned, these skills have been slowly improving and will continue to improve.

There have been tremendous advances in learning. Hundreds and even thousands of years ago, many of the brightest people had nowhere near the education or the vocabulary we have today, and they were the rulers in society. There were not many educated people a few hundred years ago, and there were far less one thousand years ago. Even today, there are many students who are the first in their family to go to college, but the percentages of people receiving education has greatly increased.

Before the invention of the printing press, books were hand-written, and only a privileged few could read. The printing press was a significant step in educating people. The number of books that were published in English was less than one thousand per decade in the early 16th century. By the 17th century, there were roughly two thousand books published in a decade. In the later 17th century, these numbers began to skyrocket.[9] As the number of books that were published increased, the literacy rate would, in turn, increase too. The idea of mass education was probably a little unnerving for those in power, since an educated public would be a threat to their control. The first set of encyclopedias that came out in the late 1700's, were seen as a threat. "They were called a War Machine, a Tower of Babel, the Gospel of Satan."[10] At one point in time, some of the volumes were locked up, and the police had orders to burn the manuscripts and impound the books.

In the early 1900's, the IQ test was invented. By definition, the average IQ is always 100, so regardless of how well educated a society becomes the average score will be 100. So, for example, the average person in the early 1900's had an IQ of 100, just like the average person today has a score of 100. In the early 1980's it was found that the average IQ score rose an average of three points per decade. This phenomenon was discovered by James Flynn and is commonly referred to as the Flynn Effect. This means that if an average teenager today went back to the year 1910, his or her IQ would be about 130. If an average person from 1910, time traveled to the present, his or her IQ would be about 70, which borders mental retardation.[11]

A likely reason for this trend is that people had considerably less education in the early 1900's. In addition to this, education itself was pretty simple, involving basic memory skills (rote learning) and generally did not involve reasoning and critical thinking. As society progressed, more people moved from jobs that required little or no education into jobs that involved more abstract thinking.

Even social etiquette has improved considerably over time. The people in the middle ages may appear down right disgusting to people today. The etiquette books of the time tackled serious issues that three-year-olds know today. Can you imagine *Miss Manners* saying such things as:

- Don't piss or defecate in the staircase, corridors, and closets, on the wall hangings, in front of ladies, or in front of doors or windows.

- Don't greet people while they are urinating or defecating.

- Don't blow your nose into your hand, sleeve, hat, or a tablecloth.

- Don't offer your used handkerchief to someone.

- "Don't carry your handkerchief in your mouth"

- "Don't pick your nose while eating"[12]

The fact is that etiquette, like any other social norm we take for granted, is learned. People were publicly naked more often. People also lacked discretion in sexual activity, men talked about their sexual exploits with their children, and prostitutes openly offered their services.[13]

Modern society is much more humane than it was centuries ago. Many modern cultures do not tolerate violent behavior today like they did in the past. If someone were to get into a fight at the workplace today, they would likely be fired on the spot. Centuries ago, slaves were a regular part of society and women were considered as property. Animals and even people were tortured as popular forms of entertainment.

Hundreds of years ago, raping and killing women was part of winning a war. Even some of the writers of the Bible showed no issues with having slaves or inflicting torture, such as blinding, stoning, or even chopping up a person – things you would most likely see in horror movies today.

Steven Pinker, *(The Better Angels of our Nature)*, explains how violence has declined throughout human history. Slowly over thousands and thousands of years, people have become more civilized. In the past few hundred years there has also been a gradual improvement in terms of human rights.

The First Major Decline in Violence

The first major decline in violence occurred when humanity moved from a nomadic living of hunting and gathering to a settled society of towns and villages. It is estimated that this alone accounted for a five-fold reduction of violence.[14] When people are not able to grow their food, they must fight for survival over what food they can get. Forensic archaeology has shown that cannibalism was more widespread in prehistoric times than previously thought.[15] It has also been shown that cannibalism likely occurred in more recent times, such as with settlers in Jamestown in the winter of 1609-1610. The bones of a 14-year-old girl show proof that she was cannibalized. George Percy, who was the colony leader, wrote of a "world of miseries" where "Nothing was spared to maintain life," he explained how a man killed then ate his pregnant wife. "Now whether she was better roasted, boiled or carbonado'd [barbequed], I know not, but of such a dish as powdered wife I never heard of."[16]

As people learned to cultivate the land, food could be grown and was more plentiful. As social groups gathered to live together, they developed rules, i.e. government, which had some control on the violence. While a common reason for warfare among tribes was vengeance, a government was able to put a stop to continued acts of individual aggression. However, while having a governing body helped reduce violence among its citizens, governments often abused their own citizens and went to war with other governments.[17]

The Advancement of Civilized Society

Another major decline in violence took place between the Middle Ages and the 20th century, in what Pinker referred to as the civilization process. With a concentrated number of people in a given area, along with a governing body to enforce the rules, people had to learn to be more civil with each other. As simple as this may sound today, learning civility was like inventing the wheel. Civility is something we are still learning. Between the 13th and 20th century, various parts of England saw anywhere from a ten-fold to one hundred-fold decrease in violence. It is estimated that in the Middle Ages, the homicide rate ranged from 4 to 100 deaths per 100,000 people, depending on location. In the 20th century the homicide rate in every Western European country was down to 1 death per 100,000 people.[18]

Centuries ago, rich people were as violent, if not more violent than poor people. People achieved higher status and rose to power through violence. As we think about the knights today, words like noble, honor, chivalry, and gallantry come to mind. But in reality, many of these people were ruthless murderers. In order to gain wealth in Medieval times, one would often take the land of others. Knights would start their own private wars, causing as much destruction as possible on the neighboring land. Peasants were maimed or killed, crops were destroyed, along with any other resources. Kings had no permanent army and had little control of the country.[19]

Political leaders not only murdered other political leaders, they frequently used torture, imprisonment, executions, starvation, and even worked their own citizens to death. Between 600 and 1800 AD, it has been estimated that about one in eight monarchs in Europe were murdered in office and a third of these murderers took over the throne. Of the forty-nine Roman emperors, thirty-four were killed by guards, high-ranking officials, or family members.[20] If you were a Roman emperor, you had nearly a 70 percent chance of being murdered.

In the 14th and 15th centuries, 26 percent of male aristocrats died from violence.[21] "Gentlemen would carry swords and would not hesitate to use them to avenge insults. They often traveled with retainers who doubled as bodyguards, so an affront or a retaliation for an affront could escalate into a bloody street fight between gangs of aristocrats (as in the opening scene of *Romeo and Juliet*)."[22] Today in western society, the vast majority of violent crimes are committed by people in the lowest socioeconomic classes.[23]

There was also a large amount of violence in entertainment, sports, religion and other parts of society. While today, we consider people who torture animals likely to be psychopaths, torturing animals was a popular form of entertainment in the middle ages. Historian Barbara Tuchman describes popular sports where players would compete by having their hands tied behind their back and would head-butt a cat to death that was nailed to a post. The challenge was to not get you cheeks ripped open or your eyes scratched out by the cat's claws. In another game, men would chase a pig and beat it to death.[24] One form of entertainment was to chain a bear to a post and watch dogs tear it apart or be killed trying. Among many other examples, people would watch a cat hoisted in a sling and slowly lowered into a fire. According to historian Norman Davies, "The spectators, including kings and queens, shrieked with laughter as the animals, howling with pain, were singed, roasted, and finally carbonized."[25]

Human torture was also common and was a part of every day life. People were burned alive, stoned to death, and tortured by being castrated or having their feet, breasts, or even nose cut off, among other things. People were dismembered or disemboweled alive. But this was not some hidden secret. Crowds of people watched with excitement and cheered as people were publically humiliated, raped, tortured, and murdered.[26]

The Coliseum in Rome is a common example where audiences were entertained for hundreds of years (between 80 AD and 523 AD) and cheered on as Gladiators and sometimes groups of people fought each other to the death. Women were even tied up naked and raped or torn apart by animals. Over this time, there were about 500,000 people who were tortured and murdered at the Coliseum as a form of entertainment.

There were many forms of sadistic torture in Medieval times. Many of these forms of torture were used in the name of religion. Torture was used to humiliate and dehumanize people and was used even for non-violent crimes such as blasphemy, criticizing the government, gossip, and adultery. A person may have been hung by his or her ankles while two people sawed downward starting at the crotch. With Judas's Cradle, which was used in the Spanish Inquisition, a person was stripped naked and bound, then suspended and lowered onto a pyramid shaped wedge that went into the anus or vagina. Over time, this would slowly tear the person's skin apart. Some people were disemboweled or burned at the stake.[27] Other people had their limbs torn from their body, which was just among many other forms of torture.

The Crusades took place between 1,095 and 1,291 and were considered to be justifiable wars. With a world population of about 400 million, one million died in the crusades between 1095 and 1208.[28] Defeated soldiers had their noses and upper lips cut off, or even had the eyes gouged out. Pinker explains that nobody today has ever met a Cathar because they were exterminated in full.[29]

When something bad happened that was unexplainable, people often blamed others. If the crops wilted, God must have been upset with them, so they focused on being more religious. Anybody who thought differently must either repent or die. It was also believed that some people engaged in black magic, sorcery, and witchcraft. Enemies were evil. Burning people for what they thought was witchcraft was common in Europe. Between the 15th and 18th centuries, French and German witch-hunters killed between 60,000 and 100,000 people who were accused of being witches. Of these people 85 percent of them were women. Accused witches were often tortured and burned at the stake.[30] The last year a woman was burned as a witch in Europe was 1749.

In the 1500's King Henry the Eighth beheaded two of his wives. The first wife, Anne Boleyn was beheaded on fabricated charges of adultery and treason because she had a son that did not survive and Henry was also attracted to one of the ladies in waiting. King Henry's third wife, Catherine Howard, was also beheaded. Because King Henry was jealous, he also had one of Catherine's former boyfriends drawn and quartered. "Drawn and quartered" is a nice way of saying that he was hung by the neck, taken down while still alive, disemboweled, castrated, decapitated, and cut into four.[31]

Henry's daughter Mary (nicknamed Bloody Marry) had 300 religious dissenters burned at the stake. She even executed her cousin, Lady Jane Grey. King Henry's other daughter Elizabeth had 123 priests drawn and quartered. She too had her cousin Mary Queen of Scots executed.[32] These people were nothing more than brutal murdering thugs who would easily qualify for one of the world's worst dictators today and sound more like characters in a Quentin Tarantino movie.

In the final years of the reign of King Henry the Eighth, there were over ten executions in London every week.[33] London's population at the time was between 100,000 and 150,000. In 2012, the United States, with a population over 300 million (and is considered to be one of the leading nations in the world that uses the death penalty), executed forty-three people.[34]

During these times it was not totally uncommon for one person to cut off another person's nose. While this was often done in vengeance, it was also an official punishment for things like heresy, treason, sodomy, or prostitution. "In one case in Nuremberg in 1520, Hanns Rigel had an affair with the wife of Hanns von Eyb. A jealous von Eby cut off the nose of Rigel's innocent wife, a supreme injustice multiplied by the fact that Rigel was sentenced to four weeks of imprisonment for adultery while von Eyb walked away scot-free."[35] These mutations were common back then, yet today, stories like these would make international news.

As society progressed, the consequences for crime and violence started to outweigh the reward. Towards the end of the Middle Ages, as trade improved, so did the economy. With this, roads improved, as well as transportation, which all lead to more trade. As people became more dependent on each other, this further led to a reduction of violence. Basically, if the peasants in the neighboring society are growing the food that you trade for, you are much less willing to kill them. The division of labor greatly increased the amount of produce, thus increasing trade. With the rise of national currencies, trade became even easier, and people relied more on each other. With trade, people could gain wealth without plundering other lands.[36]

People also learned to be fairer with each other. As people traded more and were learning fairness, they were also becoming more empathetic and understanding of their trading partner. Over time, these skills became routine, further reducing violence.[37]

As people in society rely more on each other, they are less likely to engage in violence. However, people who feel separated from this process – feeling like they don't play a role in society, feel separated from, or feel like they have nothing to share with others – are more likely to engage in crime and/or violent activity.

The Decline of Socially Sanctioned Violence

Between the 17th and 18th century, in what is known as the humanitarian revolution, the first major organized movements in human history focused on abolishing socially sanctioned forms of violence, including slavery, dueling, torture, and superstitious killing.[38] People were also becoming concerned about the humane treatment of animals. In the 19th century, the first laws were enacted that protected animals.[39]

As technology and science improved, people had better access to education and were more able to focus on pursuing happiness. It wasn't until the 18th century that governments started abolishing slavery. Among western nations, the United States was one of the last countries to abolish slavery. Along with this, there was also a movement to end the practice of debt bondage in which people who were in debt were imprisoned, enslaved, or even executed.

There was also a movement to treat prisoners more humanely. Before this time, people were frequently tortured and executed. In the late 1700's, capital punishment, such as hanging and the guillotine, were considered more humane because they resulted in a quick death. However people could be put to death for minor things such as sodomy, gossiping, stealing, even picking up sticks on the Sabbath, or in the case of children, talking back to their parents.[40]

In the early 17th century, England and Scotland abolished torture. While imprisonment was considered to be an improvement, it was not much better. Prisoners had to pay for their food. Prisons were cold and dirty with human waste, rotten food, rats, and disease. Prisoners were shackled and did hard labor when they were awake. Prisons were essentially death camps. Over time, the conditions of the prisons improved. Even executions were on the decline. Public executions were abolished and were more humane in how people were executed. In 1822, England had 222 capital offenses on the books, including poaching, counterfeiting, and robbing a rabbit warren. With the average trial length lasting only eight and a half minutes, it was likely that many innocent people were imprisoned or executed.[41]

The Decline of War

After World War II, the number of wars as well as the destructiveness of these wars decreased considerably, in part because the major powers stopped waging direct war on each other. The number of battle deaths since the late 1940's after World War II have fallen from about 500 thousand a year to about 30 thousand a year in the early 2000's. This equates to a 94 percent drop.[42]

Just because we had two world wars in the 20th century does not make this the most violent time for humanity. The only way World War II could take place with such intensity, was due to the technology we developed, mostly being able to fly, which included bombing strikes in Europe and the nuclear bombing of Hiroshima and Nagasaki, which in turn essentially ended the war.

World War II had approximately 55 million deaths, the most of any war in human history. World War I had 15 million deaths, but this was considered to be a much more gruesome war than World War II. In comparison to previous wars, the An Lushan Revolt in China in the 8th century killed 36 million people. However, when the world population at the time is adjusted to make a comparison to the mid-20th century population, it would equate to 429 million people killed. The Mongol conquest in the 13th century killed 40 million people. When adjusted to the mid-20th century population, this would equate to 278 million people killed. Pinker lists twenty-one major wars that took place throughout human history. When the death tolls of these wars were adjusted to the mid-20th century world population, World War II comes in ninth place and World War I comes in sixteenth place. Many of these wars that were more destructive are wars that many people today are not aware of.[43]

Many of the wars of the more distant past were far more brutal than they are now. While wars were smaller in size, they were more prevalent and there were many more of them. It should also be noted that between the 15th and 17th centuries, the great powers fought each other frequently – over 75 percent of the time. Between the mid 1800's and mid 1900's, the great powers were at war much less frequently – less than 20 percent of the time.[44] As surprising as this may sound, after World War II, the major powers have not fought directly with each other at all. There were a number of smaller proxy wars that involved small nations. For example, the Korean War lasted from 1950 to 1953, which involved the U.S. and China. The Cold War, which lasted from 1945 to 1991, involved the Soviet Union and the U.S., yet not even a single shot was fired.[45] As governments become more democratic and more accountable to their people, the less likely they will engage in such destructive acts, and focus more on international commerce.

There were not only more wars in the past, but there were also many more quarrels among individuals that resulted in murder.[46] People had very poor social skills and men often competed in more violent "survival of the fittest" type competition such as duels. If there is little or no government there will likely be more violence. In the middle ages, government had very little presence over such a vast amount of land. This is similar to what we think of the "Wild West," where people took the law into their own hands. Simply having a police presence or cleaning up an area and taking care of the minor crimes will help reduce crime. The less people accept the legitimacy of their government and it's laws, the more likely they will take matters into their own hands.[47]

Since the end of the Cold War in 1991, all kinds of organized conflict, including civil wars, genocides, and terrorist attacks, have declined even further throughout the world.[48] Even though we engaged in the Gulf War in the early 1990's and the War on Terror (which includes both the Afghanistan and Iraq war in the 2000's), the total number of battle deaths in these wars combined, pale in comparison to the number of battle deaths in the Korean War or the Vietnam War.

Today there are more peacekeeping forces, which have helped ease tensions by negotiating settlements. Coincidentally the numbers of civil wars have also decreased.[49] As countries have become more democratized, less corrupt, and have increased international trade, they have also become less violent. In the twentieth century, totalitarian governments killed a total of four percent of their population. Authoritarian governments killed one percent of their population, while democracies were responsible for killing 0.4 percent of their population.[50]

It would surprise most people to know that even terrorism is declining. The terrorist attack on September 11, 2001 killed nearly three thousand people. However, other than on 9/11, the number of people killed by terrorist attacks on American soil between 1970 and 2007 was 340, of which 165 were killed by Timothy McVeigh in Oklahoma City.[51] In no way is this trying to make light of what took place on 9/11, nor am I suggesting that we do not need to be vigilant, because this is a constant threat, not necessarily by other nations, but by individuals.

Around 3,350 people died on US soil from terrorist attacks from 1970 to 2013. Every year 40,000 plus people die in traffic accidents, 20,000 people die from falls, 3,000 from drowning, 3,000 from fires, and 24,000 from accidental poisoning.[52] In regards to homicide, about 18,000 people are murdered, and over 9,000 of these homicides involve a firearm. In the past 43 years, the average number of people who die per year from terrorists equates out to about 78 people per year.

Research by cognitive psychologist Gerd Gigerenzer estimated that in the year following the 9/11 attacks, 1,500 Americans, who regularly would have flown, ended up being killed in car accidents because they chose to drive instead of fly, out of a fear of terrorist attacks.[53]

You might be surprised to hear that US airlines had about 13 hijackings in the 1970s. You may have forgotten about groups responsible for bombings, hijackings, and shootings such as the Irish Republican Army, the Jewish Defense League, the Black Liberation Army, the Weather Underground, the Ulster Freedom Fighters, the Red Brigade, or the Red Army, among many others.[54]

The fact is that terrorist groups almost always fail and die off. Even if they are successful, their success is short lived. Political pressure such as economic sanctions have about a 33 percent chance of success. The actions of McVeigh, which killed 165 people including women and children, only weakened the right-wing antigovernment militia movement in the U.S.[55]

The Advancement of Human Rights

Since the Universal Declaration of Human Rights was enacted in 1948, humanity has become increasingly intolerant of aggression and violence against people.[56] Over the past several decades there have been advancements in civil rights, women's rights, children's rights, gay rights, and animal rights. It took thousands of years for us to get to this point, because before this period of time, these people had no voice.

Between the 17th and 19th century in the United States, many different religious groups and immigrant groups, such as the Irish and the Chinese, came under attack. Genocide was committed against Native Americans. There were thousands of lynchings before the late 1800's, but between the 1890's and the 1950's the number of lynchings dropped significantly.

In the 1940's and early 1950's, a majority of Americans said they were opposed to black children attending white schools. Up to the early 1960's about half of respondents said they would move away if a black family moved next door. By the 1980's, these numbers were in the single digits.[57] While in the late 1950's only 5 percent of white Americans approved of interracial marriage, by 2008, 80 percent approved. Research by political scientists Victor Asal and Amy Pate has shown that in 1950, 44 percent of governments had discriminatory policies. In 2003, only 19 percent of governments had discriminatory policies.[58]

What's interesting is that in the early 2000's with the 9/11 attacks and the London and Madrid bombings, there were no riots against Muslims. In fact, in 2008, the human rights group Human Rights First found not one clear case of fatal violence on Muslims in the West that was motivated by anti-Muslim hatred.[59]

Before the women's rights movement, women were considered to be the property of their father, and then of their husband when they married. The husband had the authority to 'discipline' his wife and had the final say. It was not considered wrong for a husband to rape his own wife.[60] Marital rape was considered an impossibility. In 1736, Sir Matthew Hale wrote in his legal treatise *History of the Pleas of the Crown*, that marital rape could not be recognized because the wife "hath given up herself un this kind unto her husband, which she cannot retract."[61]

If somebody else raped a man's wife, it was a crime committed against the man and not the wife. It was considered damage to a man's property or as theft.[62] This thinking began to change in the 18th century.

Before the mid 1970's marital rape was legal in all fifty states and it wasn't until the early 1990's that marital rape became illegal in all states.[63] In the 1970's, many Western countries repealed laws that treated women as possessions of their husbands. A man could no longer claim justifiable provocation when he killed his adulterous wife or her lover. A man could no longer legally confine his wife to the home, and it no longer was a crime for family and friends to "harbor" or give sanctuary to a wife who fled the home.[64] Before the 1980's domestic abuse was considered a private issue and a low priority for police.

Over time, more and more people were opposed to violence against women. FBI crime reports show that rape has declined over 80 percent between 1973 and 2008.[65] Surveys that measured people's attitudes towards women's rights between 1970 and 1995, showed that attitudes improved, and by the 1990's, men's attitudes towards women were actually more feminist than those of women in the 1970's.[66]

In 1968, twenty percent of men thought it was OK for a husband to slap is wife. In 1994, this attitude fell to ten percent. In 1992, women reported half the number of severe assaults committed by their husbands than in 1985. These rates fell by nearly two-thirds from 1993 to 2005.[67]

The Children's Rights Movement also made some major advancements. I've often heard people talk about the "good ol' days" where people spanked (and even slapped) their children when they did wrong. If you go back fifty years, people were more likely to spank or slap their children. But if you go back a couple of hundred years, they were even tougher on their children. One survey that was conducted in the second half of the 18th century, found that 100 percent of American children were at some point beaten with a stick, whip, or other weapon.[68]

While we are familiar with the term "spare the rod and spoil the child", there were other expressions that were used, including "better to beat your child when small than to see him hanged when grown," and "better whipt than damned".[69] In Medieval times children were beaten and whipped. Instruments such as a cat-o'-nine tails, canes, and iron rods were used to bruise and bloody the body. In 18th century England, one seven-year-old girl stole a petticoat. Do you want to know what her punishment was? She was hung…not by her parents or an angry mob, but by the justice system.[70] Even at the turn of the 20th century, German children "were regularly placed on a red-hot iron stove if stubborn, tied to their bedposts for days, thrown into cold water or snow to 'harden' them, [and] forced to kneel for hours every day against the wall on a log while the parents ate and read".[71] In no way was this limited to Europe; these abuses were worldwide in places like Egypt, Greece, China, among other places. Even fairy tales were full of tales of murder and torture. One verse even starts off with "Murdered by my mother, Eaten by my father…".[72] Many of these stories we read today are white washed.

The rates for physical abuse declined 50 percent between 1990 and 2007,[73] even at school, where mass shootings, bullying, and suicide understandably make headlines. There are postings on social media websites such as YouTube that show teens getting into fights, but these images do not portray the reality. The reality is that everything from fighting, theft, sexual assault, and robbery have all gone down.[74] The difference today is that we are much more aware of these issues.

Gay rights have come a long way too. Many governments and citizens have justified violence towards homosexuals, and some still do. While homosexuality is now legal in nearly 120 countries, it is still against the law in 80 countries and is punishable by death in seven countries.[75] In the United States, between 1970 and 2003, every state decriminalized homosexuality.

While in the past, homosexuality was hidden 'in the closet', more people feel safe to come out today. Public opinion towards gay marriage has changed greatly in just the past decade. The 2013 Supreme Court rulings on the Defense of Marriage Act and Proposition 8 were major steps in recognizing same-sex marriages.

Animal rights have taken longer to establish since animals literally cannot speak out about wrong doings and the pain they experience. In the past, many people did not think animals felt pain. Not just humans, but all sentient beings have the capacity to feel pain. Over the past few decades, there have many reforms that advanced animal rights. There have been restrictions in how animals are used in research, product testing, entertainment, and even the treatment of animals in slaughterhouses, along with the whole design of slaughterhouses.

Establishing these rights was a rebellion against the conformist establishment. As with any rebellion though, there is likely to be violence. When there was a threat to end slavery, there was a civil war. When Martin Luther King made his famous speech, some saw this as a threat to the establishment, and King was assassinated. There are not only violent responses by the establishment, but there are also violent revolts. Throughout history, there have been revolutionary overthrows or coups of governments. The level of violence is often in response to the degree of suppression. This can happen when people don't have a voice or when people feel like they are not being heard.

The 1960's, 70's, and 80's were a backlash against the conformist establishment. There were protests and riots that became violent. As the anti-establishment attitude became more popular, people developed a more negative attitude towards those in power. For a few decades, the crime rate went up considerably. In the 1990's the crime rate once again was coming back down, and despite all the stories we hear, or the images we see on TV, crime and violence are now down to historic lows.

What We Learned Over the Past Century

When World War II broke out in the 1940's the people in the United States worked together like a well-oiled machine to stop the threat. The conformity of the 1950's was a result of the need to conform during World War II. Men had the same haircuts, and women had the same laughs. Do like I do. Go to church. Eat three square meals a day. These are the rules of society, and if you thought differently, you were probably a communist. These were the days of the McCarthy Hearings.

With conformity, you are really not allowed to express yourself and show your true feelings. Don't mistake conformity with unity. Conformity is where people put themselves into a specific standard. Unity is the bringing together of different people or entities. Imagine "The Conformist States of America".

Conformity is mechanical and superficial, which is why the 1950's conformity brought on the 1960's rebellion against the 'establishment' – The rise of the Hippy generation. People were sick of "authority" and did not want to put up with it any longer. The hippy/peace/drug movement was a backlash against the authoritative tactics. This generation wanted to open peoples' minds. They lashed out against the "thought police" and the "Narks". The hippy movement was about peace, but it also was about doing your own thing. People wanted to express their individuality.

In the late 1960's and early '70's, books such as *I'm OK, You're OK* helped people understand and improve social skills. Movements sprang up, such as Transactional Analysis, and PET – Parent

Effectiveness Training, which taught parents things like effective listening skills.

The next generation (Generation X) learned from their "hippy" parents and followed their own path. They were taught to think for themselves and to be themselves. This in turn brought, among other things, a cartoon pink fingerprint character I saw on commercials from Saturday morning cartoons in the 1970's. This character, being a fingerprint would tell the viewers how they were special and unique (like a fingerprint). I wonder if this social thinking brought on the perceived selfishness of this generation. These people learned to look out for themselves and therefore were more selfish.

As this generation grew, people seemed to be shocked that we were so into ourselves. We focused on ourselves and played our video games. It was almost as if we started going too far in the other direction. In the U.S., the American dream was coming alive for some, yet we appeared to be more sad and lonely than ever.

Selfishness can only last so long and go so far before it ends up destroying society, or until people become aware. As people become aware of how their selfishness can affect others in negative ways, the more they want to help others.

Many of the problems we face are just part of the learning process. It's part of the evolution of society. As with technology, there are going to be many failures. People don't just invent things without overcoming hurtles, just like society does not advance without overcoming social hurtles.

We can blame different generations, but this is just a natural pattern. Extremely tough times call for conformity. As conformity leads to rebellion (because individuals are unique in nature), rebellion leads to a focus on oneself. While focusing on oneself is important in some ways, it also can mean selfishness in other ways, and a selfish attitude will only go so far before people realize that they need to include each other. As people become aware of the bigger picture, the more likely they will care and want to make a change.

While we have evolved both technologically and socially. In the past century, we experienced a technological revolution. It is also worth noting that, in the 1960's, people were talking about social revolution. As we look back on this, it appears that nothing ever came of it…or as so it seems.

Conclusion

The fact is that social skills are learned. Social etiquette is learned. Self-control is learned. Empathy is learned. Like how we learned to develop technology over thousands of years, it too will take centuries and even millennia to improve how we interact with each other. As our knowledge of technology grows, so does our knowledge of social skills and connectedness. Overall, more educated societies, tend to be more healthy, wealthy, and less violent.

While you still may think that humanity is more violent and worse off today, just be thankful and know that you do not live in an environment where your family is forcefully split up and you never get to see them again, or worse, you are forced to see them shot in the head, one by one. Be thankful that you have freedom of thought and religion, where you are not brutally tortured, disemboweled, or burned at the stake, for having different beliefs or think differently from that of the establishment. Be thankful you live in an environment where the greatest threat to your survival is you; i.e. your recklessness and/or disregard for your own health.

While things have greatly improved, the sad part of all this is that there is still violence today. We still live in a world that has hatred, violence, crime, and injustice…but the good news is that – We are sick and tired of it and we want to see change!

CHAPTER 4

HOW WE SEE OURSELVES
AND EACH OTHER

If we want to build a better world, we need to get a better understanding of each other. This is why companies spend millions of dollars in consumer research. In Jonah Lehrer's book *Imagine – How Creativity Works*, he writes about how Procter & Gamble wanted to improve the mop. They hired a design firm, which set up video recorders in people's homes recording them mopping their floors. What they didn't realize was that, as many people do, they cleaned their homes first, before the observers came. People often change the way they act when they known they are being watched. So people were mopping their already clean floors with a mop that did not need a whole lot of rinsing. When the observers noticed that people pre-cleaned their floors, they intentionally spilled some coffee grounds on the floor before the observation. They then realized that when people rinsed dirty mops, the process of rinsing the mop was more work than the mopping itself. In one case, they watched a woman sweep up some coffee grounds. After she finished sweeping, she then wet a paper towel to get the remaining grounds. What they realized was that instead of improving upon the mop, they needed an entirely new product. The Swiffer became such a big hit because these observers spent so much time understanding others, in this case, understanding how people mopped.[1]

The Images We Portray

While it may seem like we know people, how well do we really know each other deep down? Our interactions with others are affected by how we interpret their actions. The actions we take are also affected by how we perceive ourselves, and how we think others perceive us. Predictive Index® is a program that incorporates a simple word association test where people check off words they feel describe the way they are expected to act by others and words they believe really describe themselves. Based on this small amount of information, Predictive Index® is able to determine with a high degree of accuracy what motivates a person and how they react in certain situations. Regardless of the reality, if we think others hate us, that will affect how we act. So imagine what your life would be like if you were convinced that everybody hated you. Conversely, what would your life be like if you believed that everybody loved you?

The five people described below seem like typical people you may meet on any given day. While reading about them, you may think you like or dislike them.

- Mike is the CEO of a major corporation. He graduated at the top of his class and attended Harvard University. Mike enjoys the finer things in life, drives a high-end sports car, and he wears tailor-made suits.

- Joe is a neo-Nazi skinhead. He wears a ratty tee shirt, leather jacket with army boots, and has several tattoos to help show what he believes.

- Sara is a popular high school cheerleader, yet some peers think of her as a snobby rich bitch, because she always talks about the fun things she does, like jet setting to Paris this summer with her family.

- Doug is independent and does not need to conform to the norm. He does not care what others think of him, and prefers not to waste his time with the 'sheep' that follow the crowd.

- Janet is a practical person who likes to curl up with a good book and she fights for important causes.

Within a split second of meeting others, we are unconsciously making judgments. We notice things like how they dress, their cleanliness, or what kind of car they drive. We notice non-verbal things like their vocal pitch or demeanor. As we learn more about them, they will tell us about what they do for a living, where they live, what they like to do in their spare time, their likes and dislikes, or what music they like. People act and dress in certain ways depending on whom they are with, the occasion, the mood they are in at the moment, or how they feel overall. There are books and organizations that help people dress correctly to influence an audience. A defendant in a trial may dress like an honest, respectable citizen or a politician may be advised to wear a specific tie to convey a certain image. But this is not reality. It is just an image.

Based on this limited information, people make pre-judgments, which are a natural part of life and are critical for survival. We rely on stereotypes and generalizations, simplifying others and ourselves into various categories. But what do these categories say about what a person feels deep inside?

To fit into these categories, we wear "masks" and do what we can to associate with certain images. We wear different masks with different people. We may want to impress others by making ourselves look smarter or cooler, giving people reasons to like us. We may talk about our accomplishments or the fun things we did. A person may wear a tee shirt advertising where they've been, where they wish to go to, or what music they like. They may play the music they like loud enough to show others what they like, which also may show how they are feeling at the moment. Some people put little signs on their desks or stickers on their cars to tell us what they believe.

> "We fall into stereotypes – labeling and categorizing others in simpleminded ways, then making judgments on the basis of our prejudices. Members of different ethnic groups are lazy or dishonest, we may think. This kind of simplism robs others of their humanity,".
>
> Dr. M. Scott Peck

Masks are a way of selling ourselves. In one online survey of about 18,000 people, 73.5 percent of respondents said that they never lied on a résumé, yet it was found that 53 percent of résumé and job applications contained falsifications and 78 percent of résumés were misleading.[2]

These "masks" are ways in which we avoid showing our true selves. Hiding who you really are is much easier and less vulnerable than risking being rejected or manipulated. Some people act mean and reject others, before anybody is able to reject them. Some people act like they don't care.

When people wear masks that are cloaked in vagueness, the interpretation of these actions becomes even more distorted. Because social interaction is often superficial, people build up these false images (or masks) of themselves over the years. Wearing these masks for so much of our lives, we often do not even realize that we are wearing them. We lose touch with who we really are.

The following examples give more information on the five people described above:

- Sara does not at all think of herself as a 'snobby rich bitch'. She sees herself as nice, warm, friendly, and engaging.

- Joe wants to build a better world but he has a lot of anger in him. He wants to fall in love one day and have kids.

- Janet, like Joe wants to build a better world. She fights for human rights, animal rights, and so on.

- Doug considers himself to be a nice guy, but is very judgmental and thinks that Joe is a freak, Sara is superficial, Janet probably wants to sip her mocha while attending a poetry reading, and Mike is what's wrong with America.

- Mike describes himself as a self-starter, a real go-getter, mover and shaker, and is confident. He drives fast, is a jet setter, and he doesn't tolerate crap. His motto is that you have to pull yourself up by your own bootstraps, like he did.

While some people describe themselves in certain ways, they don't necessarily understand why they are that way. In some cases people don't realize how they behave in front of others. They may think of themselves as friendly, yet don't realize how mean or rude they can appear to others. One person I interviewed explained to me how everybody would tell her that she was negative, yet she did not think she was and was just 'telling it like it is'. I was shocked when she told me this, because she was one of the most negative people I knew. Some people may think they are 'fighting' for world peace, yet put all their energy towards being angry with the 'opposing' political party, government, or religion. Some of these people may think of themselves as loving, yet don't realize how much anger they have in them. They feel their anger is justified. Imagine how effective psychologists could be if they could pull up video footage of patients in their daily lives and compare that to what the patient says. It could also be effective for patients to see their own actions on video.

People are Not Who They Appear to Be

What we see on the outside is often not what is really going on in the inside. We don't know Mike, Joe, Sara, Doug, and Janet as well as we think we do.

- Mike did not pull himself up by his own bootstraps. He was privileged to go to a private school with a great reputation. He went into the family business, and he had no friends when he was a kid. While Mikes considers himself successful, he is now on his third marriage.

- Joe is frustrated and can never seem to make things happen. It's as if he is always in crisis mode. He loves his dog and treats her better than most guys treat their girlfriend. He is sensitive and feels alone.

- Sara's trip to Paris with her family was constant fighting and arguing as always. She wishes things would get better, but they don't. The idea of her parents getting divorced frightens her every day, but wonders if it would be for the better. She wants to win approval from people by showing everyone what a fun person she is.

- Doug felt rejected by others at a younger age, so he plays his own game by his own rules. He will be sure to reject you before you even have a chance to reject him.

- Janet is somewhat socially awkward, so she retreats into her books or the *New York Times*, while living in Los Angeles.

The reality is that some people feel bad about themselves. They feel frustrated. They don't like how they look, or they are dealing with weight issues. Some people feel isolated, alone, withdrawn, or different. Some people feel dumb and don't think they will amount to anything. Some people think they were just "born bad." Some people hate themselves. Some people are experiencing severe pain or illness. Some "normal kids" you meet at school are living out of a car at night.

Someone can come from a poor background and have a great life, while another person can have everything, yet their personal life is a wreck. Dana Plato who was a star in the 1970's hit *Different Stroke's* ended up dying of a drug overdose. Marilyn Monroe committed suicide. We write these people off as having a drug addiction or as someone who suffers from depression, as if it were out of their control. Yet we fail to understand why they became addicted to drugs, or why they were depressed.

> "Everyone sees what you appear to be,
> few experience what you really are."
> Niccolò Machiavelli
> The Prince

Some people had parents who were very controlling, who constantly criticized them, or did not pay enough attention to them. Some parents may have kids who are easy to work with, while other parents, regardless of having decent parenting skills, have kids who were very difficult to deal with. Being difficult to deal with does not make one a bad person. We think we know others, and we think we know ourselves, but if we are living in a world of false images, who are we?

If We Don't Understand People, Then We Cannot Understand Society

If you think you cannot make changes in your personal life, you are less likely to try to make a change. Instead of dealing with these problems head on, it is often easier to avoid them. But when you avoid dealing with your problems, they will just resurface in different ways. No matter how much you have it together, no matter how much money you have, and no matter how great society will ever be, we will all deal with problems throughout our lives.

Some problems seem unsolvable or out of control. Some people strive for a happy family life, yet every time things seem to start getting better, it goes back to how it was. Some people 'try their luck' at marriage, as if they were playing craps or a slot machine. The odds are a little over 50 percent of having a 'successful' marriage, but that does not account for unhappy marriages. Some people suffer from depression or are angry, but they don't know why. I suspect that in many cases, the real reason lies below all the small and large issues that have occurred over the years. In the movie *Crash*, Sandra Bullock's character was on the phone telling her friend; "I wake up like this every morning! I am angry all the time, and I don't know why." While this may simply appear to be a personal problem, this anger is very likely a part of something much bigger. In this case, her character does not even understand why she is angry all the time. A second message in this scene emphasizes the underlying problem of a lack of communication. Bullock's character is trying to open up about a problem to her friend over the phone, but the friend interrupts and says she needs to go. Both figuratively and literally the line of communication was disconnected.

The perceived problem is that some people are just angry, mean, or depressed, as if it is their disposition in life. Because there has always been bullying, we presume that there will always be bullying, as if it is human nature. With all the war and violence, it can seem that it is in our nature to destroy ourselves. It appears that this is the "reality" of life. But if we do not understand our personal problems and the problems other people face, how can we possibly solve them?

As long as we continue this illusion that we know each other, when we really don't, we will never get ahead. When we only understand our personal problems and each other on a superficial level, then we only understand society on a superficial level. If we don't understand the individual or society, then how are we to understand the problems of society? C. Wright Mills, who wrote *The Sociological Imagination*, explained that when people rationalize personal problems and social issues, they will more likely adapt to them and will be less willing to try to solve or even think about them.

The reality is that our problems are much deeper and more complex than they appear. In order to understand a person's actions, you need to understand what is happening inside that person. The more people are aware of other people's existence, the less likely they are willing to abuse others and the more they will understand each other.

Conclusion

We think we have it all figured out. We think we know each other. We think we know who is smart, who is dull, who has their life together, who our friends are and who are our enemies. But we don't have it all figured out, and we know we don't. We have false perceptions of each other and the little that we do know is just the tip of the iceberg. With superficial interactions, we build a superficial society that is made up of false images.

The reality is that people are dealing with many problems of which we are unaware. We cannot connect with each other when we hide our problems. With all the problems we face as individuals and as a society, at times, solving these problems can seem beyond our control. It appears that people just don't change. When people are not able to solve their problems, it can cause frustration where people end up taking it out on themselves and/or others.

Instead of telling you that you can solve the problems you face in life, and that you just need to try harder and be more focused, what if I told you that the reality is that some of the personal problems you face may be beyond your control? I'm not referring to unavoidable problems such as being laid off or certain health issues,

but problems that should be solvable on your own. What if I told you
that some of these problems that seem nearly impossible to solve, *are*
truly nearly impossible to solve?

What if I told you that there are greater social forces
affecting your life in a big way?

CHAPTER 5

OUR PERCEPTION OF THE PROBLEM

When trying to solve a problem, logically, we look at the source of the problem and we try to fix it. If your car is out of gas, then you would put gas into it. If you have cancer, the goal would be to eliminate the cancer.

In trying to solve our personal problems and problems in society, logically we look for the source of the problem and try to figure out a solution. In order to understand the problems of society, it is important to learn about the people that make up the society. As we learn more about people, we see that they have personal problems they are dealing with. We also realize that we don't know people as well as we think we do, and that these problems are often more complicated than they appear on the surface. Frequently, these problems are rationalized and not dealt with. Because some problems can be difficult, if not seemingly impossible to solve, this can cause frustration, where people often end up blaming others or themselves.

There are greater social forces that are affecting our lives, but what are these forces? Three major social institutions that have a major influence on us include the family, religion, and politics. In this chapter, we are not focusing on any one specific problem, but are looking at how we go about trying to solve these problems.

The Family

It is said that building a better society begins with the family. But many of the problems in society also begin with the family. Some parents don't realize how big a difference they make in their children's lives.

Parents tend to raise their children based on how they were raised. Some people were raised in violent families or in families where rudeness was common. Many violent criminals come from troubled families. How is someone to know better, if that is all they know? Even when people say they are going to raise their children differently than they were raised, they will still repeat many of the same things their parents did. It's not like parents are given a manual. What works great for one child, may not work at all for another. It can become even more difficult to raise a child when the parents get divorced.

Parents want their children to do well in school and have friends, so they can have a good life. But to accomplish this, they may put too much pressure on their children, affecting them negatively. Some parents yell at or hit their children to teach them a lesson or even blame them for 'destroying the family'. Many parents often fight with each other about how to raise their children, yet it is this fighting that ends up hurting the children the most.

While parents are responsible for their children, some people think that if the child commits a crime, the parents should be put in jail for their children's actions. But, as children grow, they spend less time with their parents. On a typical weekday, a child will be at school for about seven hours. After school, they may hang out with their friends. By the time the parents get home from work, they are rushing to prepare dinner, followed by the kids running off to their room to do their "homework". Some parents work two jobs just to stay afloat, so they have even less time with their children. If you think you know what your children are doing when you are not around, think about how many things you did, that your parents did not know about. Parents are often in disbelief and denial when they hear that their children are bullying other kids at school, breaking Christmas lights in the neighborhood, or are taking drugs.

Religion

Some people think that religion is the answer to many of society's problems. Religion plays a major part in many people's lives, providing morals and giving hope. It provides an explanation for what we do not understand. But while a fundamental value of all the great religions is love, many wars have resulted from religious differences. People who follow one religion, may think their religion is the true faith, and therefore other religions are wrong. If someone speaks from one religion, people of other religions and non-religious people will likely not listen.

Sometimes people get so focused on the little issues, that they lose focus of the greater goal – love. It is understandable that people want to help each other, but unfortunately, some people are so focused on recruiting or converting others to their religion, that they resort to scare tactics and vague threats to get people to join. It's as if they don't really trust the power of love. Most people don't respond well to threats, even vague ones. People are attracted to love and like to be around loving people. If you trust love, then all you need to do is be a loving person.

Blaming religion for causing wars is looking at the result, not the real problem. The problem lies more with how people are connecting with each other, often in negative ways.

Politics

Politics play a critical part in the structure and development of society. Without political structure, a society can fall apart. While political systems and ideas offer ways to organize the structural design of a society, there is often no one right way to go about this. Even experts cannot agree on many issues.

Because democracy involves the engagement of its citizens, political discussion should be encouraged. It is important for people to get involved, vote, and discuss important issues with each other. As C. Wright Mills said, "Freedom is...the chance to formulate the available choices, to argue over them – and then, the opportunity to choose. That is why freedom cannot exist without an enlarged role of human reason in human affairs".[1]

Unfortunately, a lot of people have a hard time discussing politics without getting angry and hostile. Differences on how to build a better society have led to violence, assassinations and even global wars. If people can only discuss politics with others whom they know have similar opinions, like with religion, the underlying problem is less about politics and more about how we communicate.

Political discussions can become uncivilized when people rely on broad generalizations and sound bites in trying to understand different opinions. People are more likely to react to negative information that imposes an immediate or potential threat, which is why political campaigns can get so negative. People will often use the opposing party or parties as a scapegoat for the problems in society. When you listen only to one point of view, other points of view may see insane. Yet most people can agree that it is important to have a tight budget, that people deserve a proper pay, and so on.

It is commonly believed that a democracy is the best political system, because it gives people the freedom to voice their opinion. But even democracies have problems. Thomas Jefferson was quoted as saying; "A democracy is nothing more than mob rule, where 51 percent of the people may take away the rights of the other 49 percent." Gandhi said that there are unjust laws as there are unjust men. "Even if your are a minority of one, the truth is the truth." So even if the vast majority of the population feels or thinks that something is right does not make it true or right. Believe it or not, dictatorships, socialism, and even anarchy have a place in the development of society. Every person has lived in a dictatorship as a young child under his or her parents' rule.

There are many societies in our world that do not have the same rules as the United States and they run just fine. Let's take, for example, the United States and Singapore. In the United States, we pride our selves on freedom. But Singapore has freedom too, just in a whole different sense. While in the U.S., people are warned not to go into certain areas of town, Singapore is a country where it is very safe for anyone to go anywhere and is one of the safest cities in the world. If someone lost their wallet or purse, chances are that the police would return it to them, along with all the money inside it. I've talked to women who were working and living in Singapore as teachers, and they loved knowing that they felt safe and free.

In the United States we have some tough laws against crime, but Singapore is much tougher. The government has no problem just chopping stuff out of TV programs or movies, without even trying to pretend that nothing happened. Big Brother is watching. Singapore is often considered to be a "fine" city, in that it has hefty fines for many things like smoking, spitting, and even chewing gum. The penalty for firing a gun is death! With these strict laws, its no wonder people feel safe, unless of course, they are the ones breaking the law.

How We Tackle Crime

Let's now look at how we go about trying to solve these problems in the scope of tackling crime. When are we too hard or too soft on crime? The answer depends on the society. Every action has a consequential reaction. The consequences of doing something against the law, results in a penalty (rather than a punishment) in the way of a fine, community service, or even jail time. With jail or prison, one is essentially taken out of society, similar to how a child is put in 'time out'.

The more we focus on punishing people, the more people will come to fear government. If we need to get tough on crime, then we need to get tough on crime, but when do we become too extreme? When are we no longer a 'free' society? The tougher on crime we get, the more freedom we lose. When we try to stop crime with threats of punishment and use scare tactics to try to keep people in line, we are using destructive forces to stop destructive forces. This may seem logical, but what good are threats of punishment when the person does not care what happens to him? If a person plans to kill himself, in the process of a violent act, the threat of the death penalty will do no good.

It is a common perception that people can have closure when the guilty are punished. But are we so focused on finding someone to blame just so we can have closure? Sometimes we get so focused on finding someone to blame, that we end up convicting innocent people of crimes they did not commit.

Amanda Knox, an American woman, was convicted in 2009 in Italy for the murder of her roommate Meredith Kercher. After she served four years in prison, her case was overturned. When she was found innocent, people proclaimed that the system worked. But I think it did not. What if Amanda's family did not have the money to appeal? She would be in jail for probably an additional twenty plus years. In addition, she had already gone to prison for four years. Let's take this a step further. What if Knox was overweight, unattractive, and suffered from depression? How innocent would she seem now?

How many innocent people are there who seem guilty beyond a reasonable doubt and are convicted? Imagine if this was your life. How would this make you feel? Regardless of a person's faith in the justice system, or in God, people have been presumed guilty and convicted of crimes they did not commit. In the United States, between 1973 and October 1, 2012, 141 people who were on death row, were either acquitted of all charges, had the charges against them dismissed by the prosecution, or were granted a complete pardon based on evidence showing their innocence. In eighteen of these cases, DNA played a substantial factor.[2] Before we were able to test for DNA, these people would have been executed.

Imagine what it would be like if your son or daughter was put to death, only to have the system tell you that they made a mistake. If you think that it would never happen to your child, just realize that it happened to someone's child, and it has happened many times throughout history.

While it may appear that crime is the underlying problem, punishing someone who committed a crime is just the reaction to the criminal action. It has very little to do with solving the actual problem. So if we are trying to solve problems in society (social problems) by getting tough on crime, no matter how tough we get on crime, the underlying problem will still be there.

If you had a leak in a pipe under your sink, to fix this problem, the first thing you might do is put a bucket under the leak to prevent more water from spilling onto the floor. The water stops leaking onto the floor but is still leaking from the pipe. The sink, pipe, and cupboard under the sink represent society structure. The water flowing through the pipe represents people. The leak represents the problem, and the "bad" water that is leaking represents the "bad" people. Now obviously the water that has traveled down this leaky path in life is not "bad" water, just like how people are not necessarily bad, but have just traveled down a path that has dealt them some bad cards in life. If you've been dealt a lot of bad cards in life, chances are you are going to be upset and get angry. You might argue that there are hardened criminals who don't change. Yes, that can be true, but this is like hard water (water that has a high mineral content). When water is "born", coming down from the "heavens", it is not hard water, but only becomes hard water, based on the environment it's in. How many hardened criminals have come into this world wielding a knife?

While you do need to fix the pipe, you don't need to do it right now because maybe there is a great football game on TV. Then there may be another football game after that, so you will probably need another bucket to hold these "criminals". In the U.S. it seems that our strategy on tackling crime is to get tough on crime. In order to deal with over crowded prisons, we react by building even more prisons, like how we temporarily solve the leak under the sink by getting more buckets. By doing this, we are only dealing with the immediate problem, but not the underlying issue.

This is clearly shown in the fact that the United States incarcerates more people than any other country in the world. According to the International Centre for Prison Studies, the U.S. prison population (per 100,000) is 716. Only 2.2 percent of countries and dependent territories have prison population rates over 500, and nearly 85 percent of countries and dependent territories have prison population rates below 300 per 100,000 people.[3]

While prisons are often called correctional centers, there is nothing correctional about them. Prisons are often violent. When there is overcrowding, some prisoners are sent out of state where they have no family, and many don't have much of a release program. Many studies have shown that people come out of prison worse off than when they went in. Between 60 and 70 percent of people incarcerated commit crimes again when they get out of prison.

How We React to the Problem

Everyday on the news we see 'random' acts of violence. So we worry and look for warning signs in people. We learn to be suspicious of strangers. We lock our doors. We carry our guns. We want to protect ourselves from all the crazy people out there, but then wonder if we ourselves are starting to go crazy. With all the problems that we hear about, the world seems to not make sense anymore.

Any time after an event like 9/11 or a mass shooting, we, as a society, want to make sure something like this never happens again, so naturally, we react. On April 20, 1999, two students, Dylan Klebold and Eric Harris went on a shooting rampage, killing twelve other students and a teacher, and then ended up killing themselves. The Columbine massacre was a tragic day for the entire country. But what did we learn from this event? We learned to be on the lookout for the next potential lunatic to go off. In reaction to school shootings, some schools have practiced mock drills that have in some cases included students playing the role of wounded victims, and in at least one case have even used a helicopter. In the Los Angeles area, schools practiced mock violent acts; where a cop dressed as a thug, comes in and holds students hostage. The program's goal was to teach kids how to deal with and cope with school shootings, just in case it ever happens again.

Going a little deeper, we learned to take a zero tolerance towards bullying with severe consequences. We started 'preventative' programs. I put quotes around "preventative" because by the time someone goes into one of these programs, it may already be far too late for them. Unfortunately students end up falling through the cracks, and these programs along with psychological counseling can only help so much. The Columbine shooters were already going through programs designed to help, but in these programs they were just manipulating the system by telling people what they wanted to hear.

Some parents tell their children that other students are unpredictable and can be dangerous.[4] Kids are growing up learning not to trust anyone, and to only look out for themselves and not others. In addition, kids learn that it is a dangerous world and schools are no exception. This type of thinking is harmful to society and encourages people not to socialize with others beyond their close friends.

Conclusion

People want to make their lives and society a better place. We turn to self-help books and psychologists, but there are so many problems and external issues that impact our lives. We turn to the family, but so many families are plagued with problems of their own. We turn to religion but there are many issues between people of different religions, non-religious people, and even people within the same church. We turn to politics but people are often so focused on what they think is the right way, that they don't try to understand each other. When you really look at an issue, there rarely is only one right way to fix it.

It does not take much to frighten people and spread rumors. Put a couple of these stories together, and it can seem like we are facing the end of the world. We hear a few stories of how the guilty go free, so we want to make sure to get extra tough on sentencing. We see a news report on political corruption and presume corruption is widespread, yet it is not. We see a crowd of "Muslims" burning the U.S. flag and think this is how most Muslims think. We see headlines like "What you don't know could kill you!"

We see these problems and we get mad. We want to find those who are responsible. We want to punish the guilty. But even if all these people who go to jail are guilty, and I suspect that the vast majority of them are, this is the result of social failure. Throwing people in prison does not build a better system or fix the underlying problem.

Many crimes go undetected, unreported, or unsolved. Only some people are caught and fewer are convicted. According to FBI statistics, in 2011 the percent of crimes that were cleared (resolved) are included on the chart below:

Murder	64.8%
Aggravated Assault	56.9%
Forcible Rape	41.2%
Robbery	28.7%
Larceny-theft	21.5%
Burglary	12.7%
Motor Vehicle Theft	11.9%

FBI 2011 Statistics[5]

I remember seeing some show on television where the announcer said things like "The hopelessness of crime!" and "We will bring you videos every week!" In sentencing, one judge is "too easy," while another judge is "very tough." On the news how often do you hear how the suspects have not been caught or are still at large? Even when suspects are caught and punished, in the case of murder, does that bring back the victim? We can use video cameras to help catch people, and thus reduce crime, but we would only be keeping people in check. If we get tough on bullying, the people who bully will just do it more discreetly. No matter how hard we try…even if cameras are on them constantly…even if they are under our control…they will still want to do it. Even if we could stop crime entirely, the reasons people commit crimes are still there…the emotions are still there.

There is still anger.

CHAPTER 6

FALSE PERCEPTIONS DESTROY LIVES

Hatred is like a disease that kills thousands of people every day. This 'disease' is far more deadly than cancer and heart disease put together. It's a disease that no scientist can cure or any politician can stop with laws. It is far more dangerous than any weapon ever created. Like other emotions, hatred, anger, and fear are contagious, and they have the power to destroy lives. These emotions can even lead to the downfall of society.

So often when we hear hateful rhetoric, we respond with hatred. When we see violence, we want to respond with violence. When we see atrocities committed by 'evil' people, we want justice – we want revenge. Victims of crime, violence, and war, want justice and revenge. A terrorist act is committed against the U.S. The U.S. retaliates and, in the process, ends up killing innocent civilians. If terrorists killed someone close to me, I would want justice, just as these innocent civilians want justice. It is pretty simplistic to just say that we need to stop the hatred and the revenge. Because if someone were to kill your family…your children…those you love, you too will give into your anger.

Similar to the energy of a giant tidal wave and the power it can unleash, hatred is a powerful force that can affect generations of people. It causes people to justify violent acts, thinking they are doing the right thing.

Hatred did not start with people like Hitler, Stalin, and Pol Pot. Hatred has been around for thousands of years, and is the same hatred that is still here today. While we may not be angry at the same things as we were centuries ago, it is still negative energy. This anger in humanity is like the coals of a fire that can still be hot the next morning. While some embers have cooled off long ago, some are still glowing red hot. Just like how some people learned hatred from their parents, who learned hatred from their parents.

When parents abuse their child, that child will likely grow up and abuse his or her child. When people are angry, they are angry and will find something to place the blame on. If you don't know who is responsible, you are more likely to just blame a group of people, be it a club, an organization, a corporation, a race, or even a country.

If you were told at a young age who the enemy was, you would believe it. When a person is around others who are negative or violent, that person will likely become negative or violent. If an entire culture is violent, a child raised in this culture will think that violence is a part of the norm. People may see change as useless or may even not notice negative energy or violence, because it is a part of the walls of reality in which they live. In cases like this, breaking the pattern of violence can be nearly impossible.

Our perceptions of people and the problems we face, is often based on the very limited perspective we have. As absolutely sure as we think we are, sometimes our perceptions are skewed or completely false. For thousands of years, people have been falsely accused of things they did not do. Millions of innocent people have been executed based on false accusations. While it is easy to label people as lazy, stupid, or evil, when you take the time to really understand them, you will realize that there is a lot more that explains their actions.

We continue to blame, but who is the enemy? It has been said that violence should only be used as a last resort to solving conflicts, but in so many cases people thought they had no other choice. Self-defense is a natural instinct. When someone is attacked, he or she will either attack back or flee. However, sometimes when people feel like they are being attacked or will be attacked, they may feel like they have no other option than resorting to violence. To get people's attention, sometimes people resort to negative tactics such as controlling, confining, suppressing, manipulation, propaganda, fear, blaming, and advocating hatred. When we try to solve problems in society by using cruel or violent ways, we are terrorizing people: we are terrorists.

How Blaming Turns to Violence

It does not take much for people to become suspicious. It can take just one incident where a person sees or hears about something and then starts imagining of how much worse it can be.

An episode of the *Twilight Zone* (*The Martians Are Due On Maple Street*), summarized how blaming can lead to violence. In the episode, people in a small town see what they think is a meteor fly overhead. Soon after this, unexplainable things start occurring such as cars starting up and then turning back off or houselights coming on then turning off. Because the townspeople do not understand why these issues are occurring they start blaming each other, which leads to frustration, anger and violence.

Between 1692 and 1693, over 150 people were arrested and at least twenty-nine people were sentenced to death, in the Salem Witch Trials. Between the 1500s and 1600s, it was believed that many problems were caused by the devil, and the blame was put onto people thought to be responsible. They were sacrificed to "better society."

Frequently people or organizations create "rumors" to discredit their competition or to convince people to join in some cause. In 1782, a letter was printed in the *Supplement to the Boston Independent Chronicle*, written by a British field officer reporting to his superior that he had some good luck working with American Indians in their fight against the colonials. He also conveyed a letter from a native war leader that lists in detail the scalping and murder of innocent old people, women and children. Hundreds of these scalps were to be sent to British royalty from the American Indians as war trophies. This was shocking news that spread throughout the colonies and eventually throughout Europe. However, there was one thing wrong with this story. There was no field officer, no letter from a field officer to his superior, nor was there a letter from a native war leader. There was no box of scalps. The *Supplement to the Boston Independent Chronicle* was not even a real newspaper. This was all an elaborate hoax perpetuated by Benjamin Franklin, a man highly regarded. This hoax was intended to help the American war effort by turning the public opinion in Europe against the British. This propaganda also perpetuated the image of American Indians as being savage, unsympathetic, and brutal.[1]

On May 4th, 1868, at Haymarket Square in Chicago, Illinois, there was a workers' strike to enact an eight-hour workday. Workers at the time were earning $1.50 per day, ($40 in today's value for nine to fourteen hours a day, six days a week, year round, without time off.) The demonstration was peaceful until someone threw a bomb killing seven police officers and wounding many others. While the evidence showed that none of the defendants on trial threw the bomb, someone had to be blamed. Eight demonstrators were convicted of conspiracy; seven were sentenced to death and one was sentenced to fifteen years in prison. Of the seven who were sentenced to death, four were hanged, one committed suicide, and two had their sentenced reduced to life in prison. They were sacrificed because people needed someone to blame…to better society.

All in the Name of Building a Better Society

When times are tough, people want to find a solution to the problem. We want to make sure that those who are responsible pay for their actions. Before the Holocaust, times were tough, there was an economic depression and people wanted to punish those who they thought were responsible. Hitler made, what he thought was a pre-emptive strike on the Jews. In Berlin of 1942, Hitler said; "This war will not come to an end the way the Jews imagine, with the extermination of the Arian people. Instead it will see the complete annihilation of the Jews."[2] Much of the public supported this, as it seemed to be the final and only solution. While people today conveniently blame Hitler for the Holocaust, this anti-Semitic rhetoric started long before he came to power. Hitler grew up in Austria, which at the time was one of the most anti-Semitic countries in western Europe.[3] Even the newspapers spread fear regarding how Christianity was under attack by the Jews. There is no doubt that this rhetoric had a major effect on Hitler and on the society. Sadly, these rumors seem to echo some of the same sentiment you may hear towards Muslims today. These false perceptions turn into destructive forces against innocent people.

The negative energy that affected Hitler spread globally. The words Hitler used convinced a nation to hate and support the murder of over six million people. It caused instability, fear, and panic across Germany. There were a number of assassination attempts on Hitler by his own military officers. Hitler's quest to conquer the rest of the world caused World War II, and in the end, Germany was destroyed. Hitler had such a build up of negative energy that he wanted Germany to suffer for losing the war and ordered his own soldiers be hunted down and killed. This negative energy lead to Hitler's suicide on April 30th, 1945. His vision was a society that was to last a thousand years. But blaming does not solve the problems of society. Regardless of how determined a person is, when their crime is against humanity, people will eventually turn against them. The higher the degree of suppression, the higher escalation of rebellion.

> ...I remember that all through history, the way of truth and love has always won. There have been tyrants and murders, and for a time they can seem invincible, but in the end they always fall, think of it, always...
>
> Gandhi

As difficult as it might be to accept, it is important to understand that Hitler wanted to create a better society. This was a man who was very passionate, intense, and emotional. He loved dogs and was a good painter. He was also abused as a child.

Many dictators had a vision to build a better society. Pol Pot was quoted as saying; "I want you to know that everything I did, I did for my country."[4] He was responsible for killing roughly one to three million people in Cambodia that had a population of just over eight million people. Hundreds of thousands of people were forced to dig mass graves and were then buried alive to save bullets.[5]

When a dictator is overthrown, there are hopes that things will improve. But this is often not the case. Idi Amin, who overthrew Milton Obote in Uganda, said that he was only going to remain in power until new elections were formed. However, he remained in power from 1971 to 1979 when he was ousted, killing approximately 300,000 people.[6] Milton Obote regained power in 1980, and killed over 100,000 people.

Have We Learned Anything From History?

We say that it is important to learn from history so that we don't make the same mistake again, but what have we learned? We learned to be on the lookout for those who are trying to destroy society, just as Hitler did. Hitler made what he considered to be a pre-emptive strike on the Jews, just as we today make pre-emptive strikes on leaders or groups in other countries.

As we were fighting against Hitler, and his ally Japan, we put Japanese Americans in "internment" camps out of fear that they were the enemy. Within a decade after the Holocaust, our own elected representatives accused thousands of Americans of being Communists or communist sympathizers. Many were arrested and tried based on accusations, even if there was no actual evidence. Many lost their jobs and some were imprisoned. Even associating with people considered to be communist was good enough to have you accused. These people were condemned to better society.

And it continues today. In the aftermath of the Columbine massacre, people looked for someone to blame. Blame was placed on the parents, on the school, down to the police department's response to the crisis, and even on the layout of the school. David Cullen, who wrote *Columbine*, said a newspaper poll found that 83 percent of those polled blamed the parents.[7] Another news poll systematically listed who was to blame for school violence, followed by percentages. Parents had the highest percentage, followed by society, media, kids, guns, and educators in that order.

Who's Most to Blame for School Violence:

Parents:	35.1%
Society:	33.3%
Media:	11.0%
Kids:	10.2%
Guns:	8.8%
Educators:	1.3%
Total Votes:	32,111

This article quoted people saying various things such as; "Parents these days need to watch their kids and know what the kids are doing in their spare time". "The parents should be held responsible and know what is going on in their own home" and "Any paid educator who claims not to know there is a problem is either incompetent or criminally negligent." This is not a criticism of the article, but more of a criticism of how we think as a society.[8]

Who is the Enemy?

We want to get rid of the "evil" people who harm our lives. But what defines a person as evil? Who are the evil people? Are people born evil? The enemy may be the "Evil Empire", the infidels, the terrorists, the gangs, racist people, and so on.

When we see people as the enemy, then naturally, we are less likely to notice anything positive about them. We see one president as having his finger on the button ready to start World War III, while we see another president as a communist who is out to take away our rights and destroy America. Just do a quick search on the Internet and there are hundreds of images of U.S. presidents, both Democrat and Republican, with Hitler mustaches, implying a similarity. While some people saw President Reagan as evil, he used the term 'Evil Empire' to describe how he saw the Soviet Union. Yet, when he visited the Soviet Union, he realized that they were people much like the people in the United States. If we believe there are people who are truly evil from birth, we can go to the hospital and figure out which babies are bad and kill them right there. But we know better. So, if people are not born evil, then the problem lies within society.

How many people have committed terrorist acts in the name of the devil? We hear people say that God is on their side, but how often have you heard people say that God is on the enemy's side? Terrorists do not see themselves as evil terrorists, but as the ones who are fighting the infidels and tyrants, defending their beliefs.

The Columbine shooters were fighting back against those who they felt were out to hurt them…they wanted what they perceived as justice. The racist says that certain races are destructive to society. The anti-racist says racists are destroying society. Religious extremists and Nazi supporters, like many other people, are only doing what they think is right. They see certain people as a threat to themselves and to society.

There are elitists of every race, religion, nation, and many other groups, who think they are superior or have the right answer, and who think negatively of those outside their group.

Going Beyond the Anger and Hatred

When animals are aggressive, there is a logical reason for their aggression. When an animal is physically hurt, that animal can become aggressive and dangerous. For example, when a horse misbehaves in some way not usual for that horse, a good horseman will first explore a possible cause of pain, such as a sore back or leg. The aggression can be due to physical irritation, or the animal may use aggression as a defense mechanism to keep away predators. The aggression can come out of fear or a perceived threat. The animal may be protecting itself, its offspring, territory/home, or a resource such as food. An animal can also be aggressive out of frustration when it is suppressed, dominated, controlled, or denied something. Animals also learn aggression in social situations.

All these traits are in people too. Like with animals, when people are in physical pain, it is pretty understandable that they may be short tempered. Pain can cause you to be irritable and mad. How many times have you cursed or yelled when you got hurt? Similarly, mental pain can also cause irritability and anger. Negative energy often comes from deeper painful emotions. When people have a really bad day, they are not always pleasant to be around. While having a bad day does not excuse meanness, next time you come across someone who is like this, you may want to think about what is going on in his or her life.

When you go beyond the hatred and anger, you will see this pain. When you look closer, you will see that some people suffered through very traumatic experiences as children, experiences most people cannot even imagine.

In his book *Apocalypse*, Charles Strozier interviewed religious extremists, who many have described their life as being unhappy, unfulfilled, and evil, before they were "reborn". Likewise, many of the stories they tell are of violence, revenge, and renewal. They believe that people are born evil, but even the "saved" will constantly struggle against the influences of the devil. "In its Christian form, fundamentalists believe that God will remake the world in a huge firestorm of destruction…"[9] These people seemed to anticipate destruction. God is furious, and will soon end it all. Birds falling from the sky, or the rise of epidemic diseases are all signs that the end is near. 1esus will triumph over evil in violent ways beyond comprehension and will keep the peace by ruling with an iron fist over a thousand years. Anyone who does wrong will be zapped and sent to the lake of fire.[10]

Raphael Ezekiel, who wrote *The Racist Mind*, explains how the white supremacist movement sees the world as a fight to the death between good and evil. They see the world as a violent place, and they see themselves as the good guys. Social isolation plays a role in racially motivated violence: "the militant white racist movement is composed of people who permanently feel in crisis."[11] This permanent feeling of crisis is a characteristic of personality disorders as defined in the Diagnostic and Statistical Manual of Mental Disorders.[12] From their perspective, life is war and everything is mired in secret causes and is not what it appears to be. There is a lot of fear and distrust, even of each other in these groups.[13]

TJ Leyden a former skinhead explained that 'skinheads' are not just angry towards different races, but also anybody who is not "white power". They have a lot of anger towards other members in their group.[14] This negative energy is a result of what they experienced in life.

As we gain a better understanding of people who are religious extremists, racists, or even people who are of different races, we learn that these "enemies" may not bad people.

Ezekiel spent a considerable amount of time working with a racist group in Detroit. Almost every member had lost a parent due to divorce or separation. Seven members reported alcoholism and six reported that there was family violence. Seven members said they served jail or prison time. There was a lot of suspicion among the membership of which almost all were male. Several were born with a medical issue at birth. There were a lot of hospital stories. These are people who are desperate, scared, stranded, isolated and lonely.[15] Their education was lacking. Being in a situation where they feel cheated in life is a motivating factor for joining a group. Many feel like they don't have much of a future and are terrified. The field notes Ezekiel took of the group over the months spoke more about fear. "These were people who at a deep level felt terror that they were about to be extinguished. They felt that their lives might disappear at any moment. They felt that they might be blown away by the next wind. The cues to this were not obvious…" "Joining a tough group made sense on the face of it if you were afraid for your survival." "…these were adolescent children from poor white families, young people from a distressed sector of the world, kids who had found a gig that lifted them from the moment from anonymity."[16]

Ezekiel noticed that many of the people in the group were rather gentle. Ezekiel even took William, one of the teens, who was interested in his work, to do some interviews with black people. Ezekiel told him; "I want you to have the experience of walking into a black home where you don't know a soul, and finding that if you just act like who you normally are, that they're going to like you."[17] Ezekiel **told** William that there's a world of people who want to have dignity and be happy, and for every person who is vicious, there's a hundred who are not.

So let me ask you this. How are we different from animals? Why is it that we understand animal behavior in a logical way and are compassionate, yet when people show the same signs, we reject and scorn them? By categorizing people as good or bad, we are labeling the person, and not the action. Many people, who we think of as evil, have done some really good things in life, and people who we think of as good, have done really bad things. We say that people have choices in life and that these people made their choices. Did people like Hitler or Stalin choose to be brutally beaten as children? One may argue that other people with similar backgrounds did not make these choices but a lot depends on specific circumstances a person faces in life.

Who am I to criticize you for what you think? I don't know what you have been through, what you have seen, and what you have heard in your life. I don't know any of this…I don't know you. Once we have built a good rapport with each other, we can begin to understand each other's lives.

If you are angry, are you really enjoying your life? Do you really think that someone who is happy in life would be full of anger? Do you think the Columbine shooters or anyone who has committed any of these rampages of violence were happy? Are child abusers happy? Are people who are often mean and cruel, happy? When people act out in violent ways or are mean to others, are they really just frustrated in life? Are they in some kind of pain – physical or emotional, which is causing their anger?

How Negative Energy Affects You

Think about how anger affects your body. You will feel it in your muscles, in your heart, and throughout your body. If you have strong intense emotions, it will affect you in strong, intense ways. Anger is like a poison. Our muscles will tense up and it becomes harder to breathe. "There is a swamp of toxic feelings, an unpleasant wash of fear and anger that seems inescapable and, subjectively, takes 'forever' to get over. At this point – full hijacking – a person's emotions are so intense, their perspective so narrow, and their thinking so confused that there is no hope of taking the other's viewpoint or settling things in a reasonable way."[18] Studies show that every time people think of people they hate, their bodies respond with anger, flooding the body with stress hormones that raise blood pressure and compromises their immune system.[19] Redford Williams, M.D. & Virginia Williams, Ph.D., who wrote the book *Anger Kills*, explain how studies have shown that hostile people are more likely to have a weaker immune system, and are more likely to die from cardiovascular disease, coronary disease, or cancer.[20]

People with hostile personalities are more likely to have problems with coworkers. They are also likely to have more stress, and less job satisfaction. In marriage, the higher levels of hostility a person has, the less marital satisfaction and the more marital conflict they are likely to report. On average, hostile people also have less social support, less marital satisfaction, more marital conflict and conflict with other family members. In addition to this, hostile people in the work place tend to have greater stress, less job satisfaction, and a more negative view of their work relationships.[21] Negative energy affects your body in negative ways. You only have so much energy, why would you spend it feeling worse?

How Much Do You Invest in Negative Energy?

Negative energy affects many people on a daily basis and can be as simple as seeing someone frowning, or a simple annoyance such as someone honking at you, or getting irritated with someone for not paying attention while they are driving. Negative energy can be in the form of cynicism, mistrust, pessimism, or having a bad attitude.

Think about your life. How much time do you spend getting angry over something? Do you get angry easily? How much negative energy do you invest in yourself? Do you make daily investments? How much negative energy runs through your body? Would a good life be full of fear, anger, and hatred? How can you be happy when you invest in so much negative energy? When has hatred made your life better? When has hatred made this world a better place? When has love made society a better place?

Investing in negative energy is like investing in a stock that only goes down. Imagine that the dollar amount you invest is represented by the number of days in your life. The average American lives 28,470 days. How many of these days do you want to invest in negative energy? The more you invest, the more likely the number of days will go down. The more you invest in positive energy, the more likely those numbers will go up.

This energy affects the cells in your body, and thus your physical health. In very real terms, you may live 22,995 days (63 years) being bitter, holding grudges, getting upset over traffic or long lines at the store. Or you may live 32,850 days (90 years), choosing to laugh more, be friendly, and make the most of your life, regardless of the hardships you face. Even if you lasted one hundred years, would you rather spend more of those years being angry?

So think about how much negative energy you invest in others…your family, your country and your world? When you focus on what's wrong with another person, you will feel negative about him or her. If you change your thoughts to what you love about that person, you will change your relationship for the better.

How often have you thought you have a right to be angry, hurt, depressed, or resentful because of the way you've been treated? Many people blame others for their anger and resentment. But if you think other people are making you angry, you need to realize that it is you who chooses what your emotions are. Give up resentments.

There may be instances where you don't even realize that you are angry. For a long time, I did not realize how negative I was until I started logging down every time I was thinking in a negative way. This was a huge wake up call for me, because it made me realize how negative I was towards myself. I realized that the only thing really stopping me was me! Even after I thought I put a big stop to this negative thinking, it still took several years to realize just how negative I was.

Sometimes people see a situation being much worse than it really is, even taking something positive and interpreting it as being negative. Sometimes people overreact to criticism, even to extreme lengths. Sometimes people can have a great day, but just one small thing happens that sours the rest of their day. Whether you think you have an anger problem or not, spend a week and write down every time you get irritated or angry over something. It may be more often than you think.

This Is Your Life

One of the great tragedies in life is what we don't know about others and what we don't reveal about ourselves. We go through our life not showing who we really are. One person I interviewed told me about how she made a "lame attempt at suicide" back in high school. This seemed to not be a big deal to her, so I asked if she ever told her parents. She said 'No', then she paused and thought about it for a second, then she said "no" again, but in a more sad/regretful tone. The suicide attempt did not bother her as much as the fact that she never told her parents. Her cry for help went unanswered because nobody heard it.

Being a parent, you may think your child is happy. But what if, deep down, they are in a lot of pain? You ask them if something is wrong, but they say they are fine. You want to do something to help, but you don't know how to reach out to them. How many times in your life have you told others that you were fine, but you clearly were not?

It is pretty easy to define yourself in one role or another, but imagine what your life would be like if things were different. You could have been born into a world where you were neglected and beaten on a regular basis. You could have been born into an environment of war, or you could have lived a wonderful life, only to have your world turned upside down on what appears to be a typical normal day. What if you were born in an environment where everybody loved you and encouraged you?

You cannot put someone in a category and then say that you know that person. When we don't know and understand each other, we get suspicious, we misunderstand, we don't relate…we don't connect. So who is the enemy? We want to demonize people who do bad things, as if they are not human. We want to think that we are not capable of doing evil things and separate ourselves from them. Millions of people have been sacrificed in the pursuit of making this world a better place. Like the generations before us, we will keep repeating the same mistakes over and over again, until we get it.

We are born into this world, we will experience life, and then we will die. There are no exceptions. For all the people who have died, we are all one. We are all connected. When you can fully understand this connection…it then is your life.

PART II:

GOING BEYOND
THESE PERCEPTIONS

So who are we? As much as we think we know each other, we really don't. We cannot understand the problem if we don't understand each other.

Regardless of whether you are from New York City, Paris, or Sao Paulo…even if you were some "great ruler" of a past civilization long forgotten, in relation to the universe, you are insignificant.

Scientists have counted well over 200 billion galaxies, and that's just what they can see. Some of these galaxies have more than three trillion stars. Our galaxy is fairly small in comparison with only approximately 200 billion stars. If our galaxy were the size of the United States, our solar system would be the size of a quarter, and the nearest star would be about two soccer-fields away. If the Sun were the size of a quarter, Pluto would be about one hundred yards away, and the nearest star would be roughly 180 miles away.

Traveling at the speed of light, it takes eighteen minutes for the light of the sun to travel to Earth. It would take three years for this light to reach the nearest star and it would take 100,000 years for it to cross the Milky Way. With the speed of the rotation of the Milky Way, the last time we were in this position of the rotation was 250 million years ago – just as the dinosaurs started roaming the earth. If you think about it, the dinosaurs circled three-fourths of our galaxy, while humanity has not even traveled a single percent of it. Earth is on the edge of an outer arm of our galaxy.

So whether you are from Tokyo or White Rock, South Dakota, you are in the boonies of the Milky Way, and your life is just a speck in an instant of time. Just one large asteroid hit can erase our entire human history. Your life could be extinguished any day, at any time – in the blink of an eye. This happens to people every day. So think about how you last interacted with those in your life, and how you will interact with them the next time you see them, if you are given that chance.

The problems you face in life are insignificant in the whole scope of it. Even events like World War II are like a bunch of little ants fighting over territory. And trust me, if and when that asteroid hits, you can tell me how important all those problems are then. So, for as small as we are in this universe, making this world a better place doesn't seem that difficult. Only when we really begin to understand each other, can we make the change.

Part II goes beyond our perceptions and looks at the underlying problem. The reality is that all these things such as success, failure, and intelligence, do not define who we are. Our emotions play a significant role in our lives and are interconnected with each other's emotions. Therefore, our problems are interconnected with each other's problems. It all comes down to these connections, and the lack of social connection is the underlying foundation for many personal problems and public issues.

Once we fully understand how this lack of connection destroys society, we can learn how to build deeper, stronger social connections, not just in our life, but also in our families and in school – two major pillars of society. In the final part of this book, we will see how all this ultimately comes together and how it will lead to a change of unimaginable scope.

CHAPTER 7:

WHY WE DO NOT
UNDERSTAND EACH OTHER

While we think we know each other, we really don't. The tragedy for so many people is that this realization often does not come until a loved one dies or until they are on their last breaths of life…precisely the reason people say to live every day like it's your last.

In order to be accepted, we try to fit ourselves into these categories. I always felt like a square peg trying to fit into a round hole, but now I know that every person is a different shaped peg, doing what he or she can to fit into a particular hole or category. Because of this, we compromise who we are. But the reality is that every person is just as complex as society.

When people attempt to define who they are, they often think about such things as their successes and failures, their level of intelligence, their beliefs, and their experiences in life. These attempts at defining ourselves fall short because there is no clear-cut line in defining who we are. You are no better than or less than anyone else. None of this defines you, because you are far more than any of this.

Labels Do Not Define You

As much as we want to, we cannot simplify people. They cannot be put into any one category. Every person is unique. People's personalities, attitudes, taste, behaviors, thoughts, and feelings, all fall on a spectrum. For example, imagine you as a blank canvas with a large pallet of colors. Every person is his or her own unique work of art. Now imagine that the colors in the painting represent different things. Let's say that autism is represented by the color red. People who are considered to be autistic will have a lot of red in their painting. Many people will have some red in their painting, but their painting would not be described as being red, as they would not be considered to be autistic. Some people may not be diagnosed as having a learning disability, yet they learn differently. For example, we have all had our dyslexic moments, and some of us more than others. Some people, who have this pretty severely, would be considered to be dyslexic.

Even things like sexual orientation are experienced in degrees, as noted in the Heterosexual-Homosexual Rating Scale classification system designed by Alfred Kinsey and his colleagues in 1948.

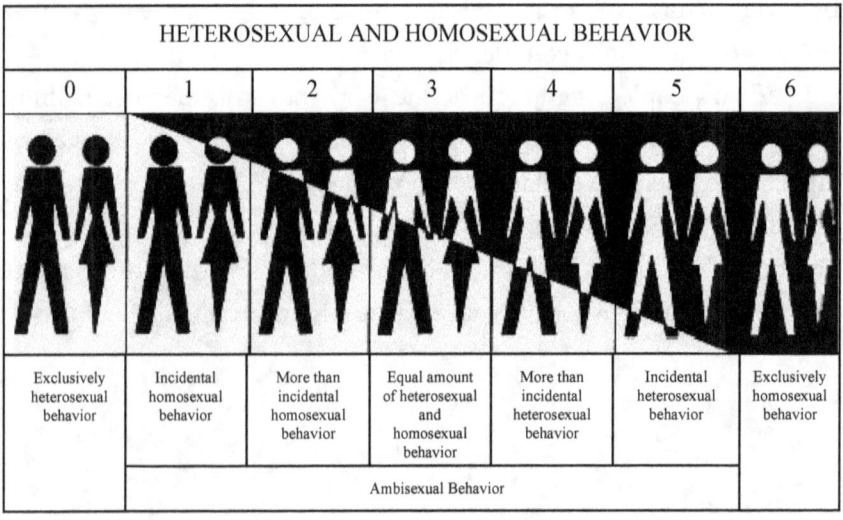

HETEROSEXUAL AND HOMOSEXUAL BEHAVIOR						
0	1	2	3	4	5	6
Exclusively heterosexual behavior	Incidental homosexual behavior	More than incidental homosexual behavior	Equal amount of heterosexual and homosexual behavior	More than incidental heterosexual behavior	Incidental heterosexual behavior	Exclusively homosexual behavior
	Ambisexual Behavior					

Through an extensive number of interviews, while most people identified themselves as being either exclusively heterosexual or homosexual, many people reported having behaviors or thoughts that at times fell between these exclusives. "It is a fundamental of taxonomy that nature rarely deals with discrete categories. Only the human mind invents categories and tries to force facts into separated pigeon-holes. The living world is a continuum in each and every one of its aspects. The sooner we learn this concerning human sexual behavior, the sooner we shall reach a sound understanding of the realities of sex."[1]

Does Intelligence or Wealth Define You?

A lot of people define themselves by how intelligent or wealthy they are. It may seem obvious that intelligence determines value. But what determines intelligence? Intelligence is much more complex than a simple IQ test, which measures only one aspect of intelligence. It has only been in recent decades that we have learned that animals are more intelligent than we thought. The fact is that people are intelligent in different ways. The question really should not be 'how smart are you?', but 'how are you smart?'.

Having a lot of knowledge is not necessarily the same as having wisdom. A book, a library, and a computer can have vast amounts of information. The information that is currently out there should be enough to 'save' the world several times over. Knowing all this information is not really useful unless you really understand how it all fits together.

One student may learn 100 percent of the information, while another student may only learn 20 percent of the information. While it would appear that the latter student is less intelligent, he or she may not test well, have a different learning style from what was taught, and/or may be more interested in that 20 percent; thinking about it in far more complex ways than just remembering facts.

Material aspects, such as wealth, do not define who we are. Money plays a critical role in providing for the basic necessities, such as food and shelter. People will do what ever it takes to survive, even commit murder, which is why all people must be covered with the basics. However, when it comes to fulfilling our desires beyond this, in many cases, buying things often bring only a temporary high. Some people use shopping to boost their spirits when they are depressed. This could be compared to using drugs. Even if you could have everything you ever wanted, you will get used to it, the high will wear off, and you will still be you. Wealth does not necessarily determine happiness. There are plenty of wealthy people who are depressed or have even committed suicide, just as there are plenty of poor people who are happy. It is not so much about how much wealth one has, but how we tend to compare ourselves to others.

Does Failure or Success Define You?

Does failure or success determine your value as a person? While it may seem quite logical that some people are more important than others, what is it that makes one person more important or better than another? You might be a successful CEO of a major corporation one day, and then fired the next day.

Gandhi was not wealthy, nor was he a king or president, yet he changed a nation and had a great effect on the world. General George C. Marshall, United States Secretary of State, was quoted as saying "Mahatma Gandhi has become the spokesperson for the conscience of all mankind. He was a man who made humility, in simple truth, more powerful than empires."

Do you define the worthiness of your children based on how 'successful' or intelligent they are? Although success feels good for many reasons, success in itself is fairly superficial. But how important is success really? While success can help build self-esteem, there are plenty of people who have been considered to be successful all their life only to live a miserable life. Some people know they are successful, yet they feel alone. Understandably people need to feel a certain degree of success, or they will eventually give up. If you are playing a game with someone where you always win, the other person may get bored or frustrated and stop playing.[2] Similarly, when people suffer from too many setbacks in life, they are more likely to give up. But when you think about it though, how do you fail at life?

Nixon's farewell speech from August 8th, 1974:

> I remember my old man. I think that they would have called him sort of a little man, a common man. He didn't consider himself that way. You know what he was? He was a streetcar motorman first, and then he was a farmer, and then he had a lemon ranch. It was the poorest lemon ranch in California, I can assure you. He sold it before they found oil on it. And then he was a grocer. But he was a great man, because he did his job, and every job counts up to the hilt, regardless of what happens.

> Nobody will ever write a book, probably, about my mother. Well, I guess all of you would say this about your mother – my mother was a saint. And I think of her, two boys dying of tuberculosis, nursing four others in order that she could take care of my older brother for three years in Arizona, and seeing each of them die, and when they died, it was like one of her own. Yes, she will have no books written about her. But she was a saint.

Love for a pet is not determined by how successful or intelligent they are. Cats and dogs do nothing but sit around the house and tell you when they want food (or treats like my cat is doing right now), which for some is always! It's not like they can even mow the lawn or go earn a paycheck. But for some reason we like to have them around, and when they die, it can be devastating.

The more you try in life, the more likely you will fail. Some of the most successful people in life have also failed a lot. When I learned to be OK with failure and stopped worrying about it, that was when I could really start enjoying my life.

When people think they are failures, trying seems pointless. But when people see failure as feedback for what they need to do, they will keep trying. When you learn from the problems and negative experiences you face in life, these experiences end up not being so bad, and are a building block important for success. As George Patton said, *"I don't measure a man's success by how high he climbs but how high he bounces when he hits bottom."* George S. Patton (1885-1945). General, U.S. Army.

Some scientists spend their entire life looking for a cure to cancer and never accomplish their goal. But they don't see this as failure. They realize that every failure is one step closer to finding a cure. Imagine if we approached our life this way. We would be living pretty amazing lives!

> "Success is not the key to happiness. Happiness is the key to success. If you love what you are doing, you will be successful."
>
> Dr. Albert Schweitzer

We may avoid failure by not trying. We may avoid problems, but these problems will continue to follow us until we understand what the real problem is and then solve it. We often make the same mistakes over and over again, and don't even realize it. There are so many people who think they can solve their problems on their own. No one knows how to solve every problem in life. Even a good leader has his/her consultants. The greatest tennis players in the world have coaches.

"Kids feel like failures when they make a mistake. Like they're not supposed to make mistakes. I like to say learning is messy. You want to take risks. And when you take risks, you fail. We teach kids three questions and it really reframes failure, as we tell them to go through the steps of what happened. What are the facts? What did I learn? And what will I do differently next time? That really gives us a new definition of failure."

Bobbi DePorter[3]

The reality is that you still move ahead when you fail. Every baby tries to walk, and every baby fails. They don't just get up and start walking around on the first try, and they don't give up. Now, think of all the times you decided not to do something because you were concerned about failing.

"We make rules that frustrate achievement. We prematurely write off people as failures. We are too much in awe of those who succeed and far too dismissive of those who fail. And, most of all, we become much too passive. We overlook just how much of a role we all play – and by 'we' I mean society – in determining who makes it and who doesn't." "…we cling to the idea that success is a simple function of individual merit and that the world in which we all grow up and the rules we choose to write as a society don't matter at all."[4]

Malcolm Gladwell,
Outliers

Colonel Sanders, who founded Kentucky Fried Chicken, dropped out of school in the seventh grade. He ran away from home because his stepfather beat him. When he was 40 years old, he made chicken for people who stopped by his service station. Eventually he had a restaurant, but that ended up failing due to an interstate that was built, thus reducing the number of customers who used to drive through the area. At age 65, he decided to take his secret recipe to potential franchisees. He received a large number of rejections before he finally got his first 'yes'. In less than ten years, he sold Kentucky Fried Chicken for $2 million.[5] It is a common saying in sales that you will get one hundred "no's" before you get your first "yes"…a big reason I would have never gone into sales!

Albert Einstein, who developed the theory of general relativity, did not learn to talk until age three. His professors in school did not hold him in high regards, nor did colleagues take him seriously. Like Einstein, Thomas Edison did not learn to talk till age three. He would have likely been considered ADHD according to today's standards. Failure also did not discourage him.

You Have the Most Important Job in the World

The President of the United States of America could arguably have the most important job in the world. Taking political party out of the equation, who is more important to you, the President of the United States or your own child? Several years ago, I asked a friend who she would shed more tears over; her pet that recently died after fifteen wonderful years, or the President, i.e. someone she really does not know personally. Her answer was clearly her pet. When you think about it, the only thing you really know about the President is the superficial bits you read in the newspaper or see on TV. What you read or see really does not say anything about a person deep down.

When thinking about who has the most important job in this world, again, one might say the President of the United States. But there is someone who has a far more important job. The answer may be surprising, because it is you. You are the president, the great leader, and the god of a multi-trillion-cell society. It is your body. It is your brain, and everything you think consciously and unconsciously.

The various kinds of cells in your body have a life span, anywhere from a few days to your entire lifetime. It is estimated that the overall average longevity of various kinds of cells equates roughly to seven to ten years. As the commander of this super-cell society, you have a very important job. These cells cannot live without you. They depend on you. When you die, they will all die within a few days.

Just as our planet has a natural defense shield, so do we. If our bodies did not have any defense, we would die. If you are diverted by all the stresses that happen in life, your body's defense will also focus on and feel this stress, and it will be weakened. With a weakened defense system, you may have a more difficult time fighting off colds, or your system may miss something more serious, such as cancer.

When I think of myself as the commander of my body, I feel in touch with every cell in my body – in my toes, legs, ears, and so on. If I am not happy, my cells are not happy, and therefore I cannot be at my maximum potential. When I am happy, my cells are happy. I love every cell in my body, and when I am aware of this and feel it, it's as if my whole body thrives with energy. Every cell counts and every cell is a part of this multi-trillion cell society, which is me.

Conclusion

For all that we, as a human race have learned, we really don't know that much about each other. How are we to learn about each other when we hide who we really are? We cannot learn from each other when we hide our problems. With superficial interactions, we build a superficial society that is made up of false images.

One thing I've learned is that no one is better than me, but no one is worse than me either. We are all on the same playing field. Every person comes into this world with his or her own unique set of circumstances, so stop trying to compare yourself to everybody else.

CHAPTER 8

HOW EMOTIONS
IMPACT YOUR LIFE

Emotions are a major part of our life, affecting everything we do. Our feelings and emotions are contagious, and are interconnected with other people's emotions, making our problems interconnected too. Our feelings are greatly affected by the environment we live in. Social influences have a major impact on how we think and act.

Many people have a difficult time communicating their feelings. They may feel uncomfortable discussing their feelings or listening to the feelings of others because they have never learned to connect on a deep level. Emotions are often discouraged or dismissed in everyday society, which encourages people to hide their feelings. Denying what you feel will affect your development.[1]

Whether we see a day as good or bad is based on our emotions and the interactions we have with other people. Someone may have cut in front of you in line or was rude to you at work. One rude comment can affect a person's entire day. However, a compliment can go just as far. I am sure you can look back on your life and remember simple events from the distant past where someone was either rude or nice to you.

Emotions Play a Major Role
Throughout Our Lives

The emotions we experience take place even before we are born. Studies have shown that when the baby is in the womb, the baby can sense the emotions of the mother. These emotions can affect the baby both physically and psychologically. What the mother thinks and feels is communicated to the unborn child through neurohormones. It has been shown that positive feelings and a sense of calm can have a positive effect on the baby.[2] Is it possible that if the mother is stressed, all the cells in her body, including the cells of the baby inside her experience this stress too?

A baby comes into this world and looks around taking everything in. When parents fight, the baby will feel this and will likely be stressed or even cry. When parents smile at the baby, the baby will often look back and smile too. How the parent interacts with his or her child can be greatly affected by how that parent is feeling.

In Danial Goleman's book *Emotional Intelligence,* he explains two situations where a mother gets up in the middle of the night to feed her crying baby.[3] In the first example, the mother comes in and happily nurses her baby for a half-hour. She smiles at the baby in an affectionate way. The baby is happy and falls back asleep. In the second example, the mother had a fight with her husband before going to bed. She has not had much sleep, and when she finally gets to sleep, she wakes up to her crying baby. The mother is tense and irritable. Instead of making constant eye contact with the baby and cooing, she is staring at the wall. The baby feels this tension, and therefore becomes tense by squirming, stiffening up, and stops nursing. The mother is upset for having to do all this work for nothing and abruptly puts the baby back in the crib. The baby cries and eventually falls asleep. While most parents probably have these moments on occasion, imagine how this would feel on a daily basis. The baby may feel unloved and will learn that others don't really care and that people cannot be counted on.

The positive and loving emotions shown by parents will have a tremendous impact on the rest of a child's life. Eating breakfast with my friend's year and a half old child, I noticed that if I didn't pay attention to him, he would just sit there and eat. While he wasn't sad, he wasn't really smiling either. So instead of continuing about my business, I decided to make his day a little more fun. I would get all excited and be silly, and then he would get all excited and clap his hands. Doing this made me realize that I would like to be more fun like this around everybody. What would happen if everyone tried to make others happy by smiling or being more fun instead of being angry? When your focus is on others, you are less focused on your own problems.

Children notice when their parents are not paying attention or feign interest while focusing on other things. When a parent continually fails to show empathy with a child's emotions, such as comforting the child when the child is sad, the child will more likely avoid expressing these emotions.[4] In one example that illustrates this was when I was with a friend while we were picking up her three-year-old son at day care. The children were singing and he would frequently turn to see if his mom was watching him. When she was watching him, he would get a big smile on his face. But when she was talking to the other parent, he seemed a little down.

Children influence and are influenced by other children. Some children have an easy time interacting with others, while other children have a more difficult time. Some children become disappointed with their performance in comparison to other students. As they approach their teenage years, and they go to bigger schools, they begin forming cliques, or maybe they don't connect at all with others. When students are not connecting with others, it is pretty easy to see where this may lead.

As teens enter adulthood, many often end up doing so many of the things their parents did, because that is what they know. The emotions from their parents and the emotions they felt in school can have a major impact on the rest of their life.

Our Emotions are Interconnected

Our emotions are contagious and are interconnected with other people's emotions. When a person yawns, you are more likely to yawn. Just the shear suggestion of it may make you feel like yawning. When one person laughs, others may start laughing too. This is like how great movies can get the audience to laugh, cheer, or cry at the same time.

Even babies sense the emotions of others. "Three-month old babies of depressed mothers…mirrored their mothers' moods while playing with them, displaying more feelings of anger and sadness, and much less spontaneous curiosity and interest, compared to infants whose mothers were not depressed."[5]

When a couple makes a strong effort to be supportive of each other and enjoy their time together, this positive energy affects not just them, but also their children as well as their extended family and friends. When people have a lot of negative energy in them, other people will likely react in a negative way.

Animals react in much the same way. Since animals don't use words to communicate, they are more sensitive to body language and energy given off by another. This is demonstrated in programs that offer people therapy with horses. When a person with a lot of internal anger tries to approach a horse, the horse will often move away from that person. The horse can read this emotion and wants to avoid it.

The emotions of others affect our everyday lives. Let's say Joe has a mean, angry boss at work, and this boss makes his job a nightmare. This makes Joe angry. When Joe gets home, his wife asks how his day went, and he replies angrily This negative energy from the boss is not only affecting Joe, but is now affecting the family through Joe's emotions. If this continues it can cause a rift between Joe and his wife, and probably the kids too. Joe, his wife, and child are all feeling depressed, angry, and frustrated. It may be a factor in divorce. Joe's child acts out in school, which affects his or her grades. The child acts out in class, and so do other children who are dealing with personal problems. This behavior affects the teacher and other students. The teacher slowly goes from being passionate about his or her job, to hating it.

Studies have shown that working in a stressful environment can cause stress on our bodies. Some doctors can tell you what companies in town create stress in the workplace by the number of stress-related illnesses they see. When the Bell Telephone companies downsized in the 80s, a significant number of secretaries and lower level workers developed stress related illnesses because they had no control over whether or where they would be working. We all know that smoking is bad for you, and we know that second-hand smoke can be bad for you too. With all the commotion over second-hand smoke, shouldn't we be just as much, if not much more concerned about "second-hand" negative energy?

The problems you face in life are going to be affected by how you are feeling emotionally and how you choose to face these problems. Your feelings will also affect how you relate with others.

Personal Problems & Public Issues are Interconnected

As much as we would like to be model spouses, parents, teachers, counselors, etc., our roles are often compromised by the problems we face in life. We feel down, because we are not performing as well as we would like to, and end up treating people based on how we are feeling at the moment. Picturesque marriages often turn into unhappy marriages with constant fighting and even divorce. Parents want to be good role models for their children, yet end up yelling at them when they do something wrong.

But many of the personal problems we deal with in life, are not necessarily just personal problems, but are also public issues. The people around us, and society as a whole, shape the way we think. This is why some personal problems can be difficult, if not seemingly impossible to solve, causing feelings of inadequacy, frustration, and anger.

While divorce may be considered to be a personal problem, if the divorce rate is high, it could be due to greater social issues. In the United States, the divorce rate shot up in the late 1960's and 1970's because states enacted a no-fault divorce bill, making the process of divorce much easier. A high divorce rate can also cause other social issues, such as an increase of single mothers who end up taking care of their children on their own, coupled, in some cases, with fathers who don't pay child support. Divorce can also have a negative impact on a child's life. This negative energy can extend from the parents and children to others such as extended family, friends, and co-workers.

There are many ways personal problems and public issues are interconnected. Let's say you are driving to work, and you spill your coffee on your shirt. This is a personal problem. Is it society's fault that you spilt your coffee? Of course not! Now let's say that you spilled the coffee you just bought, and it caused burns. Is this still your fault? Sure, you clearly must be an idiot who shouldn't be drinking coffee...but then again, we have all spilled something. Now what if the coffee you spilled caused third degree burns, and on top of that, this has happened to over seven hundred people who purchased a cup of coffee from the same company? You might be thinking that coffee is obviously hot and that these people need to be more careful, but this is clearly not a public issue.

In the lawsuit *Liebeck v. McDonald's Restaurants*,[6] a woman won against McDonnald's because she spilled the coffee she bought on herself. As it appeared, this was a case of a greedy person filing a frivolous lawsuit for millions of dollars. The summary of the story is that some woman was going up to the drive-through of a McDonald's and when she drove away, she spilled the coffee on herself and sued McDonald's for millions of dollars.

But this personal problem became a public issue. When the facts were brought to light, we learned the 79 year-old lady originally just asked McDonald's to cover her medical bills for burns that were so severe that they required skin grafting. She wasn't even the driver, and they were not even driving when she burned herself! McDonald's offered $800, thinking that this was someone trying to get away with fraud. But, it was discovered that the coffee being served was between 180 and 190 degrees. An expert even testified that even if the coffee was served above 130 degrees, it could cause third degree burns. In addition to that, McDonald's brewed this coffee between 195 degrees and 205 degrees based on the recommendations by coffee consultants who said that such a high temperature was needed to extract the full flavor of the coffee. As it turns out, liquids at 190 degrees can cause third degree burns in two to three seconds. Liquids at 180 degrees can cause third degree burns in ten to fifteen seconds, allowing enough time for you to cool it down a bit by shaking your shirt and blowing on it. Are you going to get burned? Yes, you probably will, but just ten degrees in temperature can make a difference between a minor burn and a major third degree burn.

While some people may blame lawyers, this is actually a good example of how lawyers do an important job. McDonald's probably did not know that if they lowered the temperature by ten degrees, they could have prevented hundreds and likely thousands of these scalding burns. People like their coffee hot, but have no clue about how such a small change in temperature can make such a big difference. While burn specialists may know details on temperatures of liquids and the time it takes to cause serious burns, they probably have no clue at what temperature McDonald's serves their coffee. Lawyers were able to put the information together and have the voice to say that we need to make some changes.

If this is not enough to convince you, imagine you are driving your car with your baby in the back seat. You have your hot coffee, but you carefully keep it in the cup holder except for the occasional sip. Just as you pull out of the parking lot into the intersection, another car runs a red light and hits your car from the side. Everyone is thankfully safe, but your coffee spills all over your baby. This ten degree difference may be the difference between a baby being hurt with minor superficial burns or having very serious third degree burns.

Society Affects How You Think and Feel

What seems to be purely a personal thought, decision, or action, is greatly influenced by other people and the social environment.[7] How we act, depends on whom we are with. People often follow new trends and behaviors, without even realizing it. This can be seen in how facial expressions, mannerisms, and vocal accents vary from Los Angeles to New York to London.

Greater social forces affect our individual actions, even in the case of very personal decisions such as suicide. Suicide is clearly a personal problem, but like divorce, if we have a high suicide rate, there must be something wrong with the society that needs to be fixed. Research by Emile Durkheim showed that social forces affected what appeared to be individual actions. One of Durkheim's famous studies on suicide showed that when people are oppressed, they pull together. Suicide rates will also go down in times of social crisis. For example, Jewish people had a lower suicide rate when they were oppressed than when they were not oppressed. Black children, who lived in cities that were not involved in the civil rights movement, had a higher suicide rate than those living in the south and were involved in civil rights. Although more people died in the struggle, they worked together. Durkheim concluded "…suicide rates increase as the degree of integration and regulation of the individual by the group decreases".[8, 9] The more isolated from a group a person is, the more likely that person will commit suicide. When people feel socially bonded, they are less likely to commit suicide.

People's demeanor, dress, and the words they use affect our behavior. One experiment showed that if you wear a white coat that you think is a doctor's coat you are more able to pay attention. However, if you think that the same coat is a painter's coat, there will be no change. It was also shown that one could not just look at the coat, they had do wear it. Other similar studies have shown that if a person was holding a warm drink, that person was more likely to rate other people as having a warm personality.[10]

Research has shown that people's expectations of others can have a major impact, creating a self-fulfilling prophecy. If you think someone will be mean, then you will probably treat them as if they are this way. This also applies to life in general. If you think it is going to be a tough day, then it probably will be. If you are labeled as "slow" or as having a low IQ, you will likely be treated as such and teachers may have low expectations of you.

In one experiment, groups of students tested rats in a maze to see how quickly they could get through it. The groups were told that they were given mice that were specially bred as "maze-bright" and "maze-dull". As predicted the "maze bright" mice learned the maze quicker than the "maze-dull" mice. However, there was just one problem. The mice were just mice and were not specially bred. Without realizing it, the students unconsciously influenced the "maze-bright" mice.[11, 12]

Neuroscientist Dean Buonomano, who wrote the book *Brain Bugs – How the Brain's Flaws Shape Our Lives*, explains how our brains can be primed to think about certain things. Buonomano gives the following example:

> Answer the first two questions below out loud, and then blurt out the first thing that pops into your mind in response to sentence 3:
>
> 1. In what continent is Kenya?
> 2. What are the two opposing colors in the game of chess?
> 3. Think of any animal.

Buonomano explains that by priming your mind, roughly 20 percent of people will answer "zebra" to sentence 3, and about 50 percent will say an African animal such as an elephant giraffe or lion. "...by directing your attention to Africa and the colors black and white, it is possible to manipulate your answer."[13]

This priming is a way of conditioning how we think. Psychologist Richard Solomon did a study showing how dogs are conditioned to avoid something they perceive to be real.[14] In the experiment, a dog was placed in a large cage that had two sections to it divided by a low wall the dog could easily jump over. The floor of the side that the dog was on was electrified enough to give the dog a pretty strong shock. To escape the shock, the dog would jump to the other side. Then the floor was electrified on that side, so the dog would jump back to the first side, which was no longer electrified. Solomon then used a tone that would come on ten seconds before the shock. The dog quickly learned to jump to the other side when the tone went off, before the floor was electrified. After the dog learned to do this, Solomon then would just play the tone, but not include the shock. The dog would continue to use this signal, as a way to avoid the shock, even though there was no shock. This is the same way invisible fences are used for dogs. As the dog gets close to the "fence" a sound is emitted from the collar signaling to the dog to get away before it gets shocked.

In life, we get primed and conditioned to think in certain ways. Someone who has been teased in his or her earlier years of life by a certain group of people may learn to avoid these types of people later in life, even if they are no longer like that or if these are completely different people who have never been like that. A person, who may have teased you back in elementary school, may have completely forgotten about doing it years later. A racist person may have received a "shock" from something he or she read, were told, saw, or has been treated by others.

Like in Solomon's study, it does not take many of these "shocks" to condition someone into thinking a certain way or to see walls or "fences" that are not really there. If a dog associates a light that goes on or a tone that was played as a warning sign of a shock soon to come, the dog might start assuming anything that represents a slight change, such as music being played, or a person coming in to say 'Hi', is really just an early warning sign of a shock soon to come.

With people, after experiencing a few "shocks", one may start noticing different potential warning signs. Pretty soon, one may start noticing every piece of literature, or every news story that justifies his or her beliefs. In extreme cases, a person can get so engulfed in this that it becomes their entire world, such as with religious or racist extremists. They may be convinced that everybody hates them, or that all dogs are dangerous, or that black people are trying to take over, or all white people are racist. These are the "walls of reality" in which they live. To them, these walls are very clear, and it is clear that you must obviously be blind or stupid not to see this.

Being very different from the norm, I received a small number of "shocks" from people who told me that I was an idiot or a moron, along with being one of the few kids in class who needed extra help. The actual number of times I was treated less than others was not many, but it was enough to convince me that everybody thought I lacked intelligence, to the point that I still catch myself thinking this way today!

How Group Behavior Affects Us

In some ways, our environment has an even bigger effect on us than our family. For a family moving to the United States from a completely different culture, the children, wanting to fit in, may be more influenced by what their friends are doing, and leave their old traditions behind. Studies have shown that children are better off in a good neighborhood and a troubled family than in a troubled neighborhood and a good family.[15] Community disadvantages can significantly affect criminal behavior in juveniles.[16, 17] In short, we are products of our environment and we are influenced by those around us and the greater society.

When people are in a group setting, they want to blend in. They are also less likely to say or do something when a problem arises. In some cases, a person may feel strange or uncomfortable speaking up, questioning his or her own judgment on what he or she is witnessing. The thinking is that if there is something truly wrong taking place, someone else would have already spoken up. The person may also presume that someone else will do something about it.

In the classic elevator experiment, social psychologist Solomon Asch showed that when people faced the rear of the elevator, unknowing subjects would conform to everybody else and face the rear of the elevator too.[18] Similar experiments have shown that people tend to conform to the majority view on an answer, even if the answer were completely wrong.[19] Other experiments have shown that people are less likely to react to emergencies when there are other people around who are not reacting.[20]

Group behavior can evoke strong emotions in everything from patriotism and politics to sporting events and protests. Group behavior can be so powerful that it can turn peaceful protests into violent mobs. It can turn people who would never hurt a fly into murderers.

The Jonestown Massacre

What is known today as the Jonestown massacre, Rev. Jim Jones convinced people to move down to Guyana to be a part of a cult, known as the Peoples Temple Agriculture Project. While it may be tempting to label these cult members as crazy, many were completely normal. The seemingly "normal" group they first joined, slowly became more isolated from common society and more violent. Congressman Leo Ryan went to Guyana with a TV camera crew and reporters to investigate allegations of human rights abuses. It was clear that abuse was taking place, and as they were trying to escape with over a dozen cult members who wanted to leave, other members shot at them, killing Ryan, and four others, as they were on an airstrip about to leave on a plane. Later on the same day, Jones convinced the people as a group to commit "revolutionary suicide" by drinking a cherry-flavored drink laced with cyanide. People who did not comply were murdered. On November 18, 1978, over 900 people were killed. Thirty-three members survived.

The Stanford Prison Experiment

One example of how group behavior can quickly get out of control is the Stanford Prison Experiment. In 1971, Philip Zimbardo, a psychologist at Stanford University, did a study on what the psychological effects were when college students voluntarily took on the role of a prisoner or prison guard in a simulated prison at Stanford University. What started out as a two-week experiment, became more real as time progressed, but due to the psychological abuse that took place, it was shut down within six days and should have been stopped sooner.

To make the experiment as real as possible, students who were assigned the role of prisoners were picked up at their homes by the police, handcuffed, taken into custody, fingerprinted, and put in a holding cell. They were then taken to a mock prison located in the basement of the Stanford psychology building. The prisoners were searched, stripped naked and deloused. They wore a stocking cap and a smock, which had a prisoner ID number on it. They were referred to only by their number and could only refer to each other, and themselves by their number. They also had a heavy chain shackled to their right ankle, to serve as a constant reminder that they were in prison, even when they were sleeping. The guards, on the other hand, had uniforms, mirrored sunglasses and carried batons, and were given no specific training on being guards.

Roll calls were done several times a day and during the night to show control over the prisoners. If the prisoners did anything wrong, they had to do push-ups. By the morning of the second day, the prisoners rebelled by taking off their stocking caps, ripping off their ID numbers, barricading themselves in their cells using the beds, and taunting the guards on duty. The guards called in the off duty guards, and sprayed the prisoners with fire extinguishers forcing them to move away from the doors. The guards then took away the prisoners' beds, forced them to strip naked, and put the prisoners who were in charge of the rebellion into solitary confinement.

Prisoners with good behavior were put into "privilege cells", where they were given their uniforms and beds back, were able to brush their teeth, and were given better food to be eaten in front of the other prisoners. This was all designed to break up the unified front of the prisoners. In order to confuse and make the prisoners distrustful of each other, after some time, the guards took some of the "good" prisoners and put them back in the regular cells, and took some of the "bad" prisoners and put them in the "privilege cell". Consultants to the experiment who were ex-convicts, said that similar tactics were used in real prisons to pit the prisoners against other prisoners.

Within 36 hours, Prisoner #8612 was suffering from psychological distress, showing signs of disorganized thinking, crying, and rage. The guards saw this behavior as an attempt by the prisoner to con the guards into releasing him. The prisoner was told that he was weak, making him feel like he could not quit and leave. But as #8612 mentally broke down further, he was eventually released.

Prisoner #5401 participated in the project with the intent to "expose" the project, thinking that it was designed by the school to figure out how to control student radicals. However, he like all the other prisoners fell into his role as a prisoner.

Prisoner #819 was showing signs of breaking down mentally. He was taken to a separate room and would be taken to see a doctor. However, back in the cells, the guards had the prisoners chant out loud in unison several times: "Prisoner #819 is a bad prisoner. Because of what Prisoner #819 did, my cell is a mess..." Prisoner #819 heard this and started crying uncontrollably. Zimbardo told him that he could leave. But #819 felt that he could not leave because the other prisoners said he was a bad prisoner, and he wanted to show them that he was not. Zimbardo explained; "Listen, you are not #819. You are [his name], and my name is Dr. Zimbardo. I am a psychologist, not a prison superintendent, and this is not a real prison. This is just an experiment, and those are students, not prisoners, just like you. Let's go." This was when the participant appeared to wake up out of this role.

Prisoner #416 was quoted as saying; "I began to feel that I was losing my identity, that the person that I called Clay...was distant from me…until finally I wasn't that, I was 416. I was really my number."[21]

While this was just an experiment where people were playing their designated role, this is exactly what happens in real life. People play the roles that they think people expect them to play, similar to how children put on pretend uniforms of doctors or police officers and play these roles. Yes, a doctor is a doctor, and a police officer is a police officer, but these are only jobs. Outside of these jobs, these are people like you and I.

Society Must Advance as a Whole in Order to Change

Social evolution is painstakingly slow, and there is a reason for this. The society in which you live will likely seem normal regardless of how problematic it really is. When violence is engrained in a culture, it is considered normal human behavior. Hundreds of years ago, beating your child bloody, hitting your wife, and having slaves was considered normal. Not long ago, watching cockfights, dogfights, and bullfights were just a regular part of society. It wasn't long ago when smoking was a common occurrence in bars, restaurants, in offices, and even airplanes. Now the idea of lighting up at the office or in an airplane sounds completely insane. Today we presume that bullying will always be around because it has "always been around". A person born and raised in a safe area may be surprised to see how dangerous some cities are. People who have grown up in the United States would probably be surprised by how safe places like Copenhagen, Seoul, or Singapore are.

Because personal problems and public issues are interconnected, then the entire social environment is affected by these problems. This environment has a huge impact on our lives. Imagine that you have a coin that is in some mud. The coin represents the individual, and the mud represents the environment. You take the coin out of the mud and wash it off. But if you put the coin back into the mud (the environment in which it came), it would be muddy again. This example is used when describing the difficulties of releasing someone from prison or a drug treatment program.

Now, what if the entire social system (your family, your nation, and our world) is, in a sense muddy, or flawed? Imagine that the only society you know is all within the confines of the Stanford Prison Experiment. If this is all you know, how can you even imagine life outside these walls? While the idea that society could be compared to this study may seem a little extreme, there is a lot of this that does take place in real society, that we presume is normal, and for some people, this is their life. The Stanford Prison Experiment was just an experiment, but so is life and the society we live in. We are constantly trying new approaches and are conducting research in ways to improve society.

In order to better understand these problems, we really need to understand how the entire system is interconnected. This is what we know:

- Our emotions make up a major part of our lives.

- Emotions are contagious and are therefore interconnected with other people's emotions.

- Our problems are interconnected with other people's personal problems along with greater social issues.

- Therefore, personal problems and social issues are contagious.

While the idea that social issues are contagious may seem overblown, look at the mob mentality that takes place in groups where people take issues into their own hands. Trends are contagious, so are social problems such as crime.

The Broken Windows theory put forth by social scientists Dr. James Wilson and Dr. George Kelling, explains how broken windows in a neighborhood can lead to higher crime rates. How is this? If you saw a few broken windows in an abandoned building that nobody seemed to care about, it might seem like harmless fun to take a rock and break a few more windows. If nobody else cares, why should you? If the environment is trashy and nobody is around to take care of it and enforce the law, then you can pretty much do what ever you want without fear of being caught. Since the mid 1980's, New York City has applied this theory, by cracking down on the small crimes such as graffiti, panhandling, and public intoxication. There were many critics questioning why the city was choosing to tackle small petty issues, and not tackling the bigger problems. However, by applying this theory, New York City saw a significant drop in crime.

So while issues such as crime, violence, and an overall feeling of anger and hatred can be contagious, so can other issues and general feelings, such as kindness, caring, happiness, and even love. While we look at people like Hitler as monsters, when you think about it, how many people did Hitler, himself, kill? It's possible that he actually killed no one. Is it possible that blind following, blind patriotism, and blind devotion, all based on emotional responses to one man's anger, was responsible for the killing of millions of people, along with the 50 million to over 70 million people killed in World War II.

It's All About the Connections

Our emotions and feelings, our personal problems, and greater social issues are all connected. In Chapter Six, I described how water (which represented crime) would leak from a pipe under the sink and onto the floor, destroying the cabinet (which represented social structure). We react to the water leak by trying to fix it with buckets (prisons).

Imagine now that this is not just one leaky pipe under the sink, but there are many pipes in a building that are leaking. One pipe has water flowing through it, another has milk flowing through it, and another has coolant flowing through it. What is flowing through these pipes represents different things. For example, let's say that the pipe with water flowing through it represents marriage. Now if the water (or marriage) pipe starts leaking, we have a water leak (or a marriage problem). So these leaks represent various personal problems and social issues. It really does not matter what is flowing through the pipes, because the underlying problem is that the pipes are leaking. All these problems, be them personal or social, are interconnected. Yes, we have marriage problems, bullying, and crime, but they all are the result of something more. We can say we have a problem with school shootings, but then as we look closer at a particular case, we see that the troubled youth "fell through the cracks".

With pipes, the very first thing we do is get a bucket to prevent the leak from destroying the structure. If you have a leak in the ceiling, drill a hole and let the water flow down into a bucket. If you let the water pool up in the ceiling, it could cause the entire ceiling to collapse. Similarly, if we don't address the problems in society, the social structure may collapse. These buckets represent things that solve the immediate crisis, such as marriage counseling, prisons, or even suicide prevention lines. These temporary fixes are all very important. They keep the leaks from destroying the furniture and floors (social structure). Marriage counseling can save marriages from breaking up, suicide prevention hotlines can save people's lives, and prisons can discourage criminal activity. However, these methods don't always work. People often seek marriage counseling only after it is too late. If prisons were really effective, crime should be virtually non-existent. Suicide prevention hotlines may prevent a suicide today, but who's to say that this person doesn't commit suicide a month from now?

So just like how we tackle problems in society, we are getting all these buckets to stop the leaks or problems from hitting the floor. The idea of this is insane, and it's overloading the system. People at the office are not able to do their job, because they are too busy getting more buckets and emptying the full ones. In the real world, the leaking will continue until we fix the pipes. We will continue to have marriage problems, crime, and suicides until we figure out the source of the problem.

While the leaks are the problem, the connectors that connect the pipes together are the source of these problems. When the connector is not fully connecting the pipes, we have a breakdown in the system.

Similarly, when building a computer from scratch using various parts, sometimes the different parts do not fully communicate with each other, which can cause all sorts of glitches and can even render the computer useless. This is also in relation to networking various computers. Without a network, there is no Internet.

In order to run a model train, energy must flow through the tracks. The tracks connect together using joiners. If the tracks are not fully connected, the energy will not flow and the train will not run. Sometimes plastic joiners are used to inhibit the flow of energy so that trains sitting in one area don't start moving.

Your nervous system is made up of a network of nerve cells or neurons that communicates using electrical or chemical synapses. If your nervous system does not function, you do not function. Be it pipes, electricity, electric pulses, or whatever, the point is that if there is no connection, the system does not work and may very well likely collapse. When people don't connect with each other, society fails.

In life, we are so busy with personal problems and public issues, that we have less time to get to what's really important. People want to have a happy family, yet for some, every time the family gets together, there are arguments and fights because the communication between family members is frayed. In politics, the problem is not necessarily the political structure itself, but how we are connecting with each other. If people are not connecting and do not understand each other, chances are they will be looking out for themselves and not the society as a whole. In society, we see marriage problems, crime, violence, apathy, etc., and we are trying to tackle all these problems separately with buckets, rather than working on the source – better connections.

Conclusion

Our emotions play a vital role in our lives. These emotions affect how we feel in life on a daily basis, throughout our lives. Our feelings are interconnected with other people's feelings. Because our emotions greatly affect our lives, and because they are also interconnected with other people's emotions, emotions therefore play a major role in personal problems and public issues. This is why many of our personal problems and greater public issues are all interconnected. This is why these problems can be so difficult, if not seemingly impossible to solve.

Because we don't understand other people's emotions, we don't understand each other as people. We think we know each other and we think we understand each other, but we don't. So often, we don't listen to each other. We don't even look at each other...I mean really look at each other. As Albert Schweitzer said; "We are all so much together, but we are all dying of loneliness."

It all comes down to the connections in life.

PART III:

THE LACK OF CONNECTION

Social connections are critical to the wellbeing of society. A lack of social connection, i.e. alienation, is an underlying theme in personal problems and social issues. My research focused on how alienation affects schools and marriage – two major pillars of society. I found that alienation is an underlying cause of divorce and is a major cause of problems in schools.

Chapter 9 examines what alienation is and what causes it. Chapter 10 looks at how alienation causes various personal problems and social issues.

In Part IV we will get a better understanding of deep social connection, and how we can build better connections in marriage and in the school environment. In the final part of the book we will look at the ramifications of these connections on the individual and society.

CHAPTER 9

UNDERSTANDING THE LACK OF CONNECTION

Because many of our personal problems are interconnected, when we don't recognize other people's problems, we have a more difficult time understanding our own. A lack of connection can create a lack of faith and trust in others and society. This lack of connection destroys relationships and society. This lack of connection is alienation.

Alienation is a result of social distancing between individuals. It occurs when a person does not bond with, and lacks an overall understanding of other people. The root word 'Alien' is described as being foreign, unfamiliar, strange, or not understood.[1,2] People, who have gone on shooting sprees, have often been described as being strange or unfamiliar.

People can be alienated through a lack of actual physical contact. They can be alienated mentally, which can cause various psychological disorders. People can be alienated from people of other countries, cultures, religions, or races. They can be alienated from different age groups or even from their own age group. They can be politically alienated through a lack of understanding of the political process or frustration with the system.

Many people are alienated socially and don't even realize it. A person may appear to be very social, yet feel isolated, because all of his or her friendships are on a superficial level without any real connection. A social person may be alienated from people who are socially isolated, in that he or she may not understand them.

A person can also be socially isolated from loved ones. There are plenty of couples who share the same bed, yet feel totally isolated from each other. Learning about each other is an ongoing process. People face new experiences every day that change their lives. It is only natural for people to lose touch when they stop communicating. Only through connection are people able to understand others better.

Alienation can occur between different social classes or levels of education.[3] In terms of political opinion, some people make decisions based on other opinions from a one-sided viewpoint, sound bytes, and stories they read about on the internet. As they question the accuracy of these sources, the more they appear to view all sources of information as inaccurate or misleading. True intellect involves understanding of all sides. When we truly understand others, we connect with them.[4]

Alienation & Social Issues

When it comes to social issues, people may not get involved for several reasons: they feel things are fine the way they are; they don't care; or they feel like their effort will not make a difference. Feeling powerless can bring on feelings of fear and depression. This is probably why some people are more fearful of flying than of driving, even though, statistically, driving is far more dangerous. Driving a car, you feel you are in control; as a passenger on a plane, you are powerless to do anything, except to get in the best position and pray. Like with claustrophobia, it can be frightening when you feel confined or trapped.

When people do not understand how much of a difference they make in other people's lives, the more likely they will focus on their personal needs. But when people develop a greater understanding of the problems in society, the more likely they will try to do something about it. This is a reason organizations supporting children in developing countries put a picture and story in an advertisement of only one child. They ask support for that one child…just a small donation each month. People respond when they think they can make a difference.

Being aware of and understanding what other people are dealing with in their lives can put your personal problems in perspective. A friend who was a volunteer firefighter, said that he stopped obsessing over his own problems after seeing what other people have suffered: a family losing their home; a spouse who's loved one just died from a heart attack; or even seeing body parts strewn about the road from a motorcycle accident. That was somebody's child.

Environmental issues such as over population, pollution, and global warming can only get people's involvement if they feel empowered to do so. You can list all the statistics you want, but if people feel powerless to make a difference and believe that nothing will change, then they will not bother trying.

While alienation itself is not necessarily directly associated with issues such as overpopulation, there are indirect factors that play a role. Overpopulation, for example, is a serious issue, which could have devastating consequences for humanity. With improvements in nutrition and health, the life expectancy has increased more than two-fold over the past century, which led to a sharp rise in population. But this rate is starting to slow down. As women's rights improve, more women are educated, independent, and more in control of their own bodies. This, along with birth control, means people are more likely to limit the number of children they have.[5, 6]

Alienation is a Natural State

Ever since humans first learned to communicate with each other, they have been evolving socially. Because social connections are learned, alienation is natural, but the more people connect on a deep level, the less alienated they are.

Some babies are more likely to seek out social attention, while other babies are more likely to withdraw. As we grow, we develop social connections, but not all at the same rate. People who are more withdrawn, or are rejected by others, are likely to develop social skills at a slower rate, and may feel more alienated.

Before there were rules and laws, it was survival of the fittest. So therefore, while alienation can result from class structure, class structure is also, in part, a result of alienation. Emotions came much later in time. While torturing people was a popular form of entertainment hundreds of years ago, it is regarded as a form of psychopathic behavior today.

In the natural world, every person is different and no two people are of equal strength in every area. Therefore, because alienation is natural, those with power will more likely control those who don't have power. However, the more people are connected with each other, the more likely they will help and empower each other.

When a lion attacks a zebra, the lion is not thinking about the zebra's feelings. When a cat is chasing a mouse, it is chasing it with curiosity, like how a child chases a butterfly. The only way the cat connects with the mouse is when it eats it. One person may not think twice when squashing a bug, while another person may think about the life of that bug.

"The Bambi Effect" is a term used to describe people's protest against hunting of animals, especially animals that people can relate to. In the movie *Bambi*, the fawn's mother is shot by a hunter. The movie had a profound effect on viewers, making them more aware that deer, like people, have families. The more aware we become of other peoples' or animals' feelings, the more we will feel a connection with them.

Geographical alienation is natural too. If 150 people died in your hometown from an earthquake or tornado, this would be devastating news, because you might have connections to some of these people. This would be front-page news, and the news would likely take up several pages over many days. However, if a much larger earthquake took place half way around the world, it would likely get little coverage. On September 29, 1993, there was a 6.2 earthquake in Latur-Killari, India that killed close to 10,000 people. The *New York Times* printed a story on this that was four short paragraphs. On January 26, 2001, a 7.6 earthquake struck Gujarat, India, killing just over 20,000 people. The *New York Times* printed several articles going into much greater detail.[7] While this earthquake was larger and killed twice as many people, is it possible that part of this expanded foreign coverage was due to people becoming more globally connected?

When the Boston Marathon Bomber killed three people and injured over 100 on April 18, 2013, it made headlines all over the world. On April 15, several car bombs in Iraq killed at least 75 people and injured more than 350 and barely made the news, prompting someone in Iraq to ask if only American lives were important.

Let's now say that you are reading an article that says that an earthquake in Comoros, a country off the eastern coast of Africa and north of Madagascar, killed 1,000 people and left tens of thousands of people homeless. You might think this is tragic, but wonder where this country is, and then go on to read about other news. But now let's say that you saw some footage showing the people who lost loved ones, and you see the people who are homeless and are desperate. This may even spur a huge benefit concert to help these people. If this were a country you recently traveled to, you would feel a connection and would want to learn more about what is taking place.

When looking back on past events, such as the end of a major war, or the collapse of the Berlin Wall, or the collapse of the U.S. stock market in 1929, we don't necessarily remember the articles, but we do remember the headlines and the pictures because they are a more personal connection. At the end of World War II on what is known as V-J Day (Victory over Japan), we all have seen the well-known picture of a sailor kissing a nurse. Operation Desert Storm has been described as being the first televised war. During Operation Desert Storm, some people said that we should just bomb the Middle East. Frequently when people make such statements, they don't really mean it and are saying these things out of frustration or anger. Yet when something bad happens, we want to lash out and punish the wrongdoers, even if there is collateral damage, where innocent people die in the process. But as we come to understand that people of foreign countries or even 'enemy' countries are like us, we begin to see them as people, and not just as some 'evil empire'.

In the movie *Three Kings*, Mark Wahlberg's character Troy, is caught by the Iraqis. While captured, Sa'id, the Iraqi who is torturing Troy, tells Troy how a bomb destroyed his home. His wife lost her legs due to concrete falling on them and his son died while in his bed. He then asks Troy how it would feel if he bombed his daughter. As we hear them talk, we enter Troy's imagination, seeing the image of his wife and daughter, and then we see the explosion. Troy, picturing his wife and daughter being killed from an explosion, responds to the question; "Worse than death!" For the audience, it's now easy to connect Troy's family with the Iraqi's family, along with our own family.

The more a news story pertains to our own life, the more we will relate to the story. On January 31st, 2000, at 4:19pm, Alaska Airlines, Flight 261 crashed in the ocean just west of LAX, a major airport of Los Angeles, California. News of this accident, like any plane crash, was very devastating to me. However, what made this even more devastating was that I frequently flew out of LAX on Alaska Airlines around 4:00pm in the afternoon. When flying out of LAX, most flights fly out heading west over the ocean in the same area as this crash. I realized that this could have been one of the flights I've flown before. Later, when details were coming out of the crash, oddly I felt just a slight amount of relief when I heard that the flight was not out of LAX, but out of Puerto Vallarta, Mexico, a place I knew very little about at the time.

When Steve Jobs died, I saw the following online: "The sad truth: One dies, million cry. Million die, no one cries." Along with it we see a picture of the Apple logo and Africa. While this may seem like some cold harsh reality where people just don't care, this reaction is completely natural. The reality is that in the United States alone, an aggravated assault is committed every 42 seconds, a forcible rape every 6.3 minutes, and a murder is committed every 36 minutes.[8] It is estimated that around 150,000 people in this world die every day, which equates to approximately 104 people every minute and close to two people every second![9] It is pretty safe to assume you are not crying over this, but instead are probably a little more fascinated with these statistics. Does that mean you are uncaring? No, it's because you don't know the people who are dying.

Princess Diana's death was probably one of the most mourned deaths in our world in recent history. Because Princess Diana really showed who she was as a person, people could easily identify with her. They saw her as a loving mother, a caring person, and also, a real person who had real problems like anyone else. People felt like they knew her. If Princess Diana was wearing a 'mask', it sure wasn't much of one. If she instead wore a thick mask, not showing her true self, while we still would mourn, it would not be to the same degree.

People identified with Princess Diana so much that according to *The British Journal of Psychiatry*[10], during the month following the death of Princess Diana, in England, the suicide rate increased by 17 percent, particularly for women in the same age bracket as Princess Diana, which increased by over 44 percent.

I've noticed that of the very few people out there who don't wear masks, people often describe them as being "care-free", "a breath of fresh air" and are very well-liked. They are usually kind, friendly, and very loving. They are open and honest. They see the good in things. They are truly being themselves. Unfortunately there are not many people like this, and everybody wants to be friends with them!

Conclusion

Alienation in itself is a natural phenomenon. As society developed, and as people became more educated, they were better able to communicate with each other. However, more education does not directly translate to less alienation. Some of the most brilliant people are also the most alienated. There is still a great amount of disconnect in society today. Technology has made this worse in some ways and better in others. There are so many different ways that people can be alienated. Being aware goes hand-in-hand with education. The only way to address social problems is by being aware of them and doing something about it. This is why grassroots efforts are so important – "Think globally, act locally." This connection and positive involvement will help eliminate alienation.

CHAPTER 10

HOW ALIENATION AFFECTS YOU

Alienation can result from physiological, psychological, and sociological stressors on the individual. Several studies have shown how physical deprivation, and social isolation have lead to violent and aggressive behavior in monkeys, rats, and humans. Alienation is a major factor in depression, low self-esteem, self-destruction, and personality disorders. Alienation has a major impact on everything from academics, to teen pregnancy, drug abuse, divorce, and even crime and violence. Alienation has such a huge impact on a person's psyche that it can even lead a person to suicide, when directed internally, or to murder, when directed externally. Alienation may be acted out through political extremism, religious extremism, racism, and even war. A person with high amounts of negative energy can influence people, even millions of people, to feel the same way.

Sensory Deprivation

People can be alienated from a lack of physical contact. While some may argue that physical separation and physical deprivation are separate from alienation, people connect with each other both through feelings and physical contact. Physiological aspects are not just limited to physical contact though, but also any other form of sensory deprivation. Using your senses to see someone, touch someone, hear someone's voice, talk to someone, or even smell someone, can relieve feelings of loneliness or isolation. If you are physically isolated, but can hear people encouraging you, or when talking, if you know someone can hear you, you will feel less alone. This is one reason a person might pray: "God, if you are out there and can hear me..." People transporting their pet in a kennel sometimes add a blanket or article of clothing that smells like home or the owner, which helps relieve stress for the pet. If you ever were on a long trip, you may have felt homesick for mom's cooking or even a local restaurant. A simple postcard with a brief note can go a long way.

Lisa Guenther[1] (an associate professor of Philosophy at Vanderbilt University) wrote in The *New York Times* how solitary confinement can affect people. Being physically and socially isolated from others, Guenther explains that many inmates lose touch with reality. She says that the easiest way to destroy a person mentally is likely through solitary confinement. "Deprived of meaningful human contact, otherwise healthy prisoners often come unhinged. They experience intense anxiety, paranoia, depression, memory loss, hallucinations and other perceptual distortions...Prisoners have named their experience 'living death,' the 'gray box,' or 'living in a black hole.'"

Since 95 percent of all inmates will eventually be released back into the public, this is a problem that can potentially affect all people. Guenther's article, included frightening testimony from prisoners who were interviewed by a psychiatrist in Block 10 of Walpole Penitentiary in 1982:

> I went to a standstill psychologically once — lapse of memory. I didn't talk for 15 days. I couldn't hear clearly. You can't see — you're blind — block everything out — disoriented, awareness is very bad. Did someone say he's coming out of it? I think what

I'm saying is true — not sure. I think I was drooling — a complete standstill.

I seem to see movements — real fast motions in front of me. Then seems like they're doing things behind your back — can't quite see them. Did someone just hit me? I dwell on it for hours.

Melting, everything in the cell starts moving; everything gets darker, you feel you are losing your vision.

I can't concentrate, can't read…Your mind's narcotized…sometimes can't grasp words in my mind that I know. Get stuck, have to think of another word. Memory is going. You feel you are losing something you might not get back.

One person who spent over 18 years on death row, most of them in solitary confinement, for a crime he did not commit, described his isolation as a form of "emotional torture." Two years after his exoneration and release, he still feels trapped in isolation: "I am living amongst millions of people in the world today, but most of the time I feel alone. I cry at night because of this feeling. I just want to stop feeling this way, but I haven't been able to."

Temple Grandin (*Animals In Translation*), said, "…solitary confinement is one of the worst punishments you can put them [animals] through". There are many studies that indicate that a deprivation of physical pleasure early in life, results in aggressiveness and withdrawal. When children are deprived of physical affection, they are more likely to become more violent as they grow.[2] James Prescott, a neuropsychologist, said, "deprivation of physical, sensory pleasure is the principal root cause of violence."[3]

Dr. Harry Harlow, a psychologist at the University of Wisconsin, conducted a series of studies that demonstrated how rearing monkeys in isolation, caused psychological damage. "…Harlow's experiment demonstrated that totally depriving Rhesus monkeys of their parents and peers turned them into asocial, untamable, ineffective, aggressive creatures, who fought one another and could not even reproduce their own kind".[4]

In experiments where monkeys were raised in partial isolation (where the monkey was in a bare wire cage and had no physical contact, but could see, smell, and hear other monkeys), these monkeys showed symptoms that included blank staring and self-mutilation.[5] Similarly, people who have committed mass shootings, who were reported as having blank stares include: James Holmes (2012 Colorado theater shooter), Jared Loughner (2011 Arizona shooter), Timothy McVeigh (Oklahoma City Bomber), and Jeffrey Dahmer (late 1970's, early 80's serial killer).

Monkeys raised in total isolation developed major psychological disturbances. When removed from total isolation which lasted three, six, or twelve months, the monkeys usually went into a state of "emotional shock" that included "autistic self-clutching and rocking". Two of the six monkeys raised in total isolation for three months refused to eat. One of them died five days later, while the other monkey ended up being force-fed. The results for the monkeys in isolation for six and twelve months were more debilitating. "The effects of 6 months of total social isolation were so devastating and debilitating that we had assumed initially that 12 months of isolation would not produce any additional decrement. This assumption proved to be false; 12 months of isolation almost obliterated the animals socially…". Harlow suggested "sufficiently severe and enduring early isolation reduces these animals to a social-emotional level in which the primary social responsiveness is fear."[6] With people, this fear is often acted out as anger, hatred, and even violence.

Humans experience the same responses to physical isolation. When newborn babies do not receive any human contact, they can develop health problems and even die. Dr. Saul Schanberg, a professor of pharmacology and biological psychiatry at Duke University, explained that when babies are not held, they switch over into a non-growing state. Schanberg and Dr. Stephen Butler did a study that showed that when rat pups were separated from their mother for only an hour, there were significantly lower levels of ornithine decarboxylase in the brain and heart. Ornithine decarboxylase plays a role in the growth process, and lower levels lead to the "retardation of growth and behavioral development in children known as 'psychosocial dwarfism'". When the rat pups were returned to their mother, these levels increased back to normal.[7]

Suicide on the Cellular Level

Physical deprivation can also affect the neuronal development of the brain, which can then cause psychiatric disorders later in life. These changes have been documented in rats and demonstrated in studies of humans deprived of human touch early in life.

In the development of the brain, cells are formed to perform specific functions and then die when no longer needed for that function. As the brain develops, our body creates more cells than needed. Cells that don't form synaptic connections go through apoptosis, essentially programmed cell death or "cell suicide". Cells commit apoptosis when there is a withdrawal of positive signals and delivery of negative signals. In order for cells to survive, they require continuous stimulation from other cells. When apoptosis occurs, the cell releases proteins and enzymes, which results in the shrinkage and death of the cell. In many cases, programmed cell death plays a vital role in the development of an organism. For example, when you were still in the womb, your fingers and toes were webbed together like a fin. During this time in the womb, the cells that make up this webbing go through apoptosis, so that when you are born, you have ten separate fingers and ten separate toes.

When maternal deprivation affects neuronal development, these cells go through apoptosis. One of the first studies of its kind, showed how maternal deprivation could result in the death of brain cells.[8] In the study, rat pups were separated from their mothers for a 24 hour period (in addition to shorter periods of time over a two-week period). After this period of time, their brains were examined, revealing that several types of cells in the brain were dying. One of the areas of the brain that was affected is the hippocampus, which is associated with memory, stress, and depression. Because these behavioral characteristics were difficult to reverse, it suggests that the chemistry of the brain has changed. The authors explain that previous studies showed that stress can decrease growth in adult rats.[9]

A similar study showed that prolonged separation from the mother can alter and impair brain development by increased apoptosis of neurons and glial cells, which represent the connective tissue of the nervous system. So the lack of maternal connection, results in the lack of connective tissue in the nervous system.[10]

While not necessarily related, there is a common feeling people describe when they feel rejected or not loved, as if they were withering and dying. Similarly, in Ezekiel's book, *The Racist Mind*, several of the teen interviewed felt as if their lives were about to be extinguished, as if they might disappear into non-existence. This is also similar to how I felt rejected by society. I wanted to die and be extinguished from people's memory as if I were never in this world.

Social Isolation

While a lack of physical contact can have devastating consequences, just feeling disconnected can be equally as devastating. Regardless of how physically close a person is to others, feeling isolated, lonely, excluded, rejected, or disconnected, can tear a person apart psychologically, so much so, that the individual will act out in destructive ways towards himself and/or others.

Although everyone feels lonely at times, some experience a type of loneliness in which they feel a permanent social distance from others. Some people avoid others, not because they want to be alone, but because they feel rejected or feel that they don't fit in. It may only take a few negative comments from others for that person to retreat further into isolation. We are more fragile than we think. The more a person feels rejected or unaccepted, the more alienated he or she may become. These feeling can be more severe when a person feels rejected by everyone.

Social isolation and feelings of rejection can turn natural feelings of sadness into depression or anger. It is natural for people to have enemies and to feel suspicious, anxious, and unhappy.[11] But what is not natural is when sadness lingers into "debilitating" depression and when anxiety becomes chronic.[12] Studies have shown that social isolation can contribute to family violence.[13] Social disorders can develop when we do not develop relationships. "Social rejection – or fearing it – is one of the most common causes of anxiety."[14] If you have a fear of people, a world of billions of people can feel very isolating.

It has been well documented that paying no attention to a child causes frustration and aggression in the child.[15] Being deprived of attention by a loved one can feel like rejection. When people feel deprived, they are more likely to act out violently than people who are simply unhappy.[16] People, like animals, can act out violently when they feel trapped or frustrated.[17]

Some parents pay little attention to their children and when they do discipline them, it is based more on how they feel. If the parent is in a good mood, the child could do whatever he or she wants. However, if the parent were in a bad mood, the child would be punished severely. Children raised in environments like this are more likely to feel worthless and helpless: regardless of what they do, their actions will not make a difference. They are also less likely to understand how their actions affect others. These children are more likely to get into fights, use force to get their way, are more likely to drop out of school, and more likely to have a criminal record by age thirty.[18] When they themselves become parents, they will likely repeat the same mistakes their parents made.

"The biggest disease today is not leprosy or tuberculosis, but rather the feeling of being unwanted."
                    Mother Teresa (1910 – 1997)

There are many warning signs that a child feels alienated which include; low self-esteem, behavioral problems, control issues, feelings of isolation or rejection, become socially withdrawn, having poor grades and showing little interest in school. Some children become more alienated as they get older. They are missing out on all the socialization 'games' that other kids are learning from each other. As students who are missing out get older, they fall even further behind, appearing even more different from the other students. They are more likely to have poor peer relations; get into fights, backstab, and are more likely to engage in bullying and aggressive behavior. They are also more prone to violence, showing expressions of violence in drawings and writings, uncontrolled anger, discipline problems, having a prejudicial attitude, drug use, and affiliation with gangs.[19] These problems, in turn, create a more alienating environment for all students. Several studies have suggested that vandalism and violence creates an alienating, fearful atmosphere among students and teachers.[20]

Feeling rejected by one's peers can have devastating consequences, leading to academic failure and even dropping out. Students who are most likely to drop out of school are identified as having symptoms of alienation. Students who feel socially rejected are two to eight times more likely to drop out of school than students who have friends. One study found that one in four children, who were unpopular in elementary school, dropped out of grade school.[21]

These feelings of alienation that start at an early age can extend into adulthood and even last a lifetime. For example, a survey done with former students invited to a fifty-year high school reunion found that a number of respondents, who had no interest in attending the reunion, said they hated high school. Of those attending, most said they loved their high school years. A student's positive or negative experience in high school seemed to relate directly to how included they felt. One woman said that she wanted to attend even though she felt excluded in high school. She made a point of telling another class member that she always remembered her because that classmate was always friendly toward her. She remembered this 50 years later!

"Loneliness is the ultimate poverty."
Abigail Van Buren

Crime is highly associated with alienation.[22] Teens who engage in delinquent activity and teens who have been incarcerated show signs of alienation.[23] While high rates of poverty are associated with higher crime rates, the level of social connection among people in a given community will also affect the crime rate. The mix of poverty and disconnection together have a stronger influence on crime rates than factors such as race, ethnicity, and family structure.[24]

Teen Pregnancy

Research has consistently shown that sex education leads to a reduction of teenage pregnancy. Just imagine teenagers being given a license to drive without any driver's education, experience, or supervision. The number of accidents by teen drivers would skyrocket. Beyond education, teens who get pregnant are often not the popular girls who are having sex. If you asked teenage girls who have active social lives, if they want a baby now, they would probably respond with fright, because they are still young and want to enjoy their youth. I asked some teenage girls who had active social lives, what their opinion was on getting pregnant in the next few years.

Their answers clearly showed that they absolutely did not want to get pregnant.

Being a teen mom can be alienating in itself, but if you already feel alienated from everybody else, getting pregnant might be seen as a positive thing – a source of love. It appears that girls who tend to get pregnant are the ones who are looking for some sort of connection, because they are likely to have little or no social life. They want someone to love them. These girls seem to be down on life. Several studies have shown that teenagers who become pregnant don't necessarily lack the knowledge or confidence, but tend to feel socially excluded, dislike school, and have family problems. Feeling socially excluded can result in a positive attitude towards having a baby.[25,26,27,28]

Is Mental Pain Worse than Physical Pain?

Feeling neglected can be more damaging than physical abuse.[29] Because our emotions are such a major part of our lives, it should not be surprising that psychological pain can be more painful than physical pain. Our brain registers social rejection in the same area as it does physical pain – social rejection is like a primal threat.[30] The idea that people may reject you is a very scary thought. Words, such as "broken heart", or "devastated" are used to describe mental pain. Perhaps it goes back to when people lived in tribes and being rejected from the group put you on your own. This was essentially a death sentence.

Sometimes when the psychological pain is so great, in order to help relieve the pain, people will harm themselves physically to help take the focus off the mental pain. Self-destructive behaviors such as cutting oneself are ways to help relieve that pain. This psychological pain can also be relieved through something as simple as hugging. However, when a person feels like there is no one to turn to, he or she may resort to self-harm.

How Psychological Disorders Develop

Feeling alienated can lead people to act out in seemingly irrational ways: self-mutilation, eating disorders or faking one's own rape or abduction are examples. Unfortunately, the public's reaction is to say these people are just looking for attention. When a girl in Wisconsin faked her own kidnapping, someone wrote on a website thread: "Pathetic. Young people are so starved for love and affection. They will do anything for attention. Sad. Maybe we should charge people to call the police. Then people wouldn't abuse law enforcement.".[31] While common, this reaction suggests the writer believes that [young] people are pathetic because they are in need of love and attention. Think about it. Shouldn't this be a wake up call? What if, instead of calling that person "pathetic," we took the time to respond to that call for love and attention? But how can we do that effectively?

Many people want to help, but instead of really listening, they focus on trying to fix the problem by giving advice. They may try to get the person's mind off his or her problem by saying something like "Let's go shopping!" or "Let's have a big bowl of ice cream!" in an attempt to relieve the pain. While well meaning, such quick fixes are only temporary and do not provide the psychological connection a person really needs.

Instead of giving and getting a good amount of real connection, many people settle for the fleeting moments of superficial attention. This need for real connection could explain why people get so addicted to their cell phones, email, or to social media websites. Getting a personal letter in the mail can be really exciting. Every time we get a message, via email, text, etc., we get a tiny rush of excitement – we get a little dopamine.

Dopamine is a natural chemical in the body that acts as a neurotransmitter, playing a major role in reward-motivation behavior. When dopamine is released, it gives a feeling of satisfaction or pleasure. When people feel deprived of love and attention on a continual basis, they may resort to temporary quick fixes, such as shopping, eating a big bowl of ice cream, or drinking to relieve stress, depression, or to calm anxiety.

Because rewards increase dopamine levels, people with low dopamine levels may more likely develop eating disorders, become alcoholics, compulsively spend, or become compulsive gamblers. Kleptomania, pyromania, bulimia, and obsessive-compulsive disorders also give a person a momentary dopamine rush.

Even self-mutilation releases dopamine, which may help explain why feeling pain is better than feeling numb. This is why negative attention is better than no attention. When people feel numb inside, they may turn to drugs, so they can feel something…anything. A person may take drugs to help feel some sense of normal in a life that feels out of place and full of chaos. Drugs like cocaine and heroin are known to release large amounts of dopamine artificially. When the drugs wear off, there is nothing. As our body adapts to the drugs, in order to achieve the same high, the dose will need to be increased, creating an addiction.

Bullying

Children who have anger issues are more likely to be withdrawn social outcasts who overreact to being teased or what they perceive as being teased. With these false perceptions, they presume that others are hostile or threatening, and respond by lashing out. With these overreactions, they are only ostracized further. As a student in grade school, and later as I worked with students in the classroom, I've noticed many occasions where a student does something 'under the radar,' like whisper something rude or slightly kick the chair of someone they want to tease. While the person being teased may ignore this at first, the "good" student will keep quietly doing this, until the other student lashes out. The "good" student then acts shocked when the other kid lashes out for apparently no reason. The teacher scolds the teased boy, because the "good" boy is perceived to be innocent.

Bullying is not just committed by kids who have low self-esteem or who have problems at home. Bullying is a way for students to try to gain social status and often comes from indirect anger. The natural need, especially for teenagers, to be part of the group and the opportunity for anonymous actions can lead them to expand normal "groupishness" into bullying. They are not necessarily aware of how hurtful their actions can be, nor do they understand the deeper feelings of their "victim".

On January 14, 2010, 15-year-old Phoebe Prince, a freshman at South Hadley High School in Massachusetts, was found in her family's apartment hanging in the stairway. Phoebe was bullied at school on a daily basis for weeks. Confrontations in school took place in classes, the gym, in the lunchroom, the bathroom, in the hallways, and outside of school. These bullies also spread rumors about her and tormented her online. Phoebe told a friend that: "School has been close to intolerable lately." Gus Sayer, Superintendent of South Hadley Public schools, said that Prince "was apparently a very private person, she bore a lot without talking to friends or with parents or with anybody at school." Six of the people who participated in the online bullying were charged with felonies. According to the court records, she had gone out with boys who also dated two of her alleged tormentors.[32] One of the bullies who was interviewed on the Today Show (7/8/11), said that she was trying to help out a friend. She also said that she did not know everything that Phoebe Prince was going through, and if she had known this, she would have tried to help Phoebe.[33] This is an unfortunate example that shows that while people may think they know each other, they really don't...and if they did, this never would have happened.

Violence

As children are exposed to violence, they learn to respond with violence. Anthropological studies of preliterate societies have consistently shown that the use of physical punishment (toward children) and the lack of physical affection resulted in a higher rate of violence among adults. "...the percent likelihood of a society being physically violent if it is physically affectionate toward its infants and tolerant of premarital sexual behavior is two percent".[34]

People who engage in violent behavior are more likely to have suffered from a violent past, have a chemical imbalance, or are in a situation where they feel like they are being attacked and therefore resorts to self-defense. If a child is raised in a violent environment, naturally he or she will believe that violence is how one solves problems. A majority of violent behavior comes out of a perceived need for self-defense. When a person is attacked (or feels that he or she is being attacked) mentally or physically, it is natural for that person to react in self-defense or flee the situation. When a person feels rejected by others, this form of rejection or condemnation is a form of attacking the individual. It is not necessarily social isolation that is dangerous, but the feeling of rejection or not accepted by others that can lead to violent behavior.[35] The aggression is aimed at the cause of the frustration. When these feelings of frustration and aggression become generalized towards others, acts of violence may be random.[36]

When people are severely alienated, such as people who have gone on mass shooting sprees, they are likely beyond any desire for praise or criticism. People at this level are described as being emotionless, numb, and even soulless. Having an overly negative feeling towards life, they are likely beyond anger or depression. I believe that when you are in this state, there is deadness in you and you know it…and you want to feel again. You don't just want to feel pain, you want to kill and be killed.

There are many stories where a student or adult who was socially rejected or bullied went out on a murderous rampage.[37,38] At Columbine High School in Colorado, Dylan Klebold and Eric Harris used guns and bombs, killing thirteen students and in the end, killed themselves. They were part of a clique at school called the "Trenchcoat Mafia". They were angry towards Jews, Blacks, and Hispanics, as well as some of the other cliques at school. Many students said that the violence came out of the years of taunting the boys received from other students. The school was described by students as being divided into cliques. Some students described tension between the groups.[39] Students in the Trench Coat Mafia hated athletes the most because they were more powerful and popular. They wore black trench coats, ghoulish makeup, and berets with Nazi crosses. They liked Hitler, did not like authority, and often spoke of war and guns.[40] "The Goth scene is embraced by many alienated youths who express themselves by donning black clothes and heavy makeup".[41] Columbine High was considered, by some parents, a very nice school in one of the nicest areas. Harris was described as a quiet, shy and nice student who had not caused any problems in the past. Klebold was considered smart and skilled with computers. Harris and Klebold had no prior discipline problems at school.

A person with a lack of empathy, sense of moral responsibility, or social conscience, is a person who is alienated. This antisocial behavior is classified as sociopathic behavior. A survey in the early 1970's, estimated that between 56 percent and 81 percent of all convicted felons were sociopaths.[42] Another study examined 1,200 randomly selected people and found that a significant number of those subjects who showed violent behavior also had a psychiatric disorder.[43] Several studies have shown that criminals often come from abusive or neglectful environments.[44] Some of the most violent criminals were emotionally neglected, often being moved from foster home to foster home.[45]

How a Lack of Social Support Affects People

There is plenty of research that shows that men have less social support and are more likely to be socially isolated than women. Men are also less likely to show emotions than women. Cultures throughout the world expect men to be tough and aggressive. A common perception of strength is to not show emotion or be emotionally vulnerable. On a popular dating website, the logo show an image of a male and female drawn like what you see on a typical bathroom door. The male appears to be stoic, standing up tall and strait and showing no emotion. The female on the other hand clearly shows her emotions by leaning on to the man and kicking up her leg.

All too often I have heard people talk about how women, unlike men, are emotionally unstable and even crazy. My friend's middle-school daughter told me how horrible girls were compared to guys, while I was driving her to school. I told her what she said is not really true, but she persisted, saying that women "backstab". I told her that while some women "backstab," some men just stab. I asked her how many women she has heard about who actually stabbed someone. I pointed out that every day there are reports of men stabbing, shooting, and even killing people! I was pretty angry when I told her this, because all she seems to have ever heard was how women are crazy, while men are collective, calm, and rational. Her attitude was especially amazing because her own mother was stabbed 36 times with a barbeque fork and murdered by her stepdad a few years prior to this conversation.

In cases of abuse of the wife by her husband, abusive husbands start by wanting to control the actions of their spouse, including how they dress. They start with verbal abuses, followed by over apologizing, sending flowers, protestations of their great love etc. This grows into more control, more isolating them from family and friends, and finally physical abuse, even threatening them with death. Wives were very likely to be emotionally and/or financially dependent on their husbands.[46] When a person is dependent on another person, that person will more likely accept abuse.[47] A violent spouse may blame their partner for their own outbursts of violence. In many cases, a violent spouse may be considered to be nice and show no signs of violence in public. This indicates that this is a behavior that develops over time. If gone unchecked, people may develop a habit of acting out violently.

Homicide committed by women often involves interpersonal and domestic conflicts, unlike acts of aggression or crimes that are committed by men.[48] One study which examined abused women who were incarcerated for killing their husband or boyfriend, found that women who ended up resorting to 'murder', were also more likely to have been isolated from others, compared to abused women who left the situation by going to a shelter or back to family. Data taken from forty-seven single mothers from a low socioeconomic background, showed that a lack of social support put these mothers at the greatest risk for becoming physically abusive with their children.[49]

Like with people who are recruited into gangs, terrorist recruits are not necessarily loners, but join because they have friends who joined. Jessica Stern, who serves on the Hoover Institution Task Force on National Security and Law, a lecturer at Harvard Law School, and author of *Terror in the Name of God: Why Religious Militants Kill*, explains that while many terrorists want to change society, it is more about wanting to belong.[50] A feeling of belonging and having social support are important. Umar Farouk Abdulmutallab, who is often referred to as the "Underwear Bomber," wrote in an online Islamic forum: "I have no one...to support me and I feel depressed and lonely. I do not know what to do. And then I think this loneliness leads me to other problems."[50] It is interesting to note that at Abdulmutallab's sentencing in court, he said that he was "proud to kill in the name of God". As many may think that he is evil, in actuality, he is trying to do the right thing.[51, 52, 53]

Conclusion

Monkeys raised in partial isolation resorted to self-mutilation. Monkeys raised in total isolation became aggressive, untamable, and violent, i.e. they became alienated to the full extent – they became soulless empty shells.

Is it any wonder that people who feel isolated, resort to self-destructive behaviors, develop eating disorders, cutting, and so on. Is it any wonder that people who feel completely alienated become aggressive, uncontrollable, and violent – towards themselves, and others? Our response is to point the finger and blame. We make judgments and say these people are evil. I don't think anybody would label these monkeys as evil, but instead might refer to the experimenter as evil for conducting something so "inhumane". If this is the case, then is society evil for allowing such a lack of connection in society to exist? The scientist, conducting the experiment, is trying to understand what is taking place, so we can better society. Building better connections with one another is the first step in elimination of society's greatest plague – Alienation.

PART IV:

BUILDING BETTER CONNECTIONS

Building solid social connections is a critical factor in building a powerful society. But we have never fully learned how to connect with each other. Chapter 11 explores what deep social connection means and how people can connect with each other on a deeper level. Chapter 12 examines how social connections play a critical role in marriage. Chapter 13 looks at how we can build better social connections in schools.

The final part of the book will look at the greater impact of social connections on society. It will also look at how communication and connection has evolved from the very beginning of life itself, and will answer that question of who we are.

CHAPTER 11

UNDERSTANDING CONNECTION

Gossip magazines and reality shows are popular because we want to know more about people. But the little information we get is often superficial and based on partial truths.

It can be difficult for people to open up about their emotions. Many people have told me that they feel like others do not really understand them or feel like they cannot open up to others without being judged. While we all have a need to be understood, when we are able to learn about and understand others it helps us understand our own emotions better. The point is that people desperately want to open up about who they are…their thoughts and feelings – their emotions, but they are apprehensive about this.

The interviews that I conducted often started off very superficial; but it wasn't until close to the end of the interview, or even after the camera was turned off that the respondents really started to open up. People told me things, very deep things that they do not even talk about with close friends.

In daily life, we really don't take the time to listen to each other. But in an interview, the interviewer's job is to take the time to listen to and understand the person. The interviewer will first try to establish some common ground or trust level. What is amazing is that these are total strangers that are opening up to you. It is easy for people to open up because they know the interviewer is really listening.

Communication with others is a critical life skill.[1] Only seven percent of communication involves words. Thirty-eight percent of communication is reflected in the vocal aspects such as pitch, speed, volume, and tone of voice; fifty-five percent is visual, which involves body language, gestures, and eye movement. In face-to-face communication, about 65 percent of the message is shown through what we do, and over 90 percent is non-verbal.[2]

Dr. John Gottman, who heads The Gottman Institute, could tell just from listening to a conversation of a couple in a restaurant whether or not they were headed for divorce.[3]

Understanding Social Skills

If you have a nice, friendly, honest personality, you have a greater chance at success. Doctors are discovering the value of learning how to better communicate with their patients. Research has shown that malpractice lawsuits have little to do with the number of mistakes a doctor makes. In Malcolm Gladwell's book *Blink*[4], he explains that some highly skilled doctors get sued a lot, while other doctors who make a lot of mistakes, are much less likely to get sued.

Research by Wendy Levinson has shown that half of doctors never get sued. Patients who have filed lawsuits have often said that they felt rushed and treated poorly by the doctor. Patients, who knew their doctor well or felt like the doctor listened to them and respected them, don't usually sue their doctor. Levinson's research showed that primary care physicians who had no malpractice claims against them were likely to use more humor with their patients and were more focused on educating their patients. Just examining the tone of voice was a good indicator if the doctor would get sued or not. The more dominant the doctor's voice sounded, the more likely he or she would get sued compared to doctors who sounded less dominant and showed more concern.

This demonstrates the importance of learning social skills. Why is it that doctors had to learn these social skills – something that should be common knowledge by this level of education? Why do seasoned executives need to take courses in social skills? It should tell you something that so many sign up for Dale Carnegie courses to learn self-improvement, salesmanship, corporate training, public speaking, and interpersonal skills. So why don't we teach children these skills which can be so important in their lives and success?

> "When dealing with people, remember
> you are not dealing with creatures of
> logic, but creatures of emotion."
> Dale Carnegie

Shouldn't learning social skills be as important in the curriculum as reading and math? Unfortunately many social skills, good and bad, are learned out on the playground. People, who are socially alienated from others, will have a difficult time learning what is socially acceptable and what is not. When a person in this situation makes a mistake, they are more likely to retreat back into their own world.

Lord of the Flies is a book about a group of schoolboys who get marooned on a deserted island. The students are civilized at first, then some of them resort to savagery, violence, and even murder. Some say they resorted to their savage human nature, but I believe they were never really well socialized to begin with. It does not matter if they were from a rich boarding school. Beyond the shiny exteriors of students you see in high school are people who are dealing with all sorts of issues in their lives. While the idea that comparing how we learn social skills today to *Lord of the Flies* sounds pretty exaggerated, just look at how teens and adults behave in school and the working world. Some students see school as a nightmarish social environment that is not much better than *Lord of the Flies*. A high school girl hangs herself because she was bullied. Alienated students fight back the only way they know how by shooting and killing classmates and teachers, and in turn, themselves. These are stories that we hear about again and again.

There isn't much difference between the school environment and the work environment, except that things are masked better. Gossip, manipulation, and bullying still occur in the work place.

The reality is that people often have a difficult time interacting with others. The closer people are, the more likely there will be hostile interactions. Based on this information, it would appear that people are better off not interacting with each other. But this just shows how important it is for people to learn how to connect with each other, especially in areas with a high population density.

While many people feel at least a little fear or hesitancy when talking to other people, they sure don't feel this when talking to or petting a dog. One study showed that talking to a dog and petting a dog are less physiologically arousing to a person than is talking with other people. Interactions with a dog (regardless if the person was a dog lover or was neutral toward dogs) had the most influence on lower blood pressure in the person.[5]

Some people naturally have better emotional intelligence than others. This can be affected by how socially intelligent the parents are and how those parents serve as role models. But people can learn and develop their emotional intelligence like they can learn most any other subject.

Danial Goleman, Ph.D., in *Emotional Intelligence* and *Social Intelligence*, explains that emotional intelligence involves being able to recognize and understand emotions. Emotional intelligence is important because emotions affect our thoughts, actions, bodies, and relationships. Emotional literacy helps one understand one's own emotions and the emotions of others. This knowledge is useful for building better relationships. When people are able to communicate and connect effectively, it can build a tremendous amount of confidence and trust.

Using emotional intelligence on a daily basis will be much easier once we start to learn it. All people would like to know that they are well liked and loved. With emotional intelligence, you gain the ability to better communicate with and understand people and their actions. Research documents that people who are more socially intelligent are more likely to be successful in their personal lives, social lives, and at work.

While the idea that being able to identify emotions seems simple, it is actually quite complex. There are many non-verbal signs that people may sense but do not fully pick up on. In many cases people will misinterpret these signals. After talking to someone, you may have a strange feeling that something is wrong, but not know what. You may think that the other person is being rude or deceptive, when they may just be shy or are focused on another problem.

Learning how to connect deeply with others goes beyond simply learning how to control emotions, and even goes beyond understanding emotions.

Listening

How many times have you told someone about something you believed or experienced, and before you could even finish your first sentence, he or she would already be either disagreeing with you or wanting to give you advice? How can you disagree with someone before you even hear what he or she has to say? Steven Covey, who wrote *The Seven Habits of Highly Effective People*, explains, "Most people do not listen with the intent to understand; they listen with the intent to reply. They're either speaking or preparing to speak. They're filtering everything through their own paradigms, reading their autobiography into other people's lives. 'Oh, I know exactly how you feel!' 'I went through the very same thing. Let me tell you about my experience.' "[6] Being able to listen fully is critical if you really want to communicate.

In many companies a frequent complaint from employees is that they feel like they are never heard, so they give up on saying anything and morale goes down. At one company I worked at, people in each department not only blamed the other departments, but they also blamed others in the same department. This is exactly how we operate as a society. We are always trying to find someone to blame. As a manager, I took time out of my schedule to really listen to what employees had to say. While this was more work at first, it changed the environment, making work more fun and productive for everybody. Once employees realized that I took them seriously, they started coming up with better ideas. When people feel like they are being listened to, they feel like they are more a part of the team.

After a company open house that was plagued with issues, I suggested a company meeting to figure out what we needed to fix for next year. Instead of having a meeting where people often don't speak up, I decided to have an "email meeting". I asked employees what they thought we could do better for next year. I only received about two or three responses, but instead of giving up, I edited down the responses and put their name after what they wrote. With this, I re-sent out the email and received responses from almost everybody. Too often are great ideas shot down before they are heard, because they were never heard completely. Due to the input of all employees, many customers and vendors said that the following year's open house was the best they ever saw.

Many teenagers are uncomfortable talking about their problems in life. They may feel that adults don't understand their problems or that they don't listen, which is often true. Parents may argue that their children don't tell them anything, yet may not realize that they are not really listening to their children. Many parents want to help their children feel better by giving them advice. I've seen plenty of cases where a child is trying to tell their parent something while the parent is more focused on reading the paper or checking emails. Children learn and mimic these listening skills from their parents.

Active listening helps us more fully connect with others. With active listening, we try to fully understand something from another person's point of view. People, who listen to others, have an easier time connecting with others and develop a greater empathy towards them.

The Multi-Tasking Myth

There is nothing more of a turn off than trying to talk to someone who interrupts to take a call on their cell phone or to text someone back. This is becoming more prevalent with electronics and various hand-held, communication devices. People are distracted while driving. They are being removed as jurors when they text while "listening" to a witness's testimony.

People think they can listen to you while doing other things (multi-tasking), but they can't. When people "multi-task", they are actually only taking in one thing at a time, but are switching back and forth between different tasks. Studies have shown that when people are talking in groups, like at a cocktail party, while you can listen to the person you are talking with, you cannot process what is being said in other conversations, other than certain key words or names.[7] If you decide to listen to that other conversation, you no longer are hearing the person who is talking to you.

Let's say, for example, that you are driving on the freeway, and the traffic is slowing down quickly due to an accident. If someone is in the passenger seat talking to you, seeing the traffic ahead, he or she will likely stop talking or will tell you to slow down.[8] You essentially have a second pair of eyes watching the road with you. However, when you talk to someone on the phone, while you are trying to process what is taking place ahead, the person on the phone keeps talking, having no clue what you are facing, and may not even know that you are driving.

When you are being constantly interrupted checking your email, you experience tiny amounts of stress. With these interruptions, you don't have time to process something you learned, and you will be less likely to remember it. These constant interruptions can increase levels of Cortisol, which appears to reduce memory. Cortisol is released when a person feels stress, and it also increases blood sugar. Cortisol also suppresses the immune system, which increases one's susceptibility to diseases such as diabetes, cancer, and heart disease. A person who actively listens would be gaining endorphins rather than increasing stress.[9]

Body Language

Communication is affected by how we interpret other people's body language. People, and even animals, who have a difficult time reading body language and display atypical body language, are often excluded from the group.

Non-verbal communication involves sending and receiving signals. Understanding non-verbal communication is important for one's social life and career. While some people are naturally better at communicating and interpreting these actions, this is a learned skill.

Dr. Paul Ekman, a noted psychologist who pioneered research on emotions in relation to facial expression, believes that what we show on our faces is, to a certain degree, what we are thinking. In Ekman's research on decoding different facial expressions, it was found that when a person just makes the facial expressions, it was enough to make a change in a person's mood.[10] If a person does not hide his or her expression, the expression will usually last a couple of seconds or more, clearly showing that the person is either embarrassed, excited, happy, sad, or fearful, among other feelings. However, when a person is hiding an emotion, there will very likely be at least a momentarily clue showing how a person truly feels. The reason for this is that if a person feels this way, it will show, even for a split second. While these expressions reveal the emotion a person feels, they don't say what the person is hiding or why.

When I moved back to southern California, I was temporarily staying with a friend and his girlfriend. One Friday night when she came home, she asked her boyfriend to come talk to her. I could tell that she did not have a happy look on her face, and because they were talking quietly, I could tell that it was likely because I was intruding on them for now over a week. I felt horrible about this and realized that I needed to move out as soon as possible. Then came the dreaded words; "Mark, we need to talk to you." Just as I felt the impending metaphorical axe come down on my neck, they asked me if it was OK that we not go out to the party and instead order in some Thai food and rent a movie. Being kind of worn out myself, this sounded like a great idea. When I later told them what I was thinking, they told me they loved having me there. They loved that I always did the dishes and made coffee in the morning for everyone.

Eye Contact

Perhaps most important in social interaction, is eye contact, because it goes much deeper than words, and even beyond the superficial measures we use to define our selves. Even when there are no words, such as between a mother and her baby, the looks can be some of the most powerful bonding moments in life. The eyes play a major role in facial expressions, and eye contact plays a critical role in communication. In a 2002 study published in *Developmental Psychology*, researchers found that infants followed people's eye direction, rather than head direction.[11]

People welcome eye contact when they are trying to get your attention, especially when talking to you. Eye contact shows you are interested in what the other person has to say.

Some people, especially if they are shy, have a difficult time making eye contact with other people. If you are shy, instead of worrying what the other person is thinking about you, focus on really listening to what the other person is saying, and show it by making eye contact.

There may have been times when you were a child, and you were in trouble for doing something you knew you should not have done. In these circumstances, where you were feeling shameful, you were probably looking down, because it was hard to even look at the scolding parent. Similarly with shyness, a person may feel ashamed for a defect he or she sees in him or herself.

Eye contact is a powerful communication. In the natural world, it is often considered threatening. Imagine how it would feel if you were in a forest and there was a tiger or bear watching you. In the natural world, the most logical reason for an animal to be watching another animal is either to eat it or to make sure it does not get eaten.

Similarly, in the human world, a person may stare somebody down as a form of intimidation. Likewise, when a guy is staring at a woman, she may perceive this as creepy behavior where she feels she needs to protect herself from his aggression.

It has often been said that the eyes are the windows into a person's soul. For two people to look into each other's eyes for a few minutes can be more difficult than it sounds. What is difficult is at first you are looking at someone deep down, and he or she is looking at you deep down. When you look into each other's eyes, you feel more connected. After doing this for a few minutes, you will likely develop a great amount of empathy for this person.

One program I observed[12] used an exercise where members within a team of ten to fifteen students formed into two lines with each student facing another student. While the director spoke, the students were asked to look into each other's eyes for a few minutes. After this, each student rotated to another teammate, until they did this exercise with every other person on their team. Some students nervously giggled at first, and some students ended up crying. This always appeared to be a point in the program where the level of connection between students became stronger.

Looking into each other's eyes for a couple of minutes can help build a more lasting relationship by creating deeper social connection. For any marriage, especially one that is in trouble, a good exercise would be to ask the couples to look into each other's eyes for a few minutes without talking.

Michael Ellsberg, who wrote the book *The Power of Eye Contact*, started "Eye Gazing Parties" where people would spend about two-minutes looking into the eyes of another person, and after the two minutes, they move on to the next person. Ellsberg wrote that most everyone feels some discomfort at first staring into the eyes of a stranger or a loved one because our eyes give other people instant access to how we are feeling. "Through eye gazing this happens just sitting still, seeing the depths of another person. A new world appears, with vistas you hadn't imagined. And healing. And liberation."[13] With eye contact that goes beyond the typical day-to-day eye contact, people feel like they're seen and accepted for who they are, and are able to feel all right about themselves. "The way to deeper eye contact, and to improved relations with others in general, is to accept ourselves as whole human beings, to accept our successes and failures, our areas of brilliance and our deep shortcomings. Accept it all and love it all."[14] Ellsberg notes that people have said that eye gazing permanently changed their life. When people are able to understand each other deeply, there is a feeling of oneness. "In eye gazing, you fall in love, but it's not necessarily with the other's personality. It's with something much more profound. It's almost beyond the person."[15] You see a person's deepest beauty. "Better eye contact is more like a surprise, a nice side effect of self-acceptance. The main benefit is that you'll feel better and be able to love deeper."[16]

Arthur Aron, a psychologist at Stony Brook University in New York, conducted research on what keeps people attracted to each other. In one study, he had a group of men and women form pairs. Each pair was asked to tell each other personal details about themselves and to stare into each other's eyes for two minutes. Most pairs reported feeling attracted to each other. One pair even ended up getting married.[17] Aron explains that what is taking place is that long term couples move from an addictive romantic relationship that produces dopamine, to a more bonding state that involves oxytocin. Oxytocin is a hormone that is released when we feel bonded with someone in an emotional or physical way. Oxytocin is often referred to as a "love" chemical because it is associated with eye contact, physical contact, and it helps with social connection.

Oxytocin is more prevalent in animals that mate for life. Research has shown that in prairie voles, when the oxytocin receptors are blocked, the animals were less likely to form monogamous bonds and more likely to roam. Grandin explains that oxytocin is essential to social memory, helping animals remember each other.[18] It is believed that oxytocin levels are higher in couples that have a strong long-term healthy relationship.

While oxytocin only stays in the system for a brief period of time, it is produced when a mother nurses her young, or when people hug, touch, massage, and make love. As it is released when we are with those close to us, we associate those people with these good feelings creating a bond on a chemical and psychological level.

Oxytocin also helps in lowering blood pressure, stress, and levels of cortisol. Research has shown that oxytocin may also help in treating problems such as shyness, social anxiety, and post-traumatic stress disorder. Oxytocin is even being used as a nasal spray to help treat symptoms of autism because people with autism have great difficulty building and maintaining social connections.

Touch

Research has shown that the power of touch can also have a dramatic affect on the lives of both people and animals. Just as physical deprivation can have devastating consequences on the health of the individual, touching plays an important role in good health. Touching can help ease depression and reduce stress. It can help calm babies. It has even been shown to help babies who show signs of attachment disorder. "…babies who are not held and nuzzled and hugged enough will literally stop growing and-if the situation lasts long enough, even if they are receiving proper nutrition – die. Researchers discovered this when trying to figure out why some orphanages had infant mortality rates around 30-40 percent."[19]

Research by Charles Nelson, a professor of pediatrics at Harvard Medical School and Boston Children's Hospital, has shown that neglect can greatly affects brain development, resulting in long-term mental disorders. Nelson studied children who were raised in Romania orphanages in the 1980's. Up until 1989, when the repressive Romanian government was overthrown, there were over 100,000 children raised in government institutions. It was clear that many of these children had stunted growth due to neglect. Nelson explains that when he visited these orphanages, children were left in cribs for days at a time without being held. Children were rocking back and forth as if they had autism. Toddlers were desperate for attention, reaching out to you as if they wanted to be picked up and held. The research found that many of these orphans had very low levels of brain activity. As the children grew, it was clear that their brains were physically smaller than normal healthy brains.

Izidor Ruckel, who came from a Romanian orphanage where children were beaten and neglected, wrote a book about his experience and produced a documentary on Romanian orphans. Being in the same orphanage over the years, he realized that he had power over many of the other children who had more serious disabilities. Ruckel explains that "There was no right, there was no wrong in the orphanage...You didn't know the difference because you were never taught. I was put in charge of kids and I treated them just the way they treated us. If you didn't listen to me, I'd beat you."[20] At age 11, Ruckel was adopted by an American family. Having parents who did not beat him and instead were very loving, Ruckel felt that there was something wrong with him. He wondered if he was, as he describes, "a child from hell". After many years, he is doing a lot better. Scientists believe that this has to do with the brain being able to rewire itself to compensate for problems during development.

In a series of studies conducted by Harry Harlow called *The Nature of Love*, Harlow tested baby monkeys to see if they would prefer a surrogate mother made out of wire mesh or one made of soft terry cloth. The cloth mother also had a light bulb behind it to radiate heat. "The result was a mother, soft, warm, and tender, a mother with infinite patience, a mother available twenty-four hours a day, a mother that never scolded her infant and never struck or bit her baby in anger."[21] Regardless of which surrogate offered milk, the monkeys preferred the cloth mother. Harlow explains that "We were not surprised to discover that contact comfort was an important basic affectional or love variable, but we did not expect it to overshadow so completely the variable of nursing; indeed, the disparity is so great as to suggest that the primary function of nursing as an affectional variable is that of insuring frequent and intimate body contact of the infant with the mother."[22] This is similar to how Harlow, explaining that the monkeys that were raised in isolation from their mothers, showed signs of depression, apathy, and withdrawal.

Dr. John D. Benjamin conducted studies in which rats were given the same food and living conditions. The experimental group of rats was "caressed and cuddled" while the control group of rats was "treated coldly" by not being touched. The experimental group of rats learned and grew faster than the control group. "The living organism depends to a very large extent upon the stimulation of the external world for its growth and development"[23]

In another study on heart disease, rabbits were fed a high-cholesterol diet to examine how this diet affected arteries. The results were consistent in all the groups of rabbits being tested except one group, which had 60 percent fewer symptoms. As it turns out, it was found that the student responsible for feeding this group of rabbits was hugging and petting them. This contact comfort had a powerful effect on high-cholesterol diets. The experiment was replicated several times with similar results.[24]

How Social Connections Are Beneficial to Health

Unhealthy relationships affect our physical health in negative ways, while healthy relationships affect our health in positive ways.[25] Many people who have battled cancer say the outpouring of love they received from friends and even strangers changed their life for the better and they would not trade it for anything.

> "Loneliness is epidemic, culturally
> frowned on, and completely curable."
> Martha Beck, Ph.D. Sociology

One study measured people's blood pressure when they interacted with others. Blood pressure went down when they had pleasant and soothing conversations with family or friends they enjoyed. Blood pressure would go up when they had conversations with people who were troublesome. However, blood pressure readings were highest when they had conversations with family or friends who they had a difficult relationship with. [26]

In a nine-year study, it was found that close relationships were the most important factor to a person's health.[27] People who did not have social and community ties, had a greater chance of dying than those who did. People, who were married, regardless of age or sex, had the lowest mortality rates. The lower number of social contacts people had resulted in a greater likelihood of mortality. People who belonged to a church also had a lower mortality rate, however, marital status and having close friends and relatives were more important. A major reason for this is that ties to family and close friends are more intimate than membership of a church or group association. This study, as well as several others, has shown that social networks can provide emotional support for people when they are going through difficult times.

In a study that examined health consequences of job loss showed that people who lost their jobs but had the emotional support of their spouse, had lower levels of cholesterol and were less likely to blame themselves for the job loss.[28]

Another study examined immigrant groups, their diets, and their health. People's health in these groups was shown to be higher than health averages in the United States. It was hypothesized that better health was due to diet. However, it was shown that these immigrants were healthier, not due to a better diet, but due to the support system they had.[29] These studies show that alienation (a lack of relationship/love) is a key factor in health problems and therefore longevity. Conversely, love is the most important factor in one's overall health.

Conclusion

We feel isolated because we so often hide our real feelings and have a difficult time expressing them. These feelings are a major part of our life. We want to know more about others. In some cases we do not realize this until after they die. People often avoid deeper conversations because the idea of opening up to others may be uncomfortable.

When we only hear about the great things people are doing, we start to wonder what we are doing wrong. We hear about people's great weekend, we hear about how people wrote a book in a month while working two full time jobs, all while taking care of their kids. We hear about how people pulled themselves up by their own bootstraps and made something of themselves. But these stories are often exaggerated. Rarely do we ever hear about the setbacks and failures. Some of the most successful people have also failed many times.

I've heard people say that they know someone, yet don't like them. But what do they really know? They know superficial information, and not much beyond that. When people hide who they are, we wonder what they are hiding. We become skeptical. We get judgmental. Then that person responds in the same way. If you treat someone like they are bad, they will try to live up to your expectations.

When you really focus on listening to what a person has to say, it won't take long until they open up further. When you are open and honest, and really listen to others, without even realizing it, they will do the same back, and walk away much happier. Why? Because you are connecting. When people open up about their failures and setbacks, it allows people to be more open and honest about their self. When you accept who you are and are comfortable with yourself, people will be comfortable with you.

Research by Dr. Mehl, a psychologist at the University of Arizona, has shown in a study that people who have meaningful, substantive conversations tend to be happier than people who have shallower conversations.[30]

The truth is that social skills and social connections are learned. We communicate with each other every day, yet we really do not know each other. Instead of worrying about or being upset with what people think or say, focus on trying to understand them better. Realize that there is far more going on in their life than you know. You have far more in common than you realize.

CHAPTER 12

BUILDING BETTER CONNECTIONS IN MARRIAGE

When I would tell people that alienation is at the heart of marriage failure, a number of people have told me that they knew everything about their spouse, yet they still ended up getting divorced. In the movie Mrs. Doubtfire, a husband and wife who once loved each other, end up getting divorced. The husband wants to see his kids more, so he dresses up as an old woman named Mrs. Doubtfire, in order to get a job as the children's nanny. Over time, the wife and kids grow to like this nanny. One day over tea, the ex-wife and Mrs. Doubtfire talk about marriage and the ex-wife tells Mrs. Doubtfire that her husband never knew, but so many nights she just cried herself to sleep. It was clear that the husband never knew this, even though they slept in the same bed.

While couples may know intimate details about their partners, they don't necessarily know what they are thinking or feeling. So often couples presume their partner knows what they are feeling. In many cases, people do not realize how their behavior affects their partner. In other cases, people feel that their spouse should automatically know what they are feeling.

The difference in marriage and a lot of friendships is that people can control how close they are to their friends. It is easier to hide things and when someone gets too close, they can give themselves a bit more distance. Some people manage to lie their way through life. They will lose some friends along the way who find out too much. But unlike in marriage, there is no divorce so it really isn't noticeable to others. You can only lie your way through marriage for so long.

I've spoken to many people who have said they felt like they had to "walk on eggshells" around their partner, all the while their partner never knew how their behavior was affecting them. Almost every married person who has opened up to me about their marriage, told me how their partner's behavior was bothering them, yet they never talked to their partner about it. Even when they tried to talk to their partner, they could not have a meaningful conversation without it getting verbally combative. So instead of dealing with the problem, couples often avoid talking about it, or simply avoid each other all together.

Understanding each other's feelings is a daily process. When this connection does not take place, over time, it can lead to serious problems and even divorce. This lack of relationship is an underlying cause of marriage failure.

In a study by the California Divorce Mediation Project, almost 80 percent of men and women said that they felt they were slowly "growing apart and losing a sense of closeness, and not feeling loved and appreciated."[1] John Gottman of the Gottman Institute said there is a breakdown of marital friendship. The deterioration of friendship can lead to extramarital affairs. Happy couples, for the most part, just don't cheat.[2]

The Impact of Marriage Failure

The family is a major foundation of society, but just under half of all families are broken up due to divorce, and many more families are unhappy. For the parents, divorce can feel like a major failure in life. For children, divorce may seem as if the family is no more. While a failed marriage does not mean a failed family, the health of a marriage will naturally affect the health of the family.

Regardless of the reality, children often feel responsible for the parents fighting. In one study, preschoolers were followed through age fifteen. Those who were raised in families that had a high amount of marital conflict had higher levels of stress hormones compared to other children. These children had far more instances of truancy, depression, peer rejection, behavioral problems such as aggression, and were more likely to have either low achievement or even failure at school.[3]

An unhappy marriage can be just as devastating as divorce, if not more, because there is no resolution. Some couples stay married because they feel trapped with no options. It is difficult to determine the number of married couples who are unhappy. It has been found that women, who are in physically abusive relationships, were more likely to report that they were very satisfied with their marriage.[4]

If you are in a marriage that is having problems, you will want to think about this:

1. Do you want to fix this relationship?
2. Were you in love with each other when you got married?

If you answered 'yes' to these questions, then focusing on fixing your marriage should be your number one priority.

Signs of Impending Marriage Failure

Every couple has positive and negative interactions, but the ratio of these interactions is an important factor in predicting divorce.[5] Couples who have more negative interactions are more likely to have:

- More severe marital problems
- Lower marital satisfaction
- Poorer health
- More negative and less positive emotional expressions

- A higher level of stubbornness and withdrawal from conversation
- More defensiveness
- More likely to start conflicts
- More anger

Couples who are headed for divorce tend to have less interest in their partner, less joy, and feel more negative when they talk to each other.[6] This lack of [effective] social connection is a component of alienation.

The couple may start to blame and attack each other in the form of criticism. The other partner will either avoid communicating both verbally and nonverbally, or will become defensive and attack back. Over time, these actions will build contempt and hatred between the couple. So much toxic negative energy becomes overwhelming, overriding any attempts at building positive energy, thus making it extremely difficult for the marriage to recover.

As this negative energy continues to build, a partner will focus more on the negative aspects of the relationship. Past positive experiences may be seen in a negative way. Even positive gestures may be viewed negatively, where the partner questions the motives behind the action. One or both partners will likely focus on his or her own positive contributions, while focusing on the negative things the other person does. Several studies have shown that couples noted only about 50 percent of the positive things that the spouse was doing.[7]

If you become aware of these critical warning signs in your marriage, you need to treat this as an emergency situation and should seek professional help immediately. If a couple is aware of what is taking place, they will have a better chance to turn things around by taking action.

Marriage therapy often fails because by the time a couple seeks professional help it is already too late. In one study, it was shown that couples tend to wait on average six years before seeking help. By this time, the problem has become much more serious.[8] This would be like going to a mechanic to try to fix your car engine after it has run out of oil and has locked up. Like the engine, the marriage essentially comes to a grinding halt.

While marriage therapy often shows short-term results, about 30 to 50 percent of couples relapse within two years.[9] Learning things like empathy training, active listening, or communication training, will essentially be ineffective once there is too much of a build up of negative energy.[10] Research has shown that active listening was too difficult for most couples to use and that it did not work well during times of conflict.[11] This does not mean that active listening does not work, it's just that many couples are learning this skill for the first time. Not only will active listening feel unnatural at first, it will also be difficult to do, especially in times of conflict. People should be experts at this by the time they graduate from high school.

Behavioral couples therapy has been shown through many studies to be the closest thing to an effective treatment. These therapies go beyond the conflict resolution that deal with the day-to-day problems, and instead work on building the couple's love and friendship.[12] They focus on building a positive environment on a daily basis, reducing negative energy and increasing the amount of positive energy during a conflict. When the friendship is great, conflict resolution naturally becomes easier and can even be fun.

One observation I've made is that people tend not to change unless there is a very real threat. Countries resort to war as a "last resort", yet if there is a mutually assured destruction, they miraculously find a better alternative. People who seem to not be able to lose weight, are all of a sudden more motivated when their life is at stake. I seem to never be able to lose more then a couple of pounds, unless I make a very focused effort. The first few weeks are the hardest, because it takes me that long to realize that I am not really putting much effort into it!

The same goes with marriage. People seem to go through the motions of trying to make their marriage work. They 'try', yet are not really *trying*. A threat of divorce is one thing, because people are often not serious when they make a threat. But when the threat is very real, people who really want to be together will suddenly make a much more serious effort. Too often people think that they do not need to change. They entrench their self in their perception of reality. Making real change involves self-reflection, personal change, and growth. I see so many people who are so sure of themselves that they never do change. Their personality does not grow.

What Makes Marriages Successful

A couple I knew appeared to have a typical marriage that involved a fair amount of arguing like many other couples. While I was always uncomfortable when they argued, I felt that they would stay married because after they argued, they would usually take the time to apologize and make up. But over time, the negative energy between them built up until finally they had a big argument that caused a lot of distress in their three-year-old son. This was a big wake up call for them to take a more proactive approach by making it an absolute priority to seek counseling. They did not shield this from their son and instead made sure he was aware that they were focusing on solving this.

Surprisingly, the number of conflicts a couple has, does not determine a couple's happiness.[13] Some happily married couples fight a lot, while some marriages that end in divorce have little or no conflict. The difference in the conflict of happy couples and couples who will wind up divorcing is that happy couples make amends after an argument, and by focusing on the relationship they remain happily married. When people do not make amends, they will likely continue to think about the conflict for hours, days, or even much longer. It would be like spilling something on the floor and never cleaning it up. When amends are made, these negative thoughts are replaced with positive thoughts.

People who have good marriages have approximately five times as many positive things take place during conflict. When there is no conflict, this ratio may be more like twenty to one. Couples who have an unhealthy relationship may have a ratio of 1:1 negative to positive. When there is more negativity than positivity, then the marriage is in trouble.

One study examined the brain scans of people who have been married on an average of 21 years and also considered themselves still intensely in love, and compared those scans to people who have recently fallen in love.[14] Individuals who were still in love over the years, also showed less activity in the brain associated with anxiety, fear, and obsessive behavior.[15] The study concluded that the most successful couples are couples who shared a lot and did a lot together. They were more likely to eat side-by-side, walk hand-in-hand, and begin and end each day with "I love you".

In a long-term study of 130 couples, after eight years, couples who accepted each other's influences, were much more likely to be happy. Men are less likely to accept the influences of women than women with men or other women. It was estimated that when a man does not share power with his wife, there was an 81 percent chance that the marriage would go bad.[16] It should also be noted that spouses who cooperate during therapy are most likely to benefit from it.[17]

Learning about each other's inner-most feelings, hopes, and dreams is very important, creating a feeling of fondness and admiration for each other. The more emotionally intelligent a couple is, the better able they will be to understand each other, and the more likely they will be happy, not just as a couple, but also as a family.[17] As a couple learns to connect with each other more deeply, the desire to control and change each other goes away and the less likely they will resort to blaming and getting defensive. Gottman noted that positive affection was the only variable that predicted both marital stability and happiness.

In one study, couples who were 45 years of age or older who had great sex lives, were asked why they felt their sex life was good. Almost every couple said that a great friendship made their sex life better.[19] In another study, it was shown that treated couples who became more emotionally involved with each other, experienced less hostility and coercion.[20]

Conclusion

When people get married, the marriage vows should be printed, signed, framed to serve as a daily reminder that you are committed to this marriage. It is your job to take each day and make it an amazing day.

Arguments are common in most every marriage. It is not about the number of problems a couple has, but how they deal with these problems that counts.

The legal paperwork is not what keeps you together. It is how you connect with each other. While having something in common is an important part of marriage, it really does not have much to do with why a couple would develop animosity towards each other. When a couple becomes alienated from each other, it's almost as if they see each other as strangers. The person you once married with the intent of loving for the rest of your life, you now hate. The marriage has failed.

When families break apart, this can affect the communication between the parents and the children and between the children and how they relate to their peers at school.

Too often, people end up settling for an OK marriage, as if there is nothing else they can do about it. If you are going to be spending the rest of your life with someone, you might as well make it as good as you can. Every time you get angry and yell at each other, you are emotionally cutting each other. While one incident of this is like a paper cut, over time many of these "paper cuts" can lead to negative sentiment override towards your partner. Being able to repair the relationship after these problems is critical.

Daren Fike, a business analyst who's wife suddenly passed away from leukemia, said; "I would gladly give every cent I have to spend just five more minutes with my late wife"[21] This says something important about communication, or rather the lack of. Think about it. If you are willing to give up everything to have just five minutes to be with a loved one who recently died, you may want to think about how you treat and communicate with those close to you. Unfortunately, we often don't realize it till it's too late to say the things that we wanted to say but haven't.

Imagine the following scenario: You have an argument with your wife and she decides to clear her head by going to the store. As she is driving, she is thinking about the argument, when all of a sudden she realizes the light is red and gets hit by a semi. You wonder when she will get home, but she never does. What was the last thing you said to your spouse when he or she walked out that door? The reality is that you never know if they will be coming back. People die every day, and sometimes it can be totally unexpected. It could be today, tomorrow, next month, or even when you both are very old, but it will happen. One of you will die first. I would rather know that I spent an extra ten seconds kissing my wife and making sure she knows how much I love her. I want to be sure that I made the most of our time together. Doing this is the basis of a lasting and loving marriage.

CHAPTER 13

HOW SCHOOLS CAN
FOSTER CONNECTION

Imagine what it would be like to go to a school where everybody liked you. Even if they think you are weird, they still understand you and even like you. Being new to this school district, you might come in with your prejudices about certain 'types' of people. However, because these students know that this negative energy is based on pain and fear, they don't respond to you with anger. Instead, they see right through the mask as if you were not even wearing one and instead, care about you. While this may sound impossible, it is something that is taking place now.

For many students, grades are not as important as their social standing. Getting good grades is more for the approval of their parents. The desire to be accepted can push people to do stupid things out of peer pressure. Some students will try to rationalize their situation, by retreating into their work, claiming that they don't care about social standings with others. They may justify this, thinking that they are smarter or superior, and dream about the day when their peers will be working for them later in life. Some students see themselves as anti-conformists, not caring about what others think. Regardless of all of this, people want to be liked, and they want to fit in. You may think that you don't care about social standing, but let me ask you this. How would you feel if everybody hated you? When you were in grade school, how often did you think about your social standing and reputation with other students?

When we build a socially inclusive environment in schools where students learn to understand and connect with each other, this will not just change the school environment, but will also change families, the work environment, and society overall.

Problems in the Education Environment

Many problems disrupt the flow of the learning process. In the typical classroom environment, students compete against each other. In some cases students are so focused on getting the grade that they resort to cheating, doing what ever it takes to get ahead. They memorize information not really trying to understand it. Teachers prepare students for standardized tests instead of focusing on teaching. This continues in college, with some students focused not on the learning, but on getting the degree, or getting grades that will get them into graduate school or an internship. Some people are so focused on accomplishing the tasks that they fail to see the bigger picture. Is it any wonder we have built a society focused on personal gain and greed?

People go into teaching because they want to inspire students and make a difference, but end up spending time establishing rules and dealing with the order of the school. There is no time left for building positive relationships.[1] "This attention to grades, test scores, honor rolls, and 'advanced' classes mocks our intention to create the affirming, loving environments all youngsters crave".[2] Schools will create a successful environment when they are able to create a safe, nurturing environment that develops students' natural capabilities and learning styles. Conversely, an alienating environment is destructive and less effective.[3]

Below is a fable my father showed me many years ago about why schools need to nurture individual talent.

The Animal School:
A Fable by George Reavis

Once upon a time the animals decided they must do something heroic to meet the problems of a "new world" so they organized a school. They had adopted an activity curriculum consisting of running, climbing, swimming and flying. To make it easier to administer the curriculum, all the animals took all the subjects.

The duck was excellent in swimming. In fact, better than his instructor. But he made only passing grades in flying and was very poor in running. Since he was slow in running, he had to stay after school and also drop swimming in order to practice running. This was kept up until his webbed feet were badly worn and he was only average in swimming. But average was acceptable in school so nobody worried about that, except the duck.

The rabbit started at the top of the class in running but had a nervous breakdown because of so much makeup work in swimming.

The squirrel was excellent in climbing until he developed frustration in the flying class where his teacher made him start from the ground up instead of the treetop down. He also developed a "charlie horse" from overexertion and then got a C in climbing and D in running.

The eagle was a problem child and was disciplined severely. In the climbing class, he beat all the others to the top of the tree but insisted on using his own way to get there.

Building Social Connections in Schools

It has been said that physical attraction is common, but mental connections are rare. Mental connections are rare because we haven't learned how to connect with each other. Why can't we create a society where people understand and empathize with each other rather than one purely focused on academics?

The school environment takes up a major part of our youth, and has a major impact on how we live the rest of our life. It affects how we interact at home, in the workplace, and in our interpersonal relationships.

While the family has a major impact on a child's life, a family cannot totally influence what goes on in a child's social life. Too many parents have found their child hanging by a rope or with a gunshot to the head. Wouldn't you want to know that your child enjoys school and is really connecting well with other students? When students are socially well adjusted in school, they will also be well adjusted socially at work and in marriage.

Even people who appear well socialized often lack important underlying social skills. Many people have a difficult time giving or receiving feedback without attacking or getting defensive. When people tease others, they often do not see or feel the pain they cause. When people lack advanced social skills (or social intelligence), they are more likely to get irritated, yell, or even fight. Just the fact that people get into arguments that get out of control is a clear sign that people lack social skills.

Students do not have the opportunity to really learn about each other, except on a superficial level. Many students learn to hide their personal problems from others because they do not feel safe to be open and honest about who they are. Without learning about others, they make pre-judgments based on superficial evidence (such as how one looks, dresses, or acts).

So why aren't students connecting with each other on deep levels? Why do we hear about these students who are bullied to the point where they end up committing suicide, yet every day we wake up and go about our lives. We may want to do something about it, but we don't know what to do.

In order to learn about each other on a deeper level, we need to remove the mask. While it is easy for most people to talk about their victories and successes, it is often much more difficult for people to talk about the problems they face in life. This is naturally difficult because we hide our problems just like so many animals hide their wounds and even avoid detection by camouflaging themselves. It is often difficult for people to open up when they live in a society that discourages openness. Society will not advance when the social connections that make up the society are weak. If we really want to connect, we need to understand each other's experiences in life.

Connecting as a Group: Observations from SuperCamp

Not only is it important to build an environment where people can connect on an individual level, but also on a group level. The following observations I made when I was a counselor at SuperCamp.

SuperCamp is a ten-day program that introduces students to accelerated learning academic skills and life skills. It incorporates many activities where students not only learn how to work with each other in supportive ways, they also connect with each other in very deep ways.

In the learning segment, students learn how to learn by understanding their personal learning styles as well as improving their note-taking skills, study management, and memorization skills.

With life skills, students learn to feel more confident, take responsibility for their choices, build successful relationships, think creatively and work towards life goals. They learn about having integrity, being flexible, being committed, speaking with good purpose, among other things. This is also where they learn that failure leads to success. Failure is simply feedback on what you can do to make the change.

In relationship building, students learn to communicate with others more effectively. There are also several games that are played where participants learn more about each other deeper down.

In one game, when a member of a team made an error, it was clearly shown that negative support only increased frustration, hurt feelings, and poorer results. It was also clear that members did much better when they received positive support from their teammates.

In a game that involved the entire camp there was a large circle made up of chairs facing inward. There were enough for all the students, except one. This student would stand in the center of the circle. The facilitator would make a statement, and if the statement applied to you, then you had to get up out of your seat and walk across the circle to find another seat. If you were left without a seat, you had to stand in the middle. Statements first started off easy and fun, such as "Who forgot to brush their teeth this morning?" Then some students would giggle embarrassingly and get up to find another spot. Sure enough, one student ends up standing in the middle. For the person left standing in the middle, the director would then say; "Here is a person who forgot to brush his/her teeth." As the game continued, the statements became deeper and more personal. One example was something like; "I feel like I am a disappointment to my parents." While this was still just a game, seeing the students who got up to find another seat was heartbreaking. I wish the parents of these teens could see this. As the students participated in this game, they slowly learned more about each other on a deeper level. It is one thing to make a blanket statement saying that we all deal with problems in our life and that some kids feel like a disappointment to their parents. It is something entirely different when we see individuals who feel these things.

In another game, one side of the room represented 'strongly agree' and the other side of the room represented 'strongly disagree', with the varying degrees in between. The facilitator would make a statement and the students would move to a part of the room that represented their opinion. The questions would start off very light and gradually get more serious. As expected, there will be some hurt feelings by the end of the game and there will be a serious discussion about participants' experiences. In one question on racism, one student, John, stood in the area of "strongly agree". By the end of the game, John's 'girlfriend' was understandably upset with his opinion and was not sitting with him. The point of the exercise and the discussion that ensued after the game was not about racism, but was about creating a safe environment where people can open up. When we don't have a safe environment, people censor themselves and put on masks, becoming someone they are not.

The girlfriend wanted to teach John that by thinking this way, she would not associate with him. While these actions are logical, the people who are being shunned mostly end up with hurt feelings and anger, but this does not change their opinion. For John, something in his past caused him to feel this way. When people are angry, they are angry for a reason, even if it is illogical. By the end of the discussion, his girlfriend was sitting back with him.

Naturally we make judgments based on people's actions. When people do wrong, we want to show our disapproval. However, there is a big difference in disapproval of an action and rejecting a person. As a society, we continue this belief that we can better society by seeking who's to blame. The idea is to better society by teasing, ridiculing, scolding, or hurting someone when they do something we perceive as wrong. Does inflicting physical or mental pain on someone, somehow supposed to make him or her a better person? In many cases, the person may not even understand why he or she is being attacked or alienated, which only builds more frustration and anger.

Imagine what your life would be like if you lived in a safe, supportive environment. Imagine how it would feel if you were accepted regardless of how you thought. When we incorporate social intelligence into the school environment as a whole, social intelligence will become second nature.

The Difference in Building Social Connections, Team Building, and the Sensitivity Movement

When I would bring up the topic of building social connections, people would tell me how they participated in team-building exercises at work, such as trust-falls, where one person falls back and others are supposed to catch him or her. Building social connections is much more involved than simple team-building exercises. There are plenty of stories where eager managers with good intentions, have put some of these team-building or motivational exercises together, with disastrous consequences.[4]

Building social connections should also not be mistaken for the sensitivity movements popular in the 1960's and 1970's. Dr. Brant Holmberg, who was an Associate Professor of Psychology at Central Washington University, explained that in the 1960's and 1970's, there were many programs that taught sensitivity training designed to help people express their thoughts and feelings and how they felt towards others. A focus was put on building trusting relationships that encouraged people to express themselves without fear of being rejected. However, Holmberg said, "Sadly, the sensitivity movement began to take on "touchy, feely" and "no holds barred" highly therapeutic dimensions where people were encouraged to go to nude encounter groups and belch and pass gas and do any number of bizarre antics in the name of freedom of expression and an attempt to find acceptance at every level of human behavior." There is a big difference between deep social connection, facilitated by professionals, and having a "no holds barred" freedom of expression.

Some people who were really involved in this movement saw it as a liberating, open environment where they were able to make true friends. Unfortunately, some of these people were not able to transfer what they learned to their personal lives at home and at work. Holmberg explains that they "…were very disappointed when they tried to be open and trusting in their home life and work environment only to find that people did not understand what they were attempting to do and rejected their openness and expressions of wanting to create mutually rewarding relationships."

The reality is that no matter how powerful a short-term program may be, participants still need to go back to "regular" society. Even "life-changing" experiences will fade over time, unless society advances as a whole. By incorporating social intelligence into the school environment as a whole, social intelligence will become second nature.

Programs That Build Social Connection

Schools are starting to focus more on the social environment. Some schools are trying to ease the violence by increasing the level of communication among students and adults. When students feel that they are a part of their school and feel connected with their peers and teachers, they will not be so concerned about where they stand in the social hierarchy or about how intelligent they appear in the classroom. As students become more connected with each other and see the bigger picture, the more they will see that these images are just that – images of reality, but not reality itself. Research has shown that students who are emotionally connected are less prone to anxiety, depression, drug use, suicide, dropping out of school, bullying, and violence.[5]

Some schools are focusing on building a sense of community. In one school district, principals have their lunch with the students, and not just class leaders. In another school district, teachers act as mentors to a group of students during their entire high school career, allowing students and teachers to build long-term relationships. This helps prevent students from falling through the cracks.[6]

A number of studies have demonstrated the affect of the environmental stressors on academic performance.[7,8,9,10] One study showed that a supportive school environment that had a sense of belonging, was found to be a significant predictor of the ability of students to maintain high achievement levels, in spite of stressful conditions in their lives.[11]

A study conducted by Sandra Champion[12] examined how one library has helped Hispanic student immigrants deal with the problems of alienation, literacy, and acculturation, in the U.S. culture. At Hialeah High School in Dade County, Florida, the library was redesigned to accommodate different learning styles and to be culturally diverse. In addition, a literature class was held at this learning center, which helped students learn about themselves and each other. Champion said that students must first deal with important social issues, including alienation, before they can study effectively. Champion paraphrased Henry Stack Sullivan (1953); "...the personality is almost entirely the product of interaction with other significant human beings."[13]

Students were more likely to learn from each other by problem solving, rather than asking the teacher. One teacher was quoted as saying: "It is amazing how much they learn from one another, how much they know that I have never imagined. I am learning from them!"[14] One student was quoted as saying: "I have felt so alone. I thought I was the only one with problems...Then when we talked about our personal journeys...I felt we were all in the same boat with wild opportunities, I suddenly felt full of hope".[14]

One student later shared that, upon entering the group, she felt unique in her own despair and that she alone had fears that were unspeakable. She disclosed that she felt deep concern about her sense of self worth and her sense of relatedness. Others shared similar feelings. However, students unanimously agreed that, when secrets were shared, they realized their secrets were similar to others after all, and this understanding provided a link or a connection to the group and a possibility for universally connecting with mankind.

Champion[15]

Programs such as the Jigsaw classroom,[16] which teach students to use teamwork, collaboration and Socratic questioning (questions that are used to explore and analyze complex ideas), have shown to help reduce prejudice attitudes, increase empathy, and increase confidence in students. Students develop better peer relations with each other. Students, who felt excluded, now feel more of a part of the group. Students also learned interviewing skills when asking questions about a topic. Even after five years, students who were in the jigsaw classroom still showed more empathy than those students who were not. It was also shown that having a class like this for just one hour a day was beneficial enough to decrease prejudice attitudes and increase empathy.

Learning Forum, the parent company of SuperCamp, evaluated many methods and programs that use different learning styles as well as programs that use emotional intelligence. With this research, Learning Forum has built a program for schools that focuses on life skills, relationship building, and learning how to learn.

Northwood Middle School, in California, incorporated various parts of the Learning Forum method. Students and teachers said that the school has become a close-knit community instead of an environment where cliques and authority status separate people. Peter Anderson, the principal of Northwood said that changing the atmosphere of the school was a major factor and that there is a sense of unity in the school that was not present before. One teacher said that students were responding to her on a more personal level. Other teachers, as well as parents, said that the students seemed happier. Marguerite Owens, a teacher, said, "Everyone from the janitors to the office personnel, to the faculty, and the kids, has a much more positive attitude…"[17]

Research examined the effectiveness of Learning Forum's Accelerated/Integrative Learning Model over a seven-year period[18].

The study showed that the school had an increase of 103 percent in reading scores and an 87 percent increase in math scores; 84 percent of respondents had a higher self-esteem; 80 percent felt more accepted and supported by others; 71 percent improved peer relations with others; 81 percent had more confidence; 78 percent were very pleased with their learning outcome; 70 percent participated in school more; 98 percent said that they still used the skills from the program; and 98 percent of students gave the program a favorable rating. In terms of GPA, 96.6 percent of respondents showed a one grade point jump. The research concluded that the program could be an answer to the problems that plague our schools today. Students would be more motivated and would enjoy school more. "This study has validated that even potential dropout students (1.9 and lower GPA) can learn quickly when the learning environment has been adjusted to become brain-compatible based on accelerated/integrative learning strategies". At least parts of this program are being replicated in other schools.

Understanding All People

Group dynamics play a major role in school and in life. Students are concerned about where they stand with others. A great example of group dynamics can be seen in the movie *The Breakfast Club*. In this movie, five students serve a Saturday detention at school, and each of them had to write an essay on who they think they are. These five students, all from different social cliques, develop a bond with each other over the course of the day. Unfortunately bonding moments like this rarely happen in real life. People who have had experiences like this have said they would not trade these experiences for anything. When schools are able to create an environment that fosters deep social connection among all students, as well as the faculty, issues such as bullying, fighting, suicide, and school shootings would be virtually non-existent.

With group dynamics, the size of the group plays an important role in connecting people. In a large group setting, such as a school, people will naturally form smaller groups or cliques on their own. People will seek to connect with those who are similar to them and separate themselves from those who are different. For teens, being a part of a group is important in terms of "social survival". Not being able to join a group one identifies with can be devastating. Take, for example, a girl who tries out for cheerleading with her friends. Most of her friends make it, but she doesn't and acts like it's the end of the world. Adults may think she is being overly dramatic, but she's not. While she and her friends will still be friends, her friends who made the team will be practicing together, going to games together, and hanging out together after practice and games. When she can finally join her friends, they are talking about moves and things she does not know anything about. Her sadness is not necessarily about failing to make the squad, but what that failure represents, which is a separation from friends by not being a part of the group.

In high school there are many different groups of people or 'clubs' that bond based on a superficially shared identity: the football or cheerleading team, math club, or being into Goth or the 'cool' crowd. These identifiers that give a group its identity are fairly superficial. Being good at math or being athletic only helps identify some common interests.

Students understandably want to conform to their clique, and therefore compromise who they are. If you are too different, then that clique or group may not accept you. Some people don't fit into any group and are considered outcasts.

While a shared identity is in itself superficial, bonds are strengthened as people within a group spend time with and learn more about each other.

In order to build deep social connections among a large population, such as a school, it is important to create small diverse groups of roughly eight to 16 people with no 'identifiers' that separate them from other groups. These people can then bond, not by activities, or attitudes, but by what connects them on a deeper level. As these groups come together, forming a larger group of about 100 to 150 people, individuals are then able to bond with others in the larger group. This is why a combination of small groups that are a part of a larger group is key to building social connection on a greater scale. The larger group should not get much bigger than this, as cohesion may start to break down.[19]

In a high school of 2,000 students, you might have sixteen large groups of about 125 students each. These large groups would be divided into nine teams of 12 – 14 student each, with three to four freshmen, sophomores, juniors, and seniors. Students would get to know the other students on their team on a deep level, while still learning about others in the larger group. Groups might be mixed up every quarter. In a four-year period, a student will be in 16 different teams.

Imagine what school would be like if the first week started off like this, and every school day after that was structured with an extra half hour or so where students connect with each other on a deep level.

You don't need to know every person, or every aspect of culture, or even every culture to understand human emotions. When you learn about others on a deep enough level, you will be able to understand your feelings better, develop a greater self-esteem and a higher regard for others and understand how much you share in terms of feelings and emotions. This is when you will be able to see through the mask, as if it were never there. If a person is rude, hostile, or angry, you will know that this negative energy comes from something else. They may simply not realize how their own actions affect other people or they may have suffered from something pretty traumatic, among many other things.

One of the overall observations I made at SuperCamp was that while these students came from a wide variety of backgrounds, by the end of the ten days the students (along with the staff) became a very close-knit group. These people bonded through deep personal connections. They developed a better understanding of humanity on a deeper level. It's not about memorizing statistics on a person; it's about understanding all people.

How Social Connections Benefit Society

Social connections play a vital role in society, affecting everything from families, schools, and communities, to the legal system, health care system, work force, government, and even international relations. Married couples that do not have healthy connections with each other are more likely to have more stress and are more likely to get divorced. Changing the dynamics of the school system impacts the future work force, or in some cases, future criminals and murderers. The professional work environment benefits from less dishonesty, gossip, unproductivity, disrespect, and even bullying.

For example, in the workplace, when people do a bad job, they are likely to be fired. Employers then need to spend more time in recruiting and training. When employees are fired for their behavior, they may go to a different job where they will continue to be ineffective. Some of these people go from one job to the next, constantly experiencing failure and never getting ahead. By avoiding dealing with the employee, the company does a disservice to itself, the individual, and society as a whole. As a business, it is a better investment to help make this person successful. Helping employees become great employees not only helps the company, but also produces more committed workers. In a socially educated society, the work environment will be dealing with fewer personal issues, where people can be more focused on their job.

Stress, anger, and depression can result in self-destructive behavior such as drug use and obesity. This negative energy directly affects our health and weakens the immune system. In turn, this raises health care costs.

Depression and stress in the school and work environment lowers productivity. As people get more stressed, depressed, or angry, these forms of negative energy can put undo strain on relationships.

Learning how to connect socially will relieve a tremendous amount of this stress. Even when we face daunting challenges such as cancer or the death of a loved one, it helps when you feel people are there for you.

Police brutality is still very much a problem with tremendous actual and social costs. As more police become socially intelligent, incidents of police brutality will decline, improving relations with the community. Socially intelligent people in leadership roles in government will be effective at working with other governments and improve relations. As international commerce continues to build, developing connections even further, countries will be less likely to go to war.

The financial impact of stronger connections is probably far greater than you may imagine. When a person commits a crime or violent act, this involves police, lawyers, judges, juries, selecting a jury, jury members taking time off work, jails, and prisons. According to the Bureau of Justice,[20] in the United States in 2007, we spent $74 billion on the prison system, with an average annual cost of $30,600 per inmate for 2.5 million inmates. Between 2008 and 2009 the average cost to incarcerate an inmate in the California prison system was just over $47,000.[21]

Suicide, violent crime, and murder do not just affect loved ones, but also friends, acquaintances, and the greater society. According to the website of American Foundation for Suicide Prevention, in 2010 there were 38,364 suicides that were reported, which equates to a suicide every 13.7 minutes. It was also found that 464,995 people went to the hospital for injuries due to self-harm behavior.[22] That is close to half a million people. According to the FBI, in 2010, there were an estimated 1,246,248 violent crimes in the United States,[23] and an estimated 14,788 people who were murdered.[24]

Just try to imagine how traumatizing it would be to find that your son or daughter committed suicide, or in a fit of rage, murdered someone or went on a mass-shooting spree, then committed suicide. If that isn't bad enough, most of the public ends up placing the blame on you.

So, a few thousand people die in a terrorist attack, and we spend over a trillion dollars, and cost the lives of thousands of soldiers and tens of thousands of civilians. Conversely, over 50,000 people die every single year in the United States from murder or suicide, and there are over 1.2 million violent crimes, yet we keep doing the same thing and spend vast amounts of money, year after year, without any real results. No wonder it seems that we can never get ahead. We are spending too much time on maintenance, solving and stopping crimes, and dealing with physical and mental health issues. Going back to the Pipes theory: we spend so much time finding buckets to stop the water from leaking on the floor, that we never get to the underlying problem of fixing the connections. If society were a company, we would be getting an 'F' rating.

Social Connections Are the Essence of Society

Society is essentially the sum of its social connections.[25] Social connections do not just play a vital role in society: social connections *are* society. Everything from houses, streets, and buildings, to laws and political structure, make up the physical and structural aspects of society. Religion, politics, and education, shape the flow of society.

No matter what political system is in place or what your religious beliefs are, how you treat others is most important. What good is religion if people try to control or even kill each other in the name of it? What good is the type of political structure if people use it to abuse others? Too often we have tried to build better societies by targeting the "enemy" and thus justifying violence. Too often we have abused some people in attempts to better society for others. Too often we end up working against each other, in hopes of making it better. The mission of building a better society becomes lost when the strategies to achieve that mission are counterproductive.

Social Connections are the essence of society. Therefore:

- Alienation is the antithesis (direct opposite) of society. Alienation runs counter to the underlying principals, thesis, and premise of society. One may think that the opposite of society is anarchy, but anarchy is really the opposite of government/politics. Because anarchy is not the opposite of society, politics therefore cannot be the ultimate solution for society.

- How we treat each other and connect with each other is the most important factor in building a great society. Improving our ability to make strong social connections will not just lead to a transformation of society; it will impact our lives and this world in ways that we have never imagined.

What is the sum of social relationships in your society, your family; your school; your community; and even your world? In order to understand where we, as a society, are now and where we are headed, we need to understand how we got to this point.

Conclusion

How much would you be willing to pay to have your children go to a school where they connected with their peers on a deep level? I assure you that parents whose children have committed suicide or have gone on murderous rampages, would give up everything they have if they could turn it all around.

Many people go through life only partially learning socialization skills, thinking they know how to listen, yet never really understand their children, their parents, or their spouse. When people are unable to understand others and their own problems, they develop into ineffective employees, managers, leaders, friends, and spouses.

Everybody needs to learn to connect with others on a deep level. In order to advance society as a whole, it is important to build schools where students are able to not just learn about each other, but also connect with each other. Students who have grown up in a school system like this, may not even know what bullying is, or actually be shocked to see that people act like this. While it may sound like these students are just sheltered, quite the opposite is true. It is students in regular society who are kept from the real feelings of each other. When people learn about others on a deep enough level, they become much more socially well-adjusted, understanding how their actions affect others.

Building better connections in schools will lead to happier and healthier students, along with improved academic performance. Not only that, it will build better connections in marriage and family, the work environment, and in life overall. It all comes down to the fact that social connections are the essence of society. If we incorporate this into the school system, we will make great changes to society.

As we start connecting with each other in deep, personal ways,
we naturally develop empathy.

As we develop empathy,
We naturally learn to love!

PART V:

TAKING SOCIETY TO
THE NEXT LEVEL

Our connection to each other is a learned process that has evolved over thousands of years. Deep social connection is something we are just beginning to experience as an entire society. Just like how the gradual evolution of technology turned into a revolution over the past one hundred years, the same thing is starting to happen socially. As we begin to experience other people deeply, we begin to experience life on a whole new level.

CHAPTER 14

LOVE IS THE ULTIMATE POWER

All the great religions preach the importance of love. We hear about how we should love our family and friends, love our neighbor, and even love our enemies. The concept of love has been endlessly talked about, written about, and even sung about, but the amount of social change seems to be minimal. While we spend a lot of time learning things like how to be successful in our jobs, making money, and winning, how much have we learned about love?

To say that we need to be more loving is not helpful if we do not understand *how* to be more loving. We seem to presume that people inherently understand how to love. But when people are born and raised in an unloving environment, they do not know how to be more loving. How often do you see married couples, who 'love' each other, treat each other poorly?

We have never really fully connected with each other as a whole society. But things are changing. We are able to see that people, who we thought were different from us, weren't as different as we thought. People, who we thought of as bad or evil, are not as bad as we thought. Movies have moved from two-dimensional villains to in-depth characters.

We want to connect with each other. We want to hear people's stories. We want to tell our story. We love stories about love and how the good guys triumph. In the movie *Star Wars*, we cheered when Darth Vader turned to the light side and killed the emperor, and cried when he died. When you think about it logically, Darth Vader was much worse than Hitler, and we would have demanded vengeance. But we didn't! When we see someone turn from the "dark" side of life, and embrace love, or stand for what's right, it inspires us, it strengthens us, it empowers us, and when this happens, we feel that nothing can stop us!

When we choose to love without condition, social connections and the effectiveness of a society are enhanced. As you connect with others on deeper levels, you will begin to see beyond the masks people wear. You will begin to see beyond the illusions we have built up in society. When this happens, the world will see a change that we have never seen before.

Is Alienation Simply a Lack of Love?

The damaging effects of alienation (a lack of love) have been scientifically documented as well as the benefits of feeling included, having strong social ties, having pets, touching, etc. Study after study has shown that people and animals need connection and love.

When we think about the opposite of love, we think of hate, rather than a lack of love. When people hate, there are at least feelings there. When people are alienated, there is a lack of connection. From there, all it takes is a little suspicion or a story, or even just an image, that casts a person or group of people in a negative light that arouses our fear, anger, and hatred. When people are purely alienated, it's not that they hate, but that they don't care, don't understand, or feel totally separated from the world around them.

After examining various types of alienation, evaluating and dissecting the definition of 'alienation', and how it was used in context by many sociologists including Karl Marx, C. Wright Mills, Antonio Gramsci, and Emile Durkheim, I concluded that alienation could be defined as "a lack of love". I am not saying that alienation *is* defined as a lack of love, but merely suggesting that it could be.

Defining alienation as 'a lack of love' is difficult because both 'alienation' and 'love' are vague terms. No single word defines a "lack of love," so the concept is not easily conceived. Some sources say "estrangement" best describes a lack of love. However, estrangement means to "cause (someone) to be no longer close or affectionate to someone..."[1] implying that there was once closeness. As Alfred, Lord Tennyson said, "It's better to have loved and lost, than to have never loved at all." But with alienation, there is no love. There is no connection.

One definition of love is "...a sense of underlying oneness."[2] When people do not feel connected to others, there is no sense of an "underlying oneness".

> "Next to physical survival, the greatest need of a human being is psychological survival – to be understood, to be affirmed, to be validated, to be appreciated."
> Stephen Covey[3]

If alienation is the underlying cause of personal problems and social issues, and if alienation is essentially a lack of love, then it would be logical to say that the underlying foundation of personal problems and social issues is a lack of love. It could also be argued that love (connection, bonding, etc.) is the fundamental building block of society. Although a person may not need love to survive, he or she needs love to thrive.

Understanding Love

Leo Buscaglia, who was a professor at USC, conducted a non-credit class on love. The popularity and the long waitlist to take the class showed that there were a lot of people who wanted to learn more about love, even though it was a non-credited class. Buscaglia acted more as a facilitator of the discussion than a lecturer, saying that love was exciting for everybody to learn more about.[4]

Gottman noted that the biblical term for sexual love is to "know" your partner.[5] Loving your spouse or making love to your spouse is about getting to know them (not just physically), but really learning about them on a daily basis. Could this mean that once you get to know a person on a very deep level, you love them? Loving someone does not mean that you have to have virtually everything in common. Many people don't have a lot in common with their parents, children, or pets, yet they still love them more than anything else in the world.

What is love? Is the purpose of love to build a positive and happy environment? In its most general form, love is essentially positive energy, but it is not necessarily about having a positive attitude. It is a way of thinking. Love is a choice. Love is an action. Love is learned.

It really comes down to the simple things such as; kindness, caring, respect, being nice and friendly, being considerate, giving your time, compassion, and intimacy, among other things. The smallest gestures can be the most loving gestures. Simple things such as writing a note and even just saying 'Hi!' can mean a lot. What is it about this that feels good? I received a random text from a friend that said, "We miss Uncle Mark!" I was not really their uncle, but in a sense, I was 'uncle' to their three kitties and their one-year-old son. Being referred to as 'Uncle Mark' and receiving a note saying that I was missed, was very personal and felt good, and it made all the difference in the world.

When a good friend of mine quit her job to move to the other side of the country with her husband, her coworkers made a giant poster for her that was titled "Ten Things We Will Miss About Racheal". One of these reasons really struck me. It said, "Racheal has a genuine concern for all people at all times." I think I can say that pretty much everybody has had a 'concern' for others and even a 'genuine concern', but to have a 'genuine' concern for 'all people at all times' says a lot.

When you do something, are you doing it in a loving way? If you have a loving attitude, this will affect how you interact with others. If you are focused on negative things about another person, you really are not being loving. If you are deliberately rude or mean to others, this can really impact them in a negative way. You do not just hurt people's feelings, you hurt them. If you are filled with negative energy, then you affect others negatively, and they will likely not want to be around you, maybe unless they are also full of negative energy.

How Animals Help Us Understand Love

One way to understand love is to look at examples from animals. Animals, especially mammals, like to play, have fun, and need love, like people. While some people may think this is uniquely a human trait, there are many examples of animals showing compassion for each other. For example, ducks are monogamous (in some cases mate for life) and for some, such as geese, if one is shot or hurt, a few other geese in the gaggle or group will stay behind to try to help the hurt one. There are other animals that also mate for life, such as swans, beavers, black vultures, and even some termites. While people tend to pride themselves on being faithful and monogamous, bald eagles have a far lower "divorce" rate than people.

An Ohio State University study took genetic samples of 236 coyotes in the Chicago area over a period of six years and found no evidence that the coyotes strayed from their mate. What's interesting about this is that this is an area that has a large coyote population and plenty of food, which frequently leads similar species to abandon normal monogamy.[6]

Wolves mate for life and the other wolves in the pack help to raise the pups. This makes me think that either wolves are superior to humans or that there is some hope for marriages. Perhaps a major reason so many people get divorced is because human speech is complex and leaves a lot of room for misinterpretation. People also get caught up in the false images they see or what they think they hear.

When I was young, I remember reading a news article about a German Shepherd that was left on the side of the road by it's people parents. The dog was very loyal and waited by the side of the road from them to come back. Days turned into weeks and weeks turned into months. People who owned the local restaurant gave the dog scraps. People tried to take the dog, but the dog refused to go. As winter approached, someone built a doghouse for the dog. It wasn't till about two years later did the dog allow someone to take it in. German Shepherds do not leave any of the flock behind, but people do...at least in this case.

Temple Grandin, who wrote *Animals In Translation*, explains that, "The main difference between animal emotions and human emotions is that animals don't have *mixed emotions* the way normal people do. Animals aren't ambivalent; they don't have *love-hate* relationships... That's one of the reasons humans love animals so much; animals are loyal. If an animal loves you, he loves you no matter what. He doesn't care what you look like or how much money you make. This is another connection between autism and animals: autistic people have mostly simple emotions, too. That's why normal people describe us as *innocent*. An autistic person's feelings are direct and open, just like animal feelings."[7]

I learned a lot from my pets. As so many long time lovers have concluded, it is the simple courtesies and acts of kindness that count. It is being thoughtful towards another person or animal.

Sugar, a Springer Spaniel I had growing up was always very 'talkative'. Sugar loved jogging and would wake my parents up to take her, unless it was raining that day. When Sugar would ask me to take her for a walk or jog, I often would grudgingly take her out. When I would finally give in and take her out for a walk, she would get all excited. It felt good seeing how happy she was, which made me more excited about doing this. I noticed that the more excited I was about going for a walk or jog, the more Sugar would be excited about it too.

I learned that doing simple things like spending time together were what mattered. I could buy dozens of toys for Sugar, but while they may be fun for a short time, what point is a toy if you have no one to play with? Even if you can buy your dog plenty of dog beds, your dog will still want to sleep with you.

I always enjoyed it when I would say my dog's name and see her wag her tail. When people say our name, it feels good. I think this has something to do with a feeling of connection. Someone cares enough about you to use your name. If people had tails, it would be so easy to see how much something means to someone. And when we say something that is hurtful, we would realize that it doesn't make them feel good, because their tails would be down low. But thinking about it, people would probably just hide their emotions and hide their tails.

While living in Los Angeles, I slowly built up rapport with a cat that essentially adopted me. One day, 'Kitty' showed her appreciation by bringing me a freshly killed mouse. Why would a cat bring a mouse to my door? Would a cat bring a mouse like this to just any random person? Of course not, because that would not make sense!

When staying at a friend's house for an extended period of time, there were two cats and two dogs. Every night when I would come home from work, I would give each one of them a hug when I walked through the door. What I noticed about this was that over time, when I would hug one pet, the other pets would wag their tails and wait patiently. While one may think they were wagging their tails because they would soon get a hug, I also noticed this tail wagging when I would show positive affection to another pet at a random time.

This is similar to how a baby may cry when parents are fighting or be happy when seeing signs of affection. When they do that 'Kiss Cam' at the ballpark, watching people kiss on the big screen, it seems to bring about some positive feelings within the crowd. Seeing happy scenes in a movie, or seeing positive affection in real life, makes us want to 'wag our tails', because this emotion is contagious.

However, sometimes people can feel jealous or hurt when they see these public displays of affection. Why is this? Well just imagine seeing everyone else hugging each other but nobody is hugging you.

Wouldn't you feel a little left out? That would be like all the dogs getting a treat, except the one dog that has to sit off to the side. Imagine if you were this dog and it happened all the time. All of these school shootings and other acts of violence are starting to make more sense.

Caleb, a Dalmatian at an office I worked at, hung out with me a lot. Everybody thought I gave him treats, but I never did, while most other coworkers did. Caleb liked me because I always acknowledged him when I saw him. It is funny how we sometimes have special nicknames for each other. There is something about it that feels good. I called Caleb "Carib". I do not even know why I did it, but it was just between Caleb and I. There is something about it that creates a bond, just like how close friends have nicknames for each other. This is like how a child refers to mom and dad as "mom and dad", not by their regular names. Parents get so excited when their baby calls them "mommy" or "daddy".

I learned some important lessons from Caleb. Caleb would go around and eat the food off of people's desks. You would have thought he would have learned that he was not to do this, but on the same token, you would have thought we would have learned our lesson by not leaving our food out. One day the Vice President, walked back into his office to find that Caleb just ate his sandwich, and he started yelling at Caleb. Our receptionist exclaimed; "Oh, how cute! Caleb is wagging his tail!" while Caleb was being yelled at. I wonder if this had something to do with the idea that any attention, whether it is good or bad, is better than no attention at all.

One morning on my way into work, I was very hungry and got a breakfast sandwich. I got to my desk, and just as I was about to bite into my delicious sandwich, an emergency came up, and I had to go take care of it. When I went back to my desk, my stomach sank as I realized that I left my food on the desk. Sure enough, all that was left was a chewed up wrapper on the floor. My stomach was growling at me, and I was mad! I told Caleb to get out of my office because I did not want to see him. I grudgingly got back to my work and was still very hungry. After a while, Caleb peered into my office to see if I was still upset. I refused to even look at him and shooed him away. This went on several times, but after a while of this, he peered into my office. I looked at him, and then looked back down at my work. I could tell that Caleb was still looking at me. I briefly glanced at him, but quickly looked back at my work again. He looked so sad! "All right! Come on" I said, and Caleb ran to me and was so happy to see me. It was if I was gone on a trip and just got back. Caleb did not eat any food off of anyone's desk ever again…for at least three months! What was interesting about this was that yelling at Caleb had no effect, and in some cases, he would even wag his tail, because he was getting attention. However, when I refused to even look at him and did not want him in the same room, he felt excluded or kicked out of the tribe.

It does not feel good when you feel left out. Really, when you think about it, inclusion is the name of the game. We all want to be included…well no, actually we all need to be included. To be abandoned, to be distanced, and to be excluded can be very painful. When others hate you, you in turn hate yourself.

What's important is the amount of quality time, even if it is less time overall. In cities, people surround us, yet we do not spend quality time with people. Just being in the same room or home as your spouse, children, parents, or pets, does not really count as quality time. Sometimes people are focused on doing things for someone else, but not focused on being with them. Cleaning the house, fixing the car, cooking, or even buying things for someone is considerate, but it is not spending time with each other, which is most important. Cooking together, cleaning together, and working together can be fun and more meaningful.

The less time you spend with your spouse, child, pet, or friend, the more foreign you become. When there are strong bonds, being gone for even a long time does not affect the relationship nearly as much…even when years go by. It is important to maintain closeness.

Why People Avoid Love

Some people think that love is foolish. Some have "given up" on love, or don't even "believe" in love. Giving up on love or not even believing in love would be like giving up on or not even believing in gravity or sound. Even people, who don't 'believe' in love, will admit that they want love.

Because many people, often unknowingly, have a difficult time with social skills, there tends to be hurt feelings and arguments. People may say things they later regret. Two people may connect deeply on some levels, but not fully. Over time, small irritants can turn into big ones, and negative energy continually builds.

Some people feel like they do not deserve love, or reject love because they are so used to being rejected. Just being stung once by a bee, can cause a person to be afraid of bees. Feeling rejected can cause people to be more hesitant to open up.

If people have a difficult time communicating, you really can't blame them for being afraid to open up to someone they want to have a relationship with. When people open up about deep personal feelings, there is a fear of rejection. So in order to avoid rejection, some people avoid getting into serious relationships.

Because many people don't have great social skills or are not able to connect well, when they do get into a deep relationship, hurt feelings are likely. To avoid this, some people manage to jump from romantic relationship to romantic relationship. Romantic relationships that remain superficial are doomed. It is when people develop long-term deep relationships, is oxytocin produced.

When we create a more loving world, then there is more to love, and less reason to be needy, controlling, or to claim someone as yours, as if they were property. One question you should ask yourself: Are you more focused on finding someone to love you, or are you focused on being more loving? People don't want to be controlled or be someone's possession. I've never liked those little candy hearts that say "Be Mine!" Be your what? Be your bitch? No! I am not your property, object, or possession. There is nothing romantic about that.

When you are nice and expect something in return, you are not really being loving. People I know who are loving, don't expect people to love them. It's the same as being nice. Don't do nice things with any expectations of anything in return. There are many people who may not be able to thank you now…but they will. It may be a child who is upset with you for setting down the rules, or a person who is very shy. When you love, expecting love in return, you will likely be upset when they don't.

"If we don't expect, we have all things, says Buddha. Love because you will to love. Give because you will to give. Flowers bloom because they must, not because there are people fawning over them! You live and love because you will. Because you must."[8] When you love, your loving energy is contagious, and people want to be around you. When you are interested in other people, they will be interested in you.

You love when you choose to see the beauty in something. You may also see a person's flaws, but that will not matter. Pets have flaws, but that does not matter. When you focus on loving, you focus on the good qualities.

> "When people are made to feel secure and important and appreciated, it will no longer be necessary for them to whittle down others in order to seem bigger by comparison."
>
> Virginia Arcastle[9]

We like to feel important, valued, and appreciated. Feeling included and accepted for who you are, feels very good. People like to be a part of something exclusive, because it makes them feel special – like a VIP. Successful businesses know how to make their customers and their suppliers feel important and a part of their "family". When you are in an inclusive environment, you are special.

Seeing Beyond The Mask

When we are fully connected, we will see past the masks people wear. We will see past the anger and hatred, and understand the deeper pain. Once you can see beyond those barriers…and love…I mean truly love…then you will be powerful. If someone rejects your help, you won't even feel that rejection. It just depends on how much you understand life on a deeper level. As we become more loving as a society, the more contagious this emotion will be.

One of the main underlying themes of SuperCamp was inclusion. As students understood that others were like themselves, and wanted to feel included, the more they wanted to include others. John, a student discussed in Chapter 13, wore tattered clothes, had greasy hair, and looked like, what some would consider, a 'bad' kid, which is how other campers seemed to treat him the first few days of camp. Towards the end of the ten-day program, John was fitting in and was making friends. One night we were taking a few team photos. John put up two fingers behind a fellow team member's head (the 'rabbit ears' thing). I asked him to stop, and this really frustrated him. To him, it was as if no matter what he did, it was always wrong, and this appeared to be the straw that broke the camel's back. I felt horrible about this because it was no big deal, and he was just having harmless fun.

As the whole camp came together to sing a few songs before heading off to bed, John decided to sit by himself. A few students wanted to include John by sitting by him. But John protested by getting up and storming off to sit somewhere else by himself. His non-verbal communication clearly indicated that he wanted to prove to them that he was bad, by rejecting their help. He wanted to teach them a lesson. This is the point where in regular society, the other students would have the attitude of; "Fine! Be that way." This is also the point where an adult figure might even tell the other students to leave John alone, because he probably just needed time to "cool off". But none of this happened.

After John stormed off and sat by himself again, more students got up and went to sit by him. Seeing this, he was determined to reject everyone before they could reject him. So again, he got up to sit somewhere else on his own. However, without hesitation, even more students got up and sat by John. This cycle ended when John was completely surrounded by all his peers. He realized that even if he rejected everyone, everyone still loved him 'unconditionally'. Trying to get the others to hate him did not work, nor were the other students frustrated by John's actions. This incident probably changed his entire life in a positive way. All the love in the world came out of this teen. He went around and hugged everyone with tears of joy because he was so happy. When his mom picked him up on the final day, she was shocked by how he changed.

What happened here is a good example of how when A strikes B, A anticipates B to strike back. In the movie Gandhi, Gandhi tells his friend; "Doesn't the New Testament say 'if the enemy strikes you on the right cheek, offer him the left?'" The friend responds, "Well ah, I think perhaps the phrase was used metaphorically. I don't think that…" Gandhi interrupts him and says, "I'm not so sure. I have thought about it a great deal, and I suspect he meant that you must show courage. Be willing to take a blow, several blows, to show you will not strike back, nor will you be turned aside, and when you do that, it calls on something in human nature, something that makes his hatred for you decrease and his respect increase. I think Christ grasped that, and I have seen it work."

I cannot help but think how the experience that John had, almost didn't happen. What if I did not tell John to not do the 'bunny ears' when shooting the photo? John probably would have left camp feeling accepted, but not fully convinced of it, and it could have taken just one event outside of the program to unravel a lot of what he learned. The reason this happened the way it did, was because the other students clearly saw past the superficial emotions and actions. They saw past John's anger and knew he was angry (hurt) because he felt rejected.

When the students started to see beyond the mask, it did not matter how John looked or if he was racist. It did not matter if he was sad or not. He was loved and he is loved, and that's all that counts. While what a racist person feels is very real, and what people feel as victims of racism is also very real, these are feelings and beliefs. Responding to hatred with hatred only perpetuates a cycle of hate. If a dog thinks you are mean and growls at you, naturally (if you are a dog lover) you want to show the dog that you are friendly. If you are a people lover, shouldn't you do the same?

> "We need to be loved. We need to be felt, we need to be touched, we need some sort of manifestation of love."
> Leo F. Buscaglia[10]

All people need love, especially people who have a lot of anger in them. Every person needs to be included. I don't care who you are, include everyone, and love everyone, no matter what, even if they are hateful. I assure you that peoples' hateful thoughts will diminish in time because they will be in a loving environment. The reality is that we will go far when we really begin to include and understand each other.

We Are Responsible

Your name is Adi, or at least that's what your parents nickname you.[11] Your mom is very caring, but your father is very strict, authoritative, and beats you severely. You resent how he treats you, and you also have a dislike for others who try to control you. You dream of a better world. You like painting and you love dogs. There are no rules to painting and dogs, and dogs look up to you and love you. As you grow, you think of becoming a priest. Even though you have a lot of anger towards your dad, he dies when you are in your early teens. You wish things could have been better, but it is too late for that to change. Well, at least you have your mom and you can start moving on with your life. In your later teens, your mother dies of cancer, and you are now on your own. With this, life just gets harder, and you wind up living on the streets, you are broke, and you are lonely. You have dreams of greatness, but these dreams are shattered with failure after failure. There are so many hurt feelings. There is so much fear. You are angry that things were not better. You are angry at your father for being abusive, and you are angry at him for leaving you to fend for yourself. You are angry that your mom died, and you are angry that you have nowhere to turn. You want to lash out at the world. You want to lash out at those who are responsible. While at times you just want to give up, you persevere. You are strong! You are powerful! And you will build a great society! As you grow, you see these images that show how some people are good and some people are bad. You read in the newspaper how these evil people with their beliefs in a different religion are out to take over and impose their beliefs on you. These people need to be stopped. They need to be punished. When you become the leader of The Third Reich you set out to rid society of what you perceive as evil. You "know" they are going to attack, so you strike first. You are Hitler. This is your life! (The above experiences are from actually accounts of Hitler's life.[11])

By labeling and categorizing, we frequently define people as being good or bad. We even believe some people are evil. We try to separate ourselves from people like this. We want to think of these people as monsters or not even human. We picture them looking worse than they really are to justify our actions against them. We associate heroes with images of greatness and strength, such as an eagle. But we associate those whom we think are out to harm us, with images of what we see as evil, such as rats, corruption, thievery, chaos, destruction, and violence.

People are not necessarily good or evil. They are just people. They are born into this world, and have their own unique set of circumstances. Some people are born into a world where their parents beat them…and while we may view these parents as evil, they too have their own unique set of circumstances and experiences. Some people who have been pushed too hard, ostracized, and rejected have exited quietly from life, while others have fought back.

Why do we judge people as being good or evil? Is it not our place to judge? Were people like Hitler or Pol Pot born evil? Should they have been killed when they were one or two years old? While it is easy to think that Hitler was evil; he had a lot of passion, he was a pretty good painter, and he loved dogs. Saloth Sar, the boy who later became know as Pol Pot, was considered to be gentle and kind.[12] Saloth Seng, a farmer, and Pol Pot's older brother said "He was a very polite boy; he never caused trouble".[13]

If people are not born evil, then that means that they become evil over time. If this is true, then that means we have failed as a society. We need to take responsibility for this, and we must rise up as a global society. This is our job – this is our mission. Because the essence of society is love, then we must love everyone. There are no exceptions to this.

Conclusion

How do you want your life to be? It feels great when you can make someone's day and when you make people feel good about their life. When you invest in positive energy, the trillions of cells in your body feel this – you feel this, and the people around you feel this. People crave this attention, just like pets do. If everybody needs love, then it is your job to love everybody. The purpose of a society is to help each other (to serve each other). Love your life and love everyone who comes into your life. Make life fun for others. You will have a better family life, you will be more productive, people will like you more, and you will enjoy your life more. As we all connect with and understand each other more, we start to empathize more. As we empathize more, we start to love more. The more loving we become, the more people will be influenced, and the faster this world will become a loving place.

Every day is a chance to make things better. This is your life, and it is your choice. How much did you make of this day? When this day is over, it is over. So, if you want to have a tremendous impact on other people's lives and on this world, then focus on being more loving. Because there are a lot of people out there who need love. There is a lot of sadness and hurt feelings out there...more than you may think. While people may not show it, they sure do feel it.

As of this point, we are physically together as a society, but we feel separated from each other. While things are improving, these are still the dark ages. But get ready! Because as we come together as a whole, a big change will take place – a change that will shatter these walls of reality in which we live, a change greater than you will ever imagine...a change of revolutionary proportions.

CHAPTER 15

THE REVOLUTION

When you look up at the stars while in a big city, you might be able to see a few. But when you go to the countryside and your eyes adjust to the dark, you can see hundreds of stars. What appears to be milk spilled across the sky, is actually our galaxy – the Milky Way. With a telescope, you see much more, and infinitely more with a high-powered telescope in outer space, beyond the fog of our thick atmosphere.

Our limited perception of each other and of society is similar to trying to see all those stars at night in a big city. Our understanding of each other has slowly evolved over time, and while our understanding has improved, we still have a lot to learn.

When thinking back to the beginnings of social evolution, many people probably think back to the development of language, or the beginnings of society 5,000 to 10,000 years ago. But the beginning of social evolution goes much further back.

In the evolution of technology, we are well aware of the Neolithic Revolution or the Industrial Revolution. When we think of social revolution, we usually think of political revolutions, such as the French Revolution. These revolutions had a major impact on society both politically and socially. However, there were also social revolutions of a far greater magnitude. These were not revolutions that changed society, but revolutions that changed life itself!

The Advancement of Life

Life first began on Earth more than 3.5 billion years ago, where the only life that existed were single-celled organisms. There was no concept of sight, sound, taste, smell, or even touch. These senses were roughly three billion years into the future and took hundreds of millions of years beyond that to advance. Because there was no oxygen in the atmosphere and no ozone layer, single-celled organisms could only survive in the oceans. Photosynthesis created oxygen, and oxygen with the help of ultraviolet rays, created the ozone layer.

> "[Nothing] stirred on the land, except the wind and the dust. Not a single blade of grass waved in the wind, not a single cricket chirped, not a single bird soared in the sky. All these things were tens of millions of years in the future. Even the seas were eerily still and silent, for the vertebrates too were tens of millions of years away in the future."
>
> Daniel Quinn, *Ishmael*[1]

Fossils started appearing about 540 million years ago in what's known as the Cambrian Explosion. These fossils came from life that developed hard body parts such as shells and exoskeletons. It wasn't until about 510 million years ago that plant life began to move onto the land. Fish with backbones (vertebrates) came about 500 to 450 million years ago. These vertebrates moved onto the land roughly 380 million years ago. The first sharks came about 375 million years ago. Flowering plants developed 360 million years ago and the first insects about 10 million years later. Amphibians and birds started to appear around 350 to 300 million years ago, while reptiles started developing 300 to 200 million years ago. The Mesozoic era began about 250 million years ago with the dinosaurs, and lasted 185 million years. This ended 65 million years ago, when it was estimated that a 6.2-mile wide meteorite penetrated through our atmosphere (our natural defense shield), and caused a global catastrophe with a mass extinction of life.

What many people don't realize, is that this was not the only mass extinction we faced, nor was it the largest. Over the past 500 million years, we have been hit with five mass-extinctions, and one of those was estimated to have killed 95 percent of life on Earth!

Even the continents have been through tremendous change over time. When continental drift is talked about, it is thought that the continents started off as being connected as one large "super continent" known as Pangaea. However, there were other super continents long before Pangaea. Pangaea formed a mere 300 million years ago and broke up about 180 million years ago. While anything before Pangaea is based on rough estimates, it is estimated that a previous supercontinent called Rodinia was around one billion years ago, and another supercontinent before that, known as Nuna (or Columbia) was about 1.5 billion to two billion years ago. According to this data, supercontinents form roughly every half billion years.

The Advancement of Social Connection

Since the very beginning, life has always been about connections. As society is the sum of its social connections, society essentially started when individual forms of life started communicating with each other. From that point, we have been continually learning how to better connect with and come together as life.

When I first started writing about single-celled organisms, I saw this as "pre-society." I thought that autonomous single-celled organisms could not form a society, because there was no connection or communication between cells. However, this assertion was incorrect.

Bonnie Bassler[2], a microbiology professor at Princeton University, conducted research on how bacteria communicate. A bacterium that lives in the ocean, called Vibrio Fisheri, creates light, what is known as bioluminescence. She found that when the bacteria were alone, they did not make this light, but when their population reached a certain number they would all turn on at once. How did they do this?

Individual cells communicate with each other via quorum sensing – what appears to be the most basic form of communication. Bacteria secrete protein hormone molecules and have receptors that can tell how many other cells there are by the number of these molecules that are released. A group behavior takes place only when all of these cells participate in unison.[2] This allows them to carry out tasks together that they cannot carry out on their own. All bacteria have social behaviors and also have a second specialized "language" that only like bacteria can understand. They can tell how many other bacteria are of their own kind are present, and how many are foreign. For example, a certain type of bacteria may enter the human body and will stay dormant. Once their population reaches a certain number, they can carry out an attack.

Revolutionary Stages of Life

Life itself has experienced revolutionary stages of social advancement over the course of its evolution. First, there were revolutionary changes in how cells interacted with each other. Individual cells formed into multicellular organisms. Eventually, multicellular organisms formed into larger and far more complex multicellular organisms, where whole groups of cells could be dedicated to specific functions such as sight and sound.

Second, there were revolutionary changes in how complex multicellular organisms interacted with each other. These individual organisms formed into basic groups, such as tribes or packs. Eventually, some of these groups formed into much larger and far more complex groups, such as massive ant colonies, cities, and even vast-megalopolises.

Third, there were revolutionary changes of the conscious mind. Individual conscious minds came together, forming a collective conscious or group of minds. As empathy develops, bringing together all minds, a far greater and far more complex social conscious will develop. This will just be the beginning of the next revolution of life.

In this natural process, individuals form into groups and groups form into complex groups as illustrated below.

1st Revolution	Single-celled organisms formed into multicellular organisms.
2nd Revolution	Multicellular organisms formed into complex multicellular organisms.
3nd Revolution	Individual complex multicellular organisms formed into groups such as tribes or packs.
4nd Revolution	Groups of these organisms formed into complex groups – society as we know it.
5nd Revolution	Individual minds came together into groups of minds or a collective of minds – a collective consciousness.
6nd Revolution	As these minds come together more, we are about to experience the next revolution of life – a complex group of minds or a social consciousness.

The First Revolution –
Basic Multi-Celled Organisms

For over two billion years, the only life on our planet was composed of single-celled organisms. It wasn't until about 1.5 billion years ago that something amazing took place. Some of these single-celled organisms became more than just colonies. They not only became dependent on each other, they actually became a part of each other. They formed into multi-cellular organisms, such as red algae. While basic multicellular organisms are a revolutionary leap from unicellular organisms, the first multi-celled organisms were very basic. The synergy of individual cells working together – the nature of interdependence over time, going from individual cells, evolving into a single organism composed of multiple cells was a revolution in itself.

Experiments have shown that single-celled yeast can be artificially evolved into multicellular yeast using a centrifuge. Based on this information, did life start from one single-cell of life somewhere in the universe with a trace amount of it hitting the earth, or can life start similarly to how a fire starts "from scratch", and not being lit by another fire or torch?

The Second Revolution –
Complex Multi-Celled Organisms

It wasn't until one billion years later (about 550 million years ago), that some of these multi-cellular organisms became more complex. This brought about more advanced life forms such as the sponge. Millions of years later came the jellyfish, which did not have a brain or vertebrate, but was far more complex because it had a nervous system. They also had basic organs such as ocelli, which is essentially a simple eye that can detect light.

Over millions of years, these "super cell societies," made up of millions, billions, and even trillions of cells, became far more complex. While these multicellular organisms did not have any organs or senses at first, over time, billions of cells could be dedicated to specific functions such as livers to remove toxins, and hearts to deliver oxygen and nutrients throughout the body. These super-structures, known as complex multicellular organisms even developed senses like eyesight, hearing, tasting, smelling, and touching, taking the experience of life to whole new dimensions. For the first time ever, life was becoming conscious, at least in ways that we can understand.

Complex multi-cellular organisms have a very basic form of communication that is more like an advanced version of quorum sensing. This communication operates on the same basic principle, in which pheromones, or "messenger-molecules" are released into the environment.

Deepak Chopra explains that if a plant has a virus, the plant will release hormones into the atmosphere to communicate with like plants that there is an infection. "The plant is a localized concentration of awareness in a much larger field of awareness. It knows how to share its awareness with other localized concentrations of awareness (other plants), which carry similar energy and information states (of the same species). Animals do this."[3]

In one experiment, mice were given electrical shocks and then taken out of the area. When different mice were then put into this same area, they started to panic, because they sensed the hormones that were emitted by the fear from the mice that were shocked. Chopra explains that "Every emotional state that we have has a bio-chemical milieu which is released by the body through the skin, sweat and on the breath. Our minds extend outside the body, although the consciousness of the body is within that of the mind – the mind is within something much more pervasive, and we call that field the "Spirit", which creates the mind, the body and the objective Universe."[4]

How could a multi-celled organism know to build senses such as hearing? If you have ever listened to music with the base way up, you can feel sound waves shake your body. Over millions and millions of years, cells were organizing to better feel this noise, via a thin membrane, which could vibrate easily. While it was presumed that snakes could not hear because they don't have ears, they actually have an older version of sound detection, being able to feel sound waves through their bones.

To develop these senses the cells needed to be able to communicate with other cells around the body at a faster rate. While having a nervous system was advanced at the time, these cells needed something even faster and more advanced. They needed an information super highway – they needed a central nervous system.

Only about five percent of the animal kingdom, i.e. fish, reptiles, and mammals, are more advanced, with a central nervous system composed of a brain and a vertebrate. The vertebrate, also known as a spinal column, protects the spinal cord. The spinal cord is tissue made up of nerves that carry signals to and from the brain to other parts of the body. If this connection is damaged enough so that the cells are not able to communicate with each other, the organism would not be able to move other parts of its body.

The development of the brain has come a long way. Was there a time when there was no conscience, or did even the first single-celled organisms have a conscience? If they can sense each other, then it is quite possible that they had some sort of very basic conscience. Do cells have any memory? Experiments have revealed that even single-celled slime mold, which has no brain, does have the capacity for spatial memory. Advanced types of memory developed millions of years later.

As complex organisms slowly started connecting with each other, the brain further evolved. For example, the more you use your mind and the more you use your muscles, the more they develop. The brain grew with mammals. There were improved memory skills and a capacity for a greater range of emotions. Mammals were able to learn from experience. They learned to be aware of dangerous circumstances instead of just reacting to them.

As humans came together, their brains evolved to where they could solve more complex problems. Some of these complex multi-celled organisms, mainly humans, also developed the ability to use tools, and even the ability to walk upright. But even though humans have many advantages over other animals, humans can see only a small percentage of the electromagnetic spectrum (what we see as color) and hear only a small percentage of the acoustic spectrum. Some animals developed a far better sense of smell and hearing.

Elephants can communicate in very low rumbles, lower than what humans can hear. Elephants also have a very good memory. Dogs can hear a higher range of sounds than humans can hear. Dogs also have a much keener sense of smell than humans.

Inside our bodies, there is not only a large amount of communication among our cells, but there is also communication with other organisms within our bodies. Cells in organs communicate with red blood cells that they need oxygen. Infection invading the body, signals the body to produce more white blood cells to fight it. Our bodies are not just great big trillion-cell societies, but are also massive ecosystems that host many other organisms. There are comparatively large complex multicellular organisms such as mites that live on a single eyelash their entire life. Then there are also much smaller viruses and bacteria.

While you may be under the impression that your cells are the majority and these other cells of life are the minority, actually it is the other way around. While you are the host, what you see there is not just "you". Even though you are made up of trillions of cells, only one to ten percent of these cells are actual human cells. The rest are bacterial cells that keep you alive. There are over 500 different species of bacteria living in your gut that break down the food. There are roughly a trillion bacterium cells on the skin alone that protects us from foreign bacteria. It is almost as if the human body is in a sense the society structure for all these bacteria. Your body relies on many of these organisms and they rely on you.

The Third Revolution – Groups of Organisms

The Third Revolution took place when complex organisms learned to connect with other complex organisms, forming groups, such as packs or tribes. With the power to be able to see, hear taste, smell, and feel, these complex organisms eventually were able to communicate, connect with, and even depend on other complex organisms. This connection brought about the next revolution.

With the development of the brain, animals developed a conscience beyond life forms that could not sense anything beyond the very basics. As animals communicated more, the conscious mind developed more. With this, animals were able to connect with each other in deeper ways.

When it comes to reproducing, animals such as mammals, reptiles, birds, and fish don't just get larger and split into two like single-celled organisms. Something as archaic as fish (being around for about 510 million years) don't really have sex like mammals do. In most cases, fish reproduce by means of external fertilization, where the female will release eggs into the water, and the male will release sperm into the water.

The connection between birds is much stronger than fish. In most cases, the male bird will rub up against the female. They both have a cloaca – an opening that releases waste. The male will release sperm through the cloaca into the female's cloaca. Some bird species have penises, which builds this connection between two complex-multi-celled organisms even further. Mammals have intercourse, which could be considered a little more intimate. The mother will also nurse the young in bonding ways. Unlike fish, birds and mammals feed their young, further building this bond.

Over time with communication/connection, complex organisms could form groups. These could be packs of dogs, a murder of crow, or a flock of seagulls. Similar to how basic-multi-celled organisms are not complex organisms, these groups are not complex groups. As animals evolved to work with each other, their brains continued to develop. People formed tribes, which naturally could not be very large, because there would not be enough food for everyone. While the rationale behind forming groups is protection, at least part of this may have to do with mere bonding.

About thirty thousand years prior to the beginnings of towns and villages, people started further developing communication skills. Basic cave symbols dating back about 40,000 years have been discovered. As humans became more conscious of themselves and others, they developed further complex forms of oral communication, and eventually, a written language. Before a written language, the only history people learned was from what they were told.

The Forth Revolution –
Complex Groups of Organisms (Formal Society)

The Forth Revolution took place when these packs, groups, or tribes learned skills, allowing them to form a society. Roughly about 10,000 years ago, when humans learned to cultivate the land, the next revolution took place, which allowed them to move from a hunter and gatherer life to a village. Over thousands of years, some of these small villages eventually grew into gigantic megalopolises composed of millions of people. As we are connecting with each other more, we are becoming a global society.

Today, complex societies are similar to complex organisms. People are often dedicated to specific functions, such as farming or teaching, in order to run such a large society. The heart and brain are like central business districts. Major highways are like arteries delivering people, food, or waste to various destinations. If you look down on the ground, sometimes you will see tiny ant "freeways", just as it looks when you are in a plane and can see all the cars below headed down the freeway.

The Fifth Revolution –
The Collective Conscious

As tribes turned into towns and villages, their individual minds were also coming together, bringing about a revolution of the mind. As human society developed, a collective conscious formed, which brought a revolution of shared ideas and advancements to society. But this collective conscious did not include all people to a full capacity. Only a small number of people had access to education or technology. But the more people within a society are educated, the more the society is able to advance.

As technology has improved, means of connecting have also improved. Faster travel allows us to connect with others hundreds and even thousands of miles away in relatively short periods of time. Phones speed up communication over great distances. Texting helps speed up simple communication. Television and movies play a role in helping us see what other cultures are like. We are able to connect (at least on some level) with people we have never met, even to the point of worldwide mourning of those like John F. Kennedy, Princess Diana, Steve Jobs, Mother Teresa, and Robin Williams.

As we connect more with each other, we become more concerned about each other, and the more sensitive we get to every news story we hear. We hear about a school shooting half way across the country, or we hear about a family that lost their child in a tornado, and we think about our own children. We see and think about the pain these people are going through…and we want to help.

The Next Revolution –
The Rise of the Social Conscious

Like how complex multicellular organisms are composed of billions, and even trillions of cells working together, or a society that has millions, or even billions of complex organisms working together, there is a development of a complex social consciousness made up of billions of minds connecting with each other. This is advancing from an individual conscious mind to a basic group, or collective of minds, to a more complex organization of minds, where all minds play a role, forming a higher level of thinking on a much grander scale – A social consciousness. This is advanced society.

The social revolution is the rise of the social conscious, which will take place when we are able to communicate on a much deeper level. We are just beginning to connect with each other, but this is increasing at an exponential rate. We are at the point where many people are completely unaware of what is about to take place, just as people were completely unaware of the technological revolution just before it took place. This revolution will not happen overnight. It will probably take over a hundred years to really play out…and that will be just the beginning!

In the 1950's conformity was popular. But conformity is not natural, due to the fact that every person is totally unique in nature. As more minds come together, we are realizing that all individual minds play an important role in organizations and society. Successful companies today value the input from all of their employees. Companies that operate as a team tend to be much more effective, and have happier employees. Companies that do not operate as a team are more likely to have hostile work environments where different departments blame each other and employees take out this frustration on customers. In the greater society, rebellion and coups can result from suppression.

It should be no surprise that all this 1950's conformity naturally lead to the 1960's revolt against this thinking. People taught their children that they were individuals who were unique and special. As these children grew, they believed this and focused more on themselves. As we grow, we have been self-absorbed in our own social lives. But like everything else in history, we learn from this, and we continue to evolve socially. Because social skills are learned, social evolution is natural.

While it may appear that society is on the verge of collapse, there are many signs of this revolution. There is a common theme among certain groups of people and individuals who believe that we are about to experience a major shift in social consciousness.

In the 1960's, some people were convinced that this was going to be the start of a social revolution. Looking back, we might think what these people were saying was naïve, but I think they were on to something. They felt it. They knew it.

In the world of astrology, it has been long talked about that the Age of Aquarius is approaching, being a period of peace and harmony. Some say we are just beginning to experience it, others say it will come sometime in the next one hundred years, while others believe it will be several hundred years in the future.

Noted sociologists have said that learning about each other might be the most important factor in advancing society. The development of the "social imagination" or social conscious could be a solution to problems in society. The social imagination helps people understand their own lives and society.[5] Illene Dillon, a family therapist, wrote: "In assessing the changes I have personally made, 'emotional literacy' is a cultural, personal and social revolution of unimaginable scope. Instead of violence, drugs, hate, fear, war, misery and pain, human beings will be able to live successful, happy supportive, growth-filled, intimate and loving lives."[6] Emotional literacy affects society on all social levels (individual, family, community, etc.). "Acquiring emotional literacy is relevant to everyone, and touches all fields and professions"[7] Emotional literacy can help all people and organizations, and can help solve the problems in society.[8] As people learn more about and connect with each other on a deeper level, they become more empathetic, and love becomes more natural. As one's empathy develops, the easier it becomes to understand all people in general – the social conscious of society.

> "Nothing is more powerful than an individual acting out of his or her conscience, thus helping to bring the collective conscience to life."
>
> Norman Cousins

What is taking place is a synergy of minds. Just as cells communicate and act as a unified group, just as a complex multi-celled organism operates as one, and just as many complex multicellular organisms come together creating a physical complex society, this is a coming together of all minds. This is similar to how you are the social conscience of the cells in your body.

Stephen Covey explained that synergy means that the whole is greater than the sum of its parts.

> "If you put two pieces of wood together, they will hold much more than the total of the weight held by each separately. The whole is greater than the sum of its parts." "The essence of synergy is to value differences…to build on strengths, to compensate for weaknesses." "…creating an environment that is truly fulfilling for each person, that nurtures the self-esteem and self-worth of each, that creates opportunities for each to mature into independence and then gradually into interdependence? Could synergy not create a new script for the next generation – one that is more geared to service and contribution, and is less protective, less adversarial, less selfish; one that is more open, more trusting, more giving, and…more loving…?"[9]
>
> Stephen Covey

Imagine a world where all people are able to connect with each other on a deep level. As people connect with each other more, the more they will feel connected with all people. As we advance as individuals, we advance as a whole. And as we learn about each other on a deeper level, the rise of an entire-society is beginning to take shape, that is, the rise of the social conscious will develop.

Slowly, over the course of billions of years, the consciousness of life has been awakening.

Conclusion

From the very beginning, life has been on a path of connecting with and coming together. It started off with the most basic form of communication – quorum sensing. Cells did not just join each other but became a part of each other. These cells kept advancing and while advancing their "society" they eventually developed vast megalopolises, complete with central nervous system super-highways, oxygen delivery systems, and even developed very advanced sensory to interpret things like sight and sound in the universe around them. These super-cell societies (or complex multi-cellular organisms) came together forming tribes and packs, and eventually into megalopolises of many complex multi-cellular organisms. But if that wasn't enough, some complex multi-cellular organisms developed a [more] conscious mind, and then more minds came together. As we are about to see – all minds are coming together.

While there are trillions of cells in your body that may not even be aware of you, they sure rely on you, whoever you are. So now we get down to that question I have been asking throughout this book…

Who Are You?

CHAPTER 16

UNDERSTANDING WHO
WE ARE

Has there ever been a time when you felt at one with the world? Why did you have those feelings? Did you feel this way because you were in a good mood? Or is it possible that you felt this way because you really are at one with the world? Is it possible that even though we are physically different, we really are the same on a deeper level?

So who are we, and what defines us? We looked at how people attempt to define themselves and each other. Later we looked at how these definitions are inaccurate. I wrote about different people's lives, then said how this was your life, as if what these people experienced were also a part of your life. But who are we and how are we all connected in deeper ways?

If you are the president, commander, or even the god of a multi-trillion-cell society, then where did "you" come from? If we want to build a better society, then we need to understand who we are.

What Defines A Person?

What really defines who you are? How different are we from each other once you get below the surface? People define themselves in terms of what they do for a living, the type of car they drive, and even the clothes they wear, but none of these things define who you are. Neither do factors such as intelligence, the amount of money you make, and success.

The environment we live in and the unique experiences we have in life shape our personalities. Have you ever wondered why people from a given area have a certain accent, mannerism, and even facial expression? People are affected by others around them, along with the positive and negative events they experience in life.

Our chemical/genetic makeup also shapes our personality. But this does not define who we are. A person could have a stroke, and their personality could change from being relaxed to becoming aggressive. A person could lack a certain chemical, causing them to be angry. They cannot help this. Does any of this define their personality?

Drugs, whether they are prescription or not, can affect how we think, our temperament, and our decision-making. There are parasites that can have an affect on the mind. Toxoplasma can cause affected mice and rats to behave in a way that draws attention from cats. Research by Dr. Joanne P. Webster, Director of Parasitic Diseases in the School of Public Health at Imperial College London, shows that infected rodents are even attracted to the smell of cats. Once eaten by the cat, the parasite can grow in the intestine. When it leaves the cat in the feces, it can affect other rodents and even people.[1]

Neuroscientist David Eagleman, who wrote the book *Incognito: The Secret Lives of the Brain*, believes that some criminal behavior is caused by problems with brain chemistry. Brains are like fingerprints in that they are individualized. The fact is that all people do not have the same capacity for things like decision-making or understanding future consequences.

In one well-known case in 1966, Charles Whitman, went up to the top of the University of Texas Tower in Austin, and shot and killed thirteen people. He had killed his mother and wife the night before. In a suicide note, he wrote that he wanted an autopsy done on his brain because he felt that this might have had something to do with his mind. He also had an increasing number of headaches. In the autopsy, it was found that he had a brain tumor that was impinging on his amygdalae, which affects fear and aggression.[2] This is not just some bizarre isolated case. Temple Grandin (*Animals in Translation*) noted "…a lot of prisoners who have committed violent crimes have had head injuries at some point in their lives."[3]

Eagleman explains that we are tied to our biology, and when our biology changes, so do we. He gives another example of how a man, at the age of 47, started becoming interested in child pornography. This man also had worsening headaches. He went to the doctors, and they found a massive frontal tumor. After they took out the tumor, he returned to normal. About six months later he was showing signs of pedophilia again. As it turns out, the surgeons missed a part of the tumor, which had regrown. They took this out, and he was normal again.[4]

Even your physical body and the cells that make up your body, do not define who you are. The average life expectancy for people in the United States is just over seventy-eight years, but this is much longer than the lives of the cells in your body. Sperm cells and colon cells last about three to five days. Red blood cells about 4 months and white blood cells can last from hours to years depending on the type of white blood cell. Are you merely the collective conscious of your living cells or are you a higher power? How you feel can have an effect on your cells. Stress can cause various health problems. Maternal deprivation can affect the physical development, as shown in babies.

So, what does all this say about our personalities and the choices we make? While it could be argued that in the case of Charles Whitman, or when somebody suffers brain damage from a stroke, they were not their normal selves. But what is the normal self? Does a small physical technicality of an umbilical cord getting tied around a baby's neck, causing severe brain damage, define who this person is? When a perfectly normal person becomes schizophrenic, does this define who he or she is? Are our personalities and decision-making 100 percent influenced by our environment and chemical make up?

Are our bodies merely vessels used to experience or sense the universe?

Dr. Deepak Chopra suggested that it is not matter that produces consciousness, but consciousness that produces matter. This suggests that matter (your body) and consciousness are two entirely separate things.[5] If this is true, then are we all just innocent souls who would make the same choice another person would make, if we were in their 'shoes'? What is the personality of the soul beyond the chemical makeup and environmental influences? Do only people have souls while other animals do not? Do the trillions of cells of life in our bodies have their own souls? What defines our soul?

After Death Experiences

One possible way to better understand the soul is to look at what people experience after they die. When a person dies the "trillion-cell society" shuts down, where organs, such as the heart, cease to operate. The cells in the body are still alive, but many of these cells will die within hours, minutes or even seconds unless the system is, in a sense, brought back on line. This can be done through things like CPR, or even putting the body on ice to slow down the cell death rate, while doctors try to fix the problem. There is a technology where blood goes through a by-pass machine which takes the blood out of the body, oxygenates it, and then circulates it back through the body, allowing the doctors much more time to figure out what caused the person to die. Once cells themselves die, they go through a chemical process that destroys the cell, and once destroyed, these cells cannot come back.

Dr. Sam Parnia (*Erasing Death*), one of the world's leading experts on the study of death and after-death experiences, is the director of resuscitation research at the Stony Brook University School of Medicine. Parnia's research focuses, not on people who are near death, but on people who have been pronounced dead for minutes and even hours. Parnia explains that, with people who have died and come back, there are many stories that are consistent. These people describe their experience as "absolutely real." Many people from around the world have had these experiences, even children as young as three years old.

Physicians and nurses describe how after resuscitating a person, the patient was able to tell them in detail what was taking place even though the person appeared to be dead. They saw events and heard conversations that they were able to recall with incredible accuracy, not just in the operating room, but also outside the room.

People often describe having a review of and even experiencing everything they have done in their entire life. If you are able to experience your entire life all at once, then is it arguably all in the "right now"?

Parnia explains that, in one of the most consistent experiences, people describe seeing a tunnel. In some cases it is long and dark, or like a kaleidoscope with colors on the side. People often recall a bright light at the end of the tunnel, which they interpreted as warm and welcoming. In addition to this, religious and nonreligious people alike describe a being of light containing love, mercy and compassion. There was a deep sense of all-pervading love and benevolence.[6] Many people said the after-death experience affected them in a profound positive way, especially those who say they encountered a being of light. They come out of the experience feeling less materialistic and more altruistic. One person said how he came away from the experience with a new understanding of his role as a husband, father, and friend.[7] If they hurt someone's feelings, even unintentionally, they feel the pain they caused someone else. They come back and judge their own actions, having a motivation to change their lives. One person described how he wanted to make sure he did not fail again.

Parnia also explains that people who have tried to commit suicide, tended to have frightening and disturbing experiences that were painful and distressing, and would certainly not want to go through that again. My guess is that this is not because people are going to some dark, scary hell, but more that they are experiencing the worst possible regret they could ever make in their life – taking their own life, possibly along with lives of others. We have all made regrettable decisions in our life – decisions we wish we could turn back time and choose differently. Even with these "nightmarish" decisions, some decisions are much worse if they are irreversible. Similar to the irreversible decision of committing suicide, imagine how it would feel if you hit and killed a couples' only two children, all because you took your eyes off the road to text someone.

Are We the Same Life?
Are We the Same Soul?

There appears to be no consensus of when life begins. Some people believe that life begins at conception, while others believe that life begins when one is born. Is it possible that life begins at…well, billions of years ago? Going as far back as we know, it was never new life. It was always cellular fission. One cell divides into two cells, two cells divide into four cells, and so on. As these cells divide and spread over a large area, different environments affect the chemical make up of the cell.

Let's take, for example, a male and a female who are both alive. So you have one life and another life. These two people get together, both of who are made up of trillions of cells of life. The sperm and egg are both alive…they are the life of the male and female. Both the sperm and the egg are single cells. The egg remains a single cell until fertilized by the sperm, when it then begins to split into new cells. It does not take long for these cells to form into a complex-multicellular organism. The sperm is not a separate life from the male and the egg is not a separate life from the female. It's not like I have a cup of flour and you have a cup of sugar and we mix them together and make a baby or a cat. If the cells that make up the sperm or egg are dead, then it is dead. So the sperm and egg come together:

Life + Life = Life.

They are together and are part of each other…they are still life. It's not like there was no life, and all of a sudden new life spontaneously formed. When did this become "new" life? The cells of life from the male and female came together and formed their own group.

As we see life, it is made up of separate bodies: a person, a whale, an ant, a dog, a plant, or a cell. We define ourselves as being separate lives and even separate souls, but is it possible that we are really just the same life and even the same soul? If we are separate souls, when was my soul created and when will it end?

We are under an illusion that it is different life, but if you look closer, it is not. If the largest living organism is a grove of Aspen trees that all have the same root system, what does that say about connectivity? Under a microscope, we see a few cells, but they multiply and grow. Let's zoom out a little. Now we see some mold, and after a few days we come back and we see that the mold has grown. We don't say that the mold had babies, and now there are many molds. A tree grows, and it drops some seeds. One of those seeds grows into another tree. These seeds are not dirt or rocks, but cells of life. Are the seeds a new life? The seed will grow into a new tree, but it really is not a new life. It becomes separated, but it is not new.

What about conjoined twins? Are these two separate souls? What about conjoined twins who share the same brain? Conjoined twins, Abigail and Brittany Hensel, share the same body and have just two arms and legs between them. They are two separate people and have two separate personalities.

Krista and Tatiana Hogan, are craniopagus twins, having a connection of blood vessels and share a bridge of neural tissue between their thalamus. One can feel, taste, and see what the other feels tastes, and sees, yet they have their own personalities.

Imagine that we are doing an experiment on extreme accelerated growth and the umbilical cord between the baby and mom was never cut. Obviously this line will disconnect naturally after a few days, but let's pretend that it doesn't. So the female baby grows up in a few hours and connects with a male who is also literally still attached, they have a baby who is now attached to the female. So in a sense, is this like one long plant like the grove of Aspen trees? At one end, the plant is dying, like how people and every other life form on Earth dies. At the other end is the growing part of the plant. Where do we make this separation of life…when the umbilical cord is cut, or are we just one entity of life that just continues and separates into pieces?

Anglerfish have confused scientists for decades. Little was known about the male anglerfish because they could not be found. Female anglerfish sometimes had a parasite attached to them. It was found that the parasite was the male anglerfish. While the male anglerfish is still small, he attaches himself to the female. Over time the jaw dissolves and the bloodstream of both fish fuse together. The brain and the guts either shrink or disappear entirely. The male becomes nothing more than testes that fertilize the eggs. So, what was two fish, is this now one fish?

Think of it this way. Imagine that you have a bowl of soup and another person has a bowl of the same soup. You both take a bit of your soup and put it in another bowl. It is still the same soup, maybe from two different bowls, but it is still the same. While it is the same soup, one bowl may have more noodles or more oregano, just like we all have our own unique DNA. Is death really just the big pot of soup in the sky? Is this idea of Heaven when we are all reconnected? Could it be that death is really just the other side of life?

This all leads me to wonder. Cells came together and created multi-cellular societies. Over millions of years, these multi-cellular societies formed into what we consider a single organism with a higher level of consciousness. So, is an organism, such as a person, the higher level of conscience of all the cells in his/her body? Is the social conscience of society a higher level of conscience of complex organisms? We are trillions of cells, yet we are one organism. We are trillions of organisms, yet we are one life.

Let's go a bit further. Why is it hard to look into another person's eyes for a few minutes at a time? A comment that springs up frequently is that you feel like you are looking into each other's soul. When people do look into each other's eyes for minutes at a time and get past feeling uncomfortable, why do they then feel at one with each other? When people connect with each other on a deep level, they often describe that they feel at one with each other. Why is love a "feeling of underlying oneness"?

In the book *The Art of Loving*, Erich Fromm wrote: "In essence, all human beings are identical. We are all part of One; we are One. This being so, it should not make any difference whom we love."[8] Marianne Williamson (*A Return To* Love) explains, "Psychologist Carl Jung posited the notion of the 'collective unconscious,' an innate mental structure encompassing the universal thought forms of all humanity. His idea was that if you went deeply enough into your mind, and deeply enough into mine, there is a level we all share...if you go deeply enough into your mind, and deeply enough into mine, we have the *same mind*."[9]

Dr. Goleman said, "Our experience of oneness – a sense of merging or sharing identities – increases whenever we take someone else's perspective, and strengthens the more we see things from their point of view. The moment when empathy becomes mutual has an especially rich resonance. Two tightly looped people mesh minds, even smoothly finishing sentences for each other – a sign of a vibrant relationship that marital researchers call 'high-intensity validation.' " "Such deep encounters are the moments we remember most vividly in our close relationships."[10]

> The soul is the same in all living creatures
> although the body's each is different.
>
> Hippocrates

The idea that we are the same entity of life may seem a little frightening at first. You may picture a loved one who died, and his or her individuality dissolves, absorbs, or assimilates into the whole of life, which includes a lot of scary people and other creepy life forms out there. But actually, we are the many faces of the same entity of life. The Earth is a single planet, yet there are many different parts of it. The Milky Way is a single galaxy, yet there are many facets of it. An individual cell separates into more cells. It is the same life, yet it is separate life. It is the same entity, yet it must diversify for maximum survival. It must grow and flourish. Some parts die while other parts flourish. It is the cycle of life.

The Commander

Dr. Deepak Chopra posed the question; where in your body is the commander of you, i.e., where in you do you make decisions? Some people say that where we make our decisions is in our heart, others say that it is in our brain. But where is this precisely? Research has shown where in the brain decisions are executed, but they cannot find where in the body these decisions are being made. If you choose to move your arm, where are you making that choice? They cannot find where the commander is. Deepak Chopra thinks that we cannot find the commander because the commander is everywhere and nowhere at the same time.[11]

Who is this commander? When we connect with each other on very deep levels, we feel an underlying oneness…we experience love. It could be argued that biologically we are one. If life did not begin at birth, or even conception, and that life began, based on what we know, billions of years ago, are we the same life, therefore, the same at our very core? Logically, if we are the same life, are we the same soul? If we are the same life and the same soul, then is this the same commander? If this is all the same commander, is the commander God?

God Is Life – God is Love

In the past, it was commonly believed that God was vengeful. But in reality, it was the people in society who were vengeful. As we become more loving, our image of God becomes more loving. This is not to say that we are God, but more like vessels of God. Looking at the definition of cell, could it be argued that each life (person, cat, dog, duck) is a cell of life (small compartment in a larger structure) that is a part of a larger organism? Are we the cells of life to a greater "organism" being God? Is this similar to how we are in a sense, the commander, or even god of a multi-trillion-cell society? When the social consciousness awakens, are we connecting more with the greater organism that encapsulates us all?

When I interviewed a pastor about life, he said that God is life and God is love.[12] Already knowing what the answer was, I asked him if that meant that I was God. He told me "No!" This would be like saying that one of your hairs is you. It might be your DNA, but we sure don't say, "Where's Bob? Oh there's Bob!" while pointing to a piece of hair.

Are my cells aware of me? Am I merely the social consciousness of my cells? If all I am are a bunch of cells put together in a gigantic structure (my body), then who am I the commander? I don't exist anywhere in the structure. If the cells were people, I would be to whom they pray. Some would doubt my existence. Many probably have no clue that I exist. What they do affects me, and what I do affects them. I as a whole have more influence on them then they do on me. They depend on me. They are counting on me.

While some people argue that God is male or female, it is a fact that all cells that make up life are asexual. Because this is true, then this male/female thing is just a part of the structure that makes up the complex-multicellular organism. We are used to classifying ourselves as male or female, which is fine, but when you break it down, even gender is superficial.

The perception is that we are different life, but we are not. Fire is fire, water is water, and life is life. These individual life forms are not just people, dogs, cats, and every other life form, but also the cells of life that make up that sentient being, in addition to all life throughout the universe. Is this entire combined life force God? All cells are life. All organisms are life. God is life – life is God.

Just imagine how exciting it would be to find out that there is life, any life, even cells of life on a distant planet. If we found life on another planet, even it were merely just cells of life, we would say it is a miracle nonetheless. We say that life is a miracle. The miracle is God.

Bishop John Shelby Spong wrote in the article *The Theistic God is Dead – A Casualty of Terrorism*:

> "The Epistle of John says that God is love, and whoever abides in love abides in God. Love comes to consciousness in the human experience. Love makes life possible. Love creates wholeness. When love is shared, life is enhanced, but when hatred replaces love, life is diminished. An even keener insight emerges when we reverse those biblical words. For if we can say that God is love, then surely we can say that love is God. This biblical insight proclaims that love is what God is. We thus make God visible, not by receiving an external revelation from on high, but by the human act of loving wastefully."[13]

As we have slowly gained more intelligence over billions of years, we strive to make "society" better – we strive for love – we strive for God. As we evolve as people, we work with each other in more efficient, productive ways. Isn't this like how the cells in our body work together as a whole? Going from single-celled life to complex organisms to a full revolution in how we think and connect with each other: is this the evolution of God? If we are on our path to God, as some would say, and God is life and God is love, is our path to God our path to love? Is this the highest order?

It is All Energy

Love is energy, and so is every other emotion. While it may seem that love and any other emotional energy are purely mental, not physical, how many times have you felt energized by something you saw, felt, tasted, heard, or touched? We smell barbeque and we get hungry. We hear powerful music and we get energized. We see love and we feel it in our hearts. And just when we think we don't have the strength to continue, we read a story about triumph, and we feel unstoppable!

Like the electromagnetic spectrum and the acoustic spectrum, Emotions are also on a spectrum. Because emotions are energy, on a spectrum, if God were love, then love would truly be the highest energy level.

Everything we consider to be physical is really just energy. Even when you look at the nucleus, proton, and electron, these "particles" really are not actual particles, but energy. So all life, along with everything else in this universe is pure energy. Zooming in past the single-celled organism down to the atom, the atoms in your body are more than 99.99999 percent empty space. Our star system (the Solar System) like the atom is also more than 99.99999 percent empty space. If you enlarged the atom to the size of our solar system, where the nucleus was the same size as the sun, depending on what atom we are looking at, the outermost electron would be farther away than Pluto.[14]

Because all matter is energy, larger objects are really just larger amounts of energy. Is this why there are these patterns in life and in the universe? Just as protons and electrons revolve around the nucleus, moons revolve around planets, and planets around stars. Stars revolve around galaxies and galaxies revolve around each other. Even some asteroids have their own moon. Some asteroids travel in small packs and revolve around each other. Why is this? The obvious answer is gravity. But what is gravity really?

If all matter creates gravity and all matter is energy, does love create gravity? What about negative energy? Does it actually repel like we say it does? Life revolves around love. When I say this, I mean it literally, not metaphorically. Love is an attractant, and we are attracted to love. We want to be around loving people. This is not to say that larger objects have bigger hearts, but that these larger objects are simply larger amounts of energy. If a person feels love and is very loving, then does love manifest that person's cells, and therefore would that make love essentially physical? If God is everywhere, then love is everywhere.

Conclusion

In order to help ourselves and society, we need to understand who we are, understand others, and understand society. Socrates said, "know thyself" and "the unexamined life isn't worth living." He said that without knowing yourself and examining yourself, you cannot grow. Examining your life is one of the core components of almost any philosophical system. Lao Tzu said "He who knows others is wise. He who knows himself is enlightened." Jesus said if you want to find life you need to look inside yourself. Inscribed in the Temple of Luxor it says, "The body is the house of god..."[15] and, "...know thyself...and thou shalt know the Gods." It also says, "The kingdom of heaven is within you; and whosoever shall know himself shall find it."[16]

When it comes to defining who we are, it is clear that while our environment and chemical makeup shape who we are, they do not define who we are. It appears that our conscience and our physical bodies are two separate things. While we can find where these commands are executed, we cannot find where we make the decision – we cannot find the commander.

It has been a long running debate of when life begins, being at either conception or birth. But when you look closer, it appears that there never was "new" life to begin with. It has always been the same life. Just because you can take a pitcher of water and pour some into two glasses, that does not mean you just gave birth to two glasses of water.

So if at the core, we are the same life, that means we are the same commander. If this is the same consciousness or commander, is the consciousness of life God? Just as the great religions have said that God is life, God is also love.

We are under the illusion that we are separate entities from each other and all life, just as we are under this illusion that there are solid objects all around us. Yet everything you see around you is just pure energy.

Deep down all life is the same – It is life!

We are life and we need love. Like the cells to a complex organism, are we the cells of life and God is the whole? When we realize that we are one – that we are possibly even the same entity, the social consciousness will awaken and a revolution will take place. When the social consciousness awakens, i.e. when we are at one with all life, we are at one with God. This is ultimate power!

CHAPTER 17

YOU CAN BUILD
A BETTER WORLD

After reading this book, you may still be convinced that you know your family, friends, and people in general. You may still be convinced that you understood your spouse, yet you ended up getting into a bitter divorce. You may still be convinced that the world is worse off today and that there is no way we are about to make a massive change in our global society for the better. The idea that we will revolutionize our lives and society by gaining a better understanding of each other may seem far-fetched. But there is a lot of research that backs up the information and ideas in this book. Many of these studies have been replicated tens and even hundreds of times. Volumes of books could have been written about these concepts.

When it comes to technological advancements such as reaching the moon or finding a cure to cancer, we keep trying and never give up. Yet when it comes to social advancement, such as peace talks or improving a marriage that is in trouble, we seem to give up and retreat at the slightest crack of failure. Saying that bullying will always be around because it has always been around, would be like saying that a manned mission to Mars is impossible because we have never been to Mars. Creating a world that is free of violence and war may seem idealistic, but it is possible. We have been through so much to get to this point. Too many lives have been sacrificed in the name of bettering society. We owe this to ourselves, our families and friends, and our world.

There are a lot of people who would like to help make this world a better place, but feel like they are powerless to make a difference. The good news is that you can build a better world no matter what your situation. It is simple: you just make the effort with people you interact with every day, such as your spouse, your kids, your parents, at work, at school, and in your every day interactions with strangers. How we connect with each other is learned and goes way beyond just communicating effectively.

While it may not seem like it, things are changing. We are changing. We are learning more about who we are. We are becoming more aware of other people's personal problems and therefore are more willing to help each other. We are learning empathy! Like how a soldier will help a fallen brother, when we focus on helping and inspiring each other, and we build each other up, instead of tearing each other down, we will revolutionize society. When people try to tear you down, they are hurting deep inside, beyond what you can see, and likely beyond what they understand. Just realize that if we were all aware of what challenges you were facing, you would have billions of people who would be cheering you on.

As much as we think we know people, we only know the image they portray. Our judgments and actions are based on these false images. Having little or no understanding of each other, we are unable to understand the problem. In failed attempts to try to fix the problem, we resort to blaming. We blame parents for the actions of their children and the parents blame each other. The idea that people should know better may seem obvious to you, but only if you know better. We blame opposing political parties. We get angry without really understanding the bigger picture. When we blame, we are attacking, which can lead to conflict, violence, and even war.

The reality is that we are disconnected, and when we feel disconnected or rejected by others, we either retreat into darkness or attack. Attacking and defending is something the most basic organisms have learned. Yet when people act like this, we think they are crazy. There is a reason we don't get between a momma grizzly and her cub. When people we love are attacked, we will do everything to defend them. So it should be no surprise that when we make judgments based on superficial information and point blame, we are attacking, and people will get angry.

Defining people by things like wealth, success, failure, accomplishments, and intelligence says little about them. None of this really helps us in understanding how they feel deep down. Our emotions affect every part of our life and when we do not understand what people are feeling, we do not understand them. Our emotions are not only contagious they are interconnected.

Social connections are like the neurons in the body, joiners in train tracks, or connectors that join two pipes together. When these connections are not solid, there are glitches, leaks, or even a total breakdown. No matter what political system is in place, what religion you follow, or what type of car you drive, if the connections are poor, things will not work properly. Without social connection, society fails on all levels: within the body...within the world.

Alienation affects every one of us in various ways. Our lives revolve around the connections we have with each other. Babies switch to a non-growing state when not held; Socially isolated Rhesus monkeys show blank stares, and become untamable, self-destructive, and violent; Cells that do not form synaptic connections commit apoptosis (cellular suicide); So naturally, when people feel unloved or unwanted, is it any wonder that the results will be similar?

We cut each other down. From slights to passive aggressive behavior to bullying. We yell at each other. We hurt each other. We kill and we are killed...by the millions. We hate who we are. We resort to gambling. We steal, not necessarily because we need to, but because we are just trying to feel that high that we need so bad. We hurt ourselves. We turn to drugs. We even cut ourselves...we destroy ourselves. We want to disappear from existence. We want to execute our soul.

But it so often is not until a loved one dies or when we are facing our own death does it become so clear. We want to turn back the hands of time. But it is too late. This is our fate. This is our death. This is the downfall of society. It has always been this way, and it will always be this way, or so we presume…

It is All About Connecting

By learning to connect with others in deeper ways, you will improve relations with your parents, your children, your spouse, with friends and associates, and with strangers you meet every day. As it is, we are not even good at the simple skills such as listening. If we only understand people on a superficial level then we understandably will not be that interested in listening to them. It's when we hear people's stories that we be come interested. As we gain a greater understanding of people, listening naturally becomes easier because we want to listen.

Deeper social connection such as gazing into another person's eyes for minutes at a time is more complex. I suspect that not one person I told about extensive eye contact has ever tried it. The reason for this is that it can be very uncomfortable at first. People may have staring contests to see who can win, but that is more about aggression; who's the strongest, like how a predator will eye its prey. Physical contact is important, yet you would not say that people fighting is similar to people hugging. Extensive eye contact can be uncomfortable at first because we are not used to this level of connection, even with a spouse. When people try doing it on their own, they often talk or make jokes to lighten up the experience, which actually lessens the experience of connecting on a deeper level. This is why we really need to learn skills like this in a structured setting.

Social connection needs to be taught in school. Changing the social environment, turns schools into fun, exciting learning environments where students want to learn and understand each other. As students learn about each other and learn to include each other, they naturally will want to include each other. When you empathize with people, you want to include them, you want to help them. People who are well-socialized and are friendly, are more likely to succeed in the work environment.

You marry with every intention of being with this person for the rest of your life, so you should make it as good as you can. It is not about the number of conflicts you have, but if and how you make amends after an argument. People with good marriages will have more positive things that take place during an argument. When they are not fighting, they say about twenty times more positive things than negative. Couples who have as many or more negative things to say as positive things are creating a negative relationship. Marriages with great sex lives have great friendships. When it comes down to it, positive affection is the only variable that predicts both marital stability and happiness. A lot of this comes down to emotional intelligence.

If your marriage is in trouble, don't wait to fix it, because the problem will only get worse. Spend time learning about your spouse's deeper feelings. When you stop showing interest, he/she will lose interest. Spend several minutes at a time looking into each other's eyes. Once you really start connecting, and build up the positive energy, it will get much easier. Realize that every hurtful comment you say is like a paper cut. It hurts, but will not do any long term damage if you clean and heal the wound.

It is important to know that accidents happen in the blink of an eye, and loved ones (or yourself) may die at any time. Don't ever take it for granted that they will be there tomorrow. You will be with this person for the rest of your life, so you might as well set a goal every day to make that a great day. Would you rather spend this time being mean to each other, or would you rather make it a great day?

This all comes down to love. We choose to love. Regardless of how abusive of a past you experienced, you are capable of loving and being loved. As complicated as we make out love to be, it is really quite simple. However, it can be quite difficult if your only role models are people who are not very loving. Love is learned. It comes down to being kind, friendly, caring, and considerate. It is about taking time to do something for someone else. Even a quick message to say 'hi'. Having a genuine concern for all people at all times says it all. By having a loving attitude, you will affect people in a loving way. If you have negative energy in you, people will notice.

Alienation is the antithesis of society. Alienation is also a lack of love. When you connect deeply with someone, you will be able to see beyond the mask – you will see someone just like you. The more we learn to love as a society, the quicker this contagious energy will spread. You can make life fun for others. People and animals crave this attention. When you have positive energy in you, people feel it.

We Can Choose How We Face Challenges

Many people have tried very hard to make a change in their lives, but gave up because it was too difficult. You make a big change, but then go back to your old routine without even realizing it. It is easy to think that people just don't change. Habits are difficult to permanently change, so we often think we failed. If you are used to doing things one way, it will take you a while for you to consistently do it another way. There will be many setbacks, but the more something becomes a habit, the more it will become a part of you. It's like walking one hundred steps in one direction and ninety-nine steps back. Just be patient and don't get discouraged. You may have a hundred setbacks before the change becomes permanent.

You can worry about your problems, but the fact remains that you will face problems throughout your life. It is not the number of problems you have, but how you deal with these problems that counts. So if you are going to deal with problems throughout your life, you might as well change the way you handle these problems. See these problems as challenges.

As a Team Leader at SuperCamp, I explained to other staff that the next day, the ropes course, was going to be the toughest day of the program. Hot weather was predicted and students would likely get cranky in the afternoon. One of the other experienced Team Leaders said that the way I was explaining this, I was setting myself up for failure. While what I said was accurate, this made me realize that I could change the way I would see the following day. Why do people climb Mt. Everest? Are they being punished for committing a crime? No, they do it for the challenge. Changing how I saw the next day, I went to bed excited. In the morning, I was pumped up, ready to tackle the day. On a typical ropes course, you have events that take place high in the air. You also have a lot of smaller events that take place on the ground, which are not as exciting. For every one of these events, I would make up a story to make the game more exciting. Because I showed so much enthusiasm and excitement, my team was enthusiastic and excited. By lunchtime, it was already hot out, and the entire camp was excited to get to the air-conditioned cafeteria. But as soon as my team finished eating, they wanted to go back outside to do more on the course, while the other teams were content to stay inside. By the end of the day, when everybody is usually worn out, my team wanted to do more of the ground events. They were the last team off the course. We went back to the dorms tired, yet still having fun. Changing my way of looking at something, made what I initially saw as a long grueling day into a great day, not just for me, but also for the entire team.

People who have made extraordinary accomplishments in this world, owe it to a lifetime of failures. We fail every day finding a cure to diseases, yet despite the seemingly endless number of failures, when we do find a cure, it is huge. Usually though, many of these massive discoveries are due to the many small successes that lead to it. With success, anybody can feel confident. But it is failure that really tests your confidence. One of greatest feelings I have is when, despite constant failures and setbacks, I feel unstoppable. In the great society, it will not matter how many times you fail or how successful you are – because you are loved.

So imagine what your life could be like if you changed your habit of thinking. When things get very difficult, you can change your perceptions of these situations and accomplish amazing things.

Your Life Is Your Journey

We come into this life to experience the universe around us. Like curious puppies, we take it in with excitement. But for many people, as they grow older, life becomes a predictable routine: "been there and done that". But there is so much more out there to experience and to learn. Recapture the joy of exploration and learning you had as a child.

> Joy is a great teacher, and so is despair, wonder, confusion, hope, disillusionment, life, and even death. To deny yourself any of those – any aspect – is not experiencing life totally. I don't know any other culture in the world where so many of us go through life without experiencing life. We don't understand pain and death. A child isn't even allowed to be around death. Leo's parents did not protect him from life. The kids were a part of everything; the joy, music, wonder, pain, and despair. Papa would come home and would say; "We don't have any more money…what are we going to do about it?" Then the whole family would pitch in to help out. By doing this, they experienced togetherness.
>
> Leo Buscaglia Ph.D.

Sometimes we focus so much on the destination that we lose track of the journey. Our life is the journey. We will reach our destination when we die. Your life is like a game. The gun fires and you are born. You start off and are experiencing this game of life for the first time. In this game, you are not competing against anybody. It is simply a game, and is full of excitement and challenges. If there is no challenge in the game, then you are not really experiencing life…you are not actively participating in the game.

Some people start their game with very little, making their game more of a challenge. It is as if they chose to play their game on a higher difficulty mode before they were born. Some of the challenges you face are going to be easy, and some are going to take you to the absolute limit. There may be times that you are ready to throw in the towel and give up. But regardless of what disadvantages you have, such as a physical or mental disability, or how little wealth you have, just realize that no matter how tough things are, or will get, these experiences are a part of your game.

Some of the most inspirational moments in life are when you get knocked down and feel defeated, only to find the strength to get back on your feet and keep going. Even if you fail in the end, your courage gives others courage. Some of the toughest times in your life, when you face humiliation, terror, or even death, you may look back on as amazing experiences that changed your life, experiences that you would never trade because of the impact they had on you.

It's not about how fast you go, just as long as you stay in the game. The goal is not about crossing a finish line, but about the journey you take. You cannot fail at life. You just live and go as far as you can. The game ends when you die. This is unavoidable. It could be in several decades or it could be today. The more afraid of dying you are, the more afraid you will be to live your life. Death is a part of life. It is important to accept death, so you can live your life.

When your game is over, everyone who finished their game will be there to congratulate you. When you die, you might look back on your life, and regardless of how difficult it was, you will be in awe of the whole experience.

So you have two choices. You can choose to play the game, and have some amazing experiences, or you can opt out and choose to die. If you choose to live, then take on the challenge and give it everything you got. But if you give up and leave your game early, you will wish that you stayed in…because this is the most exciting game ever. This is your life.

The Time Is Now

Your journey through life will go by quickly, and the older you get, the faster it will seem to go by. For the time you have, would you rather spend more time getting angry or would you rather spend more time loving? If you had a chance to re-live your life, what would you do differently? I am guessing you would take more chances.

Wade Davis, who wrote *The Wayfinders – Why Ancient Wisdom Matters in the Modern World*, explains that in, 670 original dialects of Australia, there is no word for time. The past, present, and future are all woven into a multi-dimensional space. It is the eternal now.

In the movie *2001: A Space Odyssey*, at the very end, the main character, Dave witnesses himself as an old man, yet he is the old man. As an old man, he then sees himself on his deathbed, yet at the same moment, he is on his deathbed. He is also on the verge of being born.

We know that we are currently in the present – we are always in the present, not the past or the future. Remember back to a time you were looking forward to something that would take place in the distant future. Maybe you were a kid looking forward to Christmas, or you were getting ready to go on an exciting trip. You remember the feelings, the temperature, the smells, others who were with you. While this was a future event, it was also a current event, and now, a past event…something that happened a long time ago.

I remember very clearly spending time with my dogs and cats knowing that they would die in the future. They are dead now, and my time with them was in the past. But the fact remains that they are a part of my existence. They exist! This is why I so often speak of them in the present tense.

These moments are also in the past, as well as in the future. Because it is always now, at this moment, you are experiencing your death, but you are also experiencing your first breaths of life. You are experiencing your first crush…and your first kiss. If you pick up this book and read this section on your deathbed in the future, it will be now…it is all right now! I am writing this right now and you are reading this right now. So instead of waiting in anticipation for the next event, realize that the event of life is right now.

We are All Connected – We are One

All this time, we have been on a journey of connecting with each other...in a sense to become whole again. Realize that others are neither better than nor less than you. We are all on the same level.

We can label life as a dog, duck, goat, or person. But what is life at the deepest level? We are not necessarily many different lives, but are all the same life just in separate bodies. New life does not just spontaneously generate. When the complex multi-cellular organism procreates, it involves bringing together the cells of two complex multi-cellular organisms. These cells, through fission, create a separate organism.

Based on the evidence, the most logical conclusion is that while we are separate forms of life, we are still the same life. I am composed of trillions of cells of life, of which most of these cells are not even "my" cells! Yet I, along with trillions of other complex multi-cellular organisms, are cells or vessels of life to the greater whole of life. This entity – life, is what many refer to as God. So, we are vessels of life, we are vessels of God – we are all God's creatures.

Even if decisions are made within the body of billions and even trillions of cells, where in these cells are we choosing to make a choice? While our bodies are made up of matter, the commander is nowhere to be found, and therefore must be separate from the body. So is it possible that while death is commonly seen as the opposite of life, could death really be life in its wholeness – the big pot of soup in the sky?

The more I see, not just beyond the images and masks people wear, but also beyond the environmental influences around us and the physical/chemical composition of the body that we think define who we are, the more love I feel towards everyone and life as a whole. I don't see enemies. I see life. When people do horrible things to each other, I realize that we need to do more as a society.

So you have a very important job. You are the God of a multi-trillion cell society. You cells may not know who you are, but they are sure counting on you. People are counting on you. People need your help…and there will be many times where you will need their help.

Living above the line is about responsibility, freedom, and choice. Living below the line is about denial, labeling, quitting, and justifying our actions. How are you living your life? When you think about actions you take, ask yourself if you are living above or below the line. When you do something that is wrong or have to justify your actions, these actions are probably below the line. So try living above the line. Have integrity, own up to responsibility, and take control of your life!

Are you working against society or are you helping it? When you are rude to people, you are hurting them. When you yell at people, you are hurting them. This negative energy is bad for their health as well as your own. Even little slights could be compared to someone poking you with their finger, which can get irritating quickly. If you have the intelligence to not do this to a lion, why would you do this to a person?

We have come to a crossroads. We can either continue to make the same excuses or we can choose to live above the line. We can choose to love. No matter how impossible the idea may seem the challenge is here. If our hatred wins, we will ultimately end up destroying ourselves. But when love wins, this energy will be the start of the revolution. Love your life…love all life…and through your attitude, you will affect others.

With love, we are a part of something greater. As we learn to love, imagine where we will take this world in the next one hundred years and even in the next one thousand years. Today's triumphs will be the norm of tomorrow, and tomorrow's triumphs will be what we see as impossible today. When we are operating as a whole – we can get beyond the "small stuff" in life and focus on more important issues.

The Revolution is about connection.
It's about choosing to love.

When we fully connect with each other,
We love each other.

When we love each other,
We are willing to die for each other,
Therefore, nothing will stop us.

WE ARE LIFE

WE ARE THE ULTIMATE POWER!

NOTES

CHAPTER 2

1. I first read about this in Grandin & Johnson, *Animals in translation*, 24. I watched one of the many videos on the internet and while I already was anticipating seeing the gorilla, when I focused on passing of the ball, I could see how people would miss this.

CHAPTER 3

1. Moffett, "Tracking a 'sisterhood' of traveling ants" [Audio blog interview by D. Davies]. Additional information came from the following book: *Adventures among ants: A global safari with a cast of trillions*, by Moffett.
2. My notes on this were from a discussion with Dr. Paul Apodaca in 2010.
3. Pinker, *The better angels of our nature*, 22.
4. Ibid., 61. A study by Steven Pinker & Bennett Haselton.
5. Ibid., 697.
6. The headline is from *The Guardian*, This information was well documented in many newspapers. It should also be noted that the articles I read, all showed how this was based on a natural phenomenon.
7. It does not take much to panic people. The following links retrieved on July 31, 2014 make the case that these are almost all entirely rumors. Here are a few sources/links:

a. Best, Joel; Gerald T. Horiuchi. "The razor blad in the apple: the social construction of urban legends." *Social Problems*. Vol. 32, No. 5, Jun. (1985). Abstract viewed on July 31, 2014. http://www.jstor.org/discover/10.2307/800777?uid =3739560&uid=2129&uid=2&uid=70&uid=4&uid= 3739256&sid=21104428478007

b. http://urbanlegends.about.com/od/halloween/a/Is-Halloween-Candy-Tampering-A-Myth.htm

c. http://www.snopes.com/horrors/mayhem/needles.asp

d. http://www.snopes.com/horrors/robbery/kidney.asp

e. http://www.snopes.com/horrors/robbery/kidney2.asp

f. http://www.hoax-slayer.com/kidney-stealing-hoax.html

g. http://urbanlegends.about.com/od/horrors/a/kidney_thieves.htm

In India in the early 1990's, there appears to have been a doctor who was doing this:

h. http://abcnews.go.com/Health/story?id=4224506

i. http://www.nytimes.com/2008/01/30/world/asia/30kidney.html?_r=0 Article Title: Kidney Thefts Shock India.

8. Regarding Car Death Per Year. Car Accident Statistics, Stats, Auto, Fatal, Drunk Driving. *Car Accident Statistics, Stats, Auto, Fatal, Drunk Driving*. Retrieved May 4, 2013, from http://www.car-accidents.com/pages/stats.html *Regarding Airline passengers per year.* Several Websites in regards to airline deaths. Data Elements. (n.d.). *Data Elements*. Retrieved May 5, 2013, from: http://www.transtats.bts.gov/Data_Elements.aspx?Data =1

9. Pinker, *The better angels of our nature*, 173.

10. Koning, "The eleventh edition".

11.   Pinker, *The better angels of our nature*, 651.
12.   Ibid., 69-70. Original source: *The Civilizing Process: Sociogenetic and Psycogenetic Investigation*, by Norbert Elias.
13.   Ibid., 71.
14.   Ibid., 51.
15.   Ibid., 45.
16.   Chumley, "New evidence: Starving Jamestown settlers resorted to cannibalism".
17.   Pinker, *The better angels of our nature*, 34.
18.   Ibid., 60.
19.   Ibid., 67.
20.   Ibid., 159.
21.   Ibid., 81-82.
22.   Ibid., 81.
23.   Ibid., 82.
24.   Ibid., 67-68.
25.   Ibid., 145.
26.   Ibid., 132.
27.   Ibid.
28.   Ibid., 140.
29.   Ibid., 30-31.
30.   Ibid., 137.
31.   Ibid., 19.
32.   Ibid., 18-19.
33.   Ibid., 149.
34.   Spielmann, "Capital Punishment: U.S. Ranks 5th On Global Execution Scale, Amnesty International Reports".
35.   Pinker, *The better angels of our nature*, 68.
36.   Ibid., 76.
37.   Ibid., 78.
38.   Ibid., xxiv.
39.   Ibid., 148.
40.   Ibid., 149.
41.   Ibid., 146, 149.
42.   Ibid., 302.
43.   Ibid., 195.

44. Ibid., 224.
45. Ibid., 250.
46. Ibid., 210-211.
47. Ibid., 96.
48. Ibid., xxiv, 296-297.
49. Ibid., 314.
50. Ibid., 337.
51. Ibid., 344.
52. Ibid., 345.
53. Ibid. 345.
54. Ibid., 347.
55. Ibid., 348-349.
56. Ibid., xxiv-xxv.
57. Ibid., 390.
58. Ibid., 389.
59. Ibid., 388.
60. Ibid., 397.
61. Hale, "The history of the please of the crown".
62. Pinker, *The better angels of our nature*, 397.
63. Ibid., 400.
64. Ibid., 407.
65. Ibid., 402.
66. Ibid., 404.
67. Ibid., 408, 410-411.
68. Ibid., 429.
69. Ibid.
70. Ibid.
71. Ibid.
72. Ibid., 430.
73. Ibid., 440.
74. Ibid., 442.
75. Ibid., .447, 449

CHAPTER 4

1. Lehrer, *Imagine: How creativity works.* First heard about from: NPR: Fresh Air 3/21/12 at 14:00 minutes.
2. http://www.statisticbrain.com/resume-falsification-statistics/ Source: Accu-Screen, Inc., ADP, The Society of Human Resource Managers, Research Date (from website): 7.16.2012. I looked up on 8/2/13. Not sure if this is AccuScreen *(www.accuscreen.com)* or *The Society for Human Resource Management (not Managers) http://www.shrm.org*

CHAPTER 5

1. Mills, *The sociological imagination*, 174.
2. Death Penalty Information Center. Another websites to look at: The Innocence Project.
3. *International Centre for Prison Studies.*
4. Healy, "Back to school - surrounded by safeguards".
5. Federal Bureau of Investigation. "Crime in the United States 2011 – clearances".

CHAPTER 6

1. This was originally cited from Dr. Paul Apodaca. This information came from the book: *The Life of Joseph Brandt – Thayendanega* by William Leete Stone and was published in 1838 by George Dearborn and Co, New York and was republished in 2005 for Elbiron Classic Series by Adamant Media Corp ISBN 1-4021-0930-X Hardcover. The letter is in Appendix 1 of the book.
   Additional information was found on the following website: http://www.museumofhoaxes.com/hoax/archive/permalink /benjamin_franklin
2. From the 2005 documentary *Hitler in Colour*, that was directed by David Batty. About 1 minute, 30 seconds into the movie.

This was quoted from a few different websites:
http://listverse.com/2011/06/13/20-quotes-of-evil-leaders/

3. From an email conversation with Aaron Breitbart of the Simon Wiesenthal Center in Los Angeles, California on 8/1/14. This is also the location of the Museum of Tolerance, which I highly recommend going to.]
4. http://en.wikipedia.org/wiki/Pol_Pot
5. http://en.wikipedia.org/wiki/Pol_Pot
6. http://www.scaruffi.com/politics/dictat.html
7. Cullen, *Columbine*, 340.
8. Based on my recollection, I think this was from an ABC News poll, possibly found in the Los Angeles Times.
9. Strozier, *Apocalypse*, 2.
10. Ibid., 147.
11. Ezekiel, *The racist mind,* xviii.
12. *Diagnostic and statistical manual of mental disorders.* 629
13. Ezekiel, *The racist mind.*
14. Leyden, "Q & A and Letters about TJ".
15. Ezekiel, *The racist mind*, 155.
16. Ibid., 156.
17. Ibid., 234.
18. Goleman, *Emotional intelligence*, 139.
19. Goleman, *Social intelligence*, 308.
20. Williams, *Anger kills*, 51, 58.
21. Ibid., 40-41.

CHAPTER 7

1. Kinsey, *Sexual Behavior in the Human Male.*
2. Many video games are designed for you to get a little further the more you play. Eventually, you win the game and then move on to the next one. These challenging successes keep you coming back for more. There is a physical/psychological effect from success. There is a temporary high people will feel when they win a game or when they win a bet, which can get addicting. This is a similar high when a person temporarily

escapes his/her problems by shopping or getting high on drugs or cigarettes.

3. Kellgren, "Revealing the genius in our teens – an interview with SuperCamp cofounder Bobbi DePorter".

4. Gladwell, *Outliers*, 32.

5. http://en.wikipedia.org/wiki/Colonel_Sanders

CHAPTER 8

1. Hoy, "Dimensions of student alienation and characteristics of public high schools", 38-52.

2. Goodlatte, "A Mother's Emotions Affect Her Unborn Child".

   Additional Information:

   a. Blanchard, K. (2011, November 14). Babies in the womb can sense mom's emotions. *Babies in the Womb Can Sense Mom's Emotions*. Retrieved September 1, 2013, from http://www.emaxhealth.com/1020/babies-womb-can-sense-moms-emotions

   b. Chopra, D. (2005). *Magical beginnings, enchanted lives*. London: Rider.

   c. Curt A. Sandman, Elysia P. Davis, and Laura M. Glynn of the University of California-Irvine.

3. Goleman, *Emotional intelligence*, 194.

4. Ibid., 101.

5. Ibid.

6. Cain, "And now, the rest of the story…about the McDonald's coffee lawsuit".

7. McQuarie & Denisoff, *Readings in contemporary sociological theory*.

8. Durkheim, *Suicide*. Confirmed in: Emile Durkheim (1858-1917). (2002, December 13). *Emile Durkheim*. Retrieved September 1, 2013, from http://www.emile-durkheim.com/

9. Farganis, J. (1996). *Readings in social theory: The classic tradition to post-modernism* (p. 75). New York: McGraw-Hill.

10. Blakeslee, "Mind games: sometimes a white coat isn't just a white coat".
11. Rosenthal & Fode, "The effect of experimenter bias on the performance of the albino rat", 183-189.
    Also:
12. Rosenthal & Jacobson, "Teachers' expectancies: Determinants of pupils' IQ gains", 115-118.
13. Buonomano, *Brain bugs*, 20.
14. Solomon, "Traumatic avoidance learning: acquisition in normal dogs".
15. Gladwell, *The tipping point*, 167.
    Additional information at: *The Nurture Assumption: Why children turn out the way they do.* By Judith Rich Harris.
16. Hay et al., "The Impact of Community Disadvantage on the Relationship between the Family and Juvenile Crime", 326-356.
17. Latané & Darley, "Group inhibition of bystander intervention in emergencies", 215-221.
18. Asch, "Studies of independence and conformity: A minority of one against a unanimous majority".
19. Asch, "Effects of group pressure on the modification and distortion of judgments."
20. Latané & Darley, *The unresponsive bystander: Why doesn't he help?*
21. Zimbardo, *"A Simulation Study of the Psychology of Imprisonment".* For more information on this study, please visit the home page at http://www.prisonexp.org/.

CHAPTER 9

1. *The American Heritage Stedman's medical dictionary.* Original Source: *The American Heritage Stedman's Medical Dictionary.*
2. Seeman, "On the meaning of alienation [Abstract]", 783-791.
3. Boggs, *The two revolutions*, 159.
4. Bocock, *Hegemony*, 37.
5. Connelly, *Fatal misconception.*
6. Zehner, *Green Illusions.*

7. Earthquake.usgs.gov "Historic World Earthquakes".
8. FBI, "2011 Crime clock statistics".
9. www.worldpopulationbalance.org/faq, "World Population Balance".
10. Hawton et al., "Effect of death of Diana, princess of Wales on suicide and deliberate self-harm", 463-466.

CHAPTER 10

1. Guenther, "The Living Death of Solitary Confinement".
2. Haynie, "Deprivation of body pleasure", 287-297.
3. Prescott, "Body Pleasure and the Origins of Violence".
4. Gunn, *Violence*, 114.
5. Reinhardt & Stevens, "Social housing of previously single-caged macaques", 307-328.
6. Harlow, "Total Social Isolation in Monkeys", 94.
7. Montagu, *Touching: The human significance of the skin*, 199-201.
8. Levine et al., "Maternal deprivation induces neuronal death". This study was not published at the time of retrieval. However, it appears that several later studies confirmed the results of this study. Spoke with Dr. Mark Smith on December 3, 1997.
9. *Ibid.*
10. Chocyk et al., "Maternal separation affects the number, proliferation and apoptosis of glia cells...", 1-11.
11. Wright, "The evolution of despair", 50-57.
12. Rivera, *Violence*.
13. Straus, Gelles, & Smith, "Physical violence in American families".
14. Goleman, *Social intelligence*, 114.
15. Gentry, "Effect Of Time-Out From Positive Reinforcement On Aggressive Behavior In Young Children", 283-288.
16. Rivera, *Violence*, 43.
17. Haynie, "Deprivation of body pleasure: Origins of violent behavior?" 289.
18. Goleman, *Social intelligence*, 196-197.

19. U.S. Department of Education, "Early warning timely response: a guide to safe schools".
20. Taylor, 1980
21. Goleman, *Emotional Intelligence*, 250.
22. Schaff, *Alienation as a social phenomenon.*
23. Krueger et al., "Personality traits are linked to crime among men and women", 328-338.
24. Goleman, *Social intelligence*, 291.
25. Bonell et al., "The effect of dislike of school on risk of teenage pregnancy", 871-6.
26. Haldre et al., "Individual and familial factors associated with teenage pregnancy", 266-270.
27. Bower, "Females show strong capacity for aggression", 359.
28. Harden & Grunton, "Teenage pregnancy and social disadvantage".
29. Goleman, *Emotional intelligence*, 195. Original study: Damage from neglect: M. Erickson et al., "The Relationship Between Quality of Attachment and Behavior Problems in Preschool in a High-Risk Sample", in I. Betherton and E. Waters, eds., *Monographs of the Society of Research in Child Development* 50, series no. 209.
30. Goleman, *Social intelligence*, 113.
31. "Secular Board", http://professing.proboards.com/index.cgi?board=temporal
32. O'Neill et al., "Court filing reveals taunted teen's anguish in final hours".
33. Today, "A mother's grief: The Phoebe Prince bullying case".
34. Haynie, "Deprivation of body pleasure: Origins of violent behavior?" 292.
35. Rivera, *Violence*, 50.
36. Ibid.
37. Bridis, "Alienated teenagers".
38. Pilcher, "Six Georgia high school students shot".
39. Cart, "Recalling the slain and their slayers".
40. Foster, "A look at the 'Trenchcoat Mafia'".
41. Gold, "Gothic subculture not to blame for violence".

42. Guze, Goodwin, and Crane, "Criminality and psychiatric disorders", 583-591.
43. Bland & Orn, "Family violence and psychiatric disorder", 129-137.
44. Montagu, *Touching*, 229.
45. Goleman, *Emotional intelligence*, 102.
46. Straus, Gelles, & Smith, "Physical violence in American families".
47. Grant & Curry, "Women murderers and victims of abuse in a southern state", 73-83.
48. Loper & Cornell, "Homicide by juvenile girls", 323-336.
49. Moncher, "Social isolation and child-abuse risk", 421-433.
50. Stern, "5 Myths about who becomes a terrorist".
51. Ryan, "Underwear bomber Abdulmutallab".
52. Cozzarelli & Karafa, "Cultural Estrangement and Terror Management Theory", 253-267.
53. Gottschalk & Gottschalk, "Authoritarianism and pathological hatred".

CHAPTER 11

1. Covey, *The 7 habits of highly effective people*, 237.
2. Womack & Womack, *Speak to me!*.
3. From my recollection, Dr. Gottman said this at a workshop in Seattle, Washington that I attended.
4. Gladwell, Blink, 41-42.
   Also: Levinson, "Physician-patient communication", 553-559.
5. Vormbrock, & Grossberg, "Cardiovascular effects of human-pet dog interactions", 509-517.
6. Covey, *The 7 habits of highly effective people*, 239.
7. Richel, "Digital Overload: Your Brain on Gadgets".
8. Ibid.
9. Ibid.
10. Ekman, "Why Are Micro Expressions Important?".

11. A 2002 study published in *Developmental Psychology*, researchers found that infants followed people's eye direction, rather than head direction.

12. These were observations I made at SuperCamp that I attended in 1988 and worked as a Team Leader on four separate occasions in the early 1990's.

13. Ellsberg, *The power of eye contact*, 190.

14. Ibid., 206.

15. Ibid., 191.

16. Ibid., 207.

17. Slater, "Romantic Love Information, Serotonin Level Facts".

18. Grandin & Johnson, *Animals in translation*, 106.

19. Szalavitz & Perry, "Born for love: Empathy, the brain, and human connections".

20. Hamilton, "Orphans' lonely beginnings reveal how parents shape a child's brain".

21. Harlow, "The nature of love", 676.

22. Ibid., 677.

23. Montagu, *Touching*, 238.

24. This study was found in the following: Williamson, *A Return to Love;* Chopra, *Quantum Healing*, 33; and Montagu, *Touching* 34.

25. Goleman, *Social intelligence*, 5.

26. Goleman, *Social intelligence*, 228.

27. Berkman & Syme, "Social networks, host resistance, and morality", 186–204.

28. Gore, "The effect of social support in moderating the health consequences of unemployment", 157-165.

29. Berkman & Breslow, "Health and the ways of living: The Alameda County Study."

30. Rabin, "Talk Deeply, Be Happy?"

CHAPTER 12

1. Gottman, *Clinical Manual for Marital Therapy*, 13.
2. Gottman & Silver, *The seven principles for making marriage work*.
3. Gottman & Silver, *The seven principles for making marriage work*.
4. Ibid.
5. Gottman & Levenson, "Marital processes predictive of later dissolution", 221-233.
6   Ibid.
7   Robinson & Price, "Pleasurable behavior in marital interaction", 117-118.
8   Gottman & Silver, *The seven principles for making marriage work*.
9   Jacobson & Addis, "Research on couple therapy: What do we know? Where are we going?", 85-93.
    While not included, additional research examined includes: Snyder, "Predicting couples' response to marital therapy; A comparison of short and long-term predictors".
10 Hahlweg et al., "The Munich marital therapy study." 3-26.
11 Ibid.
12 Gottman & Silver, *The seven principles for making marriage work*.
13 Gottman & Levenson, "Marital processes predictive of later dissolution", 221-233.
14 Fisher, Aron, & Brown, "Romantic love: An fmri study of a neural mechanism for mate choice", 58-62.
15 Social Cognitive and Affective Neuroscience, "Neural correlates of long-term intense romantic love".
16 Gottman & Silver, *The seven principles for making marriage work*, 100.
17 Holtzworth-Munroe et al., "Relationship between behavioral marital therapy outcome and process variables", 658-662.
18 Gottman & Silver, *The seven principles for making marriage work*, 100.
19 Zilbergeld, *The New Male Sexuality*.
20 Johnson, *The Blackwell dictionary of sociology*".
21 Zappone, "Millionaire in the making: Daren Fike".

CHAPTER 13

1. Schultz, *Annual editions: Education,* 140.
2. Shapiro, "Killing kids: The new culture of destruction", 23-25.
3. Marshak, "Re-humanizing our children", 7-12.
4. Noguchi, ""Paintballing the boss: office team-building exercises gone bad".
5. Goleman, *Social intelligence,* 282.
6. Healy, "Back to school-surrounded by safeguards"
7. National Research Council, "Losing generations: Adolescents in high risk settings".
8. Alva, "Academic invulnerability among Mexican-American students", 18-34.
9. Goodenow, "School motivation, engagement, and sense of belonging among urban adolescent students", 349-364.
10. Hernandez, "The Role of Protective Factors In the School Resilience of Mexican American High School Students".
11. Gonzalez & Padilla, "The Academic resilience of Mexican American high school students", 301-317.
12. Champion, "The adolescent quest for meaning through multicultural reading", 462(31).
13. Ibid., 462
14. Ibid.
15. Ibid.
16. Gilbert, "A conversation with Elliot Aronson".
   In 1971, Dr. Elliot Aronson, who was the head of the social psychology department at the University of Texas, Austin, and author, was asked to help with problems that came with desegregation. Dr. Aronson, along with graduate students, designed a classroom that would encourage students to work with each other instead of against each other. In the Jigsaw classroom, students are divided into groups of five to six students. Each student in the group is responsible for learning about a different section of what they are studying. For example, if the classroom was learning about Abraham Lincoln, one student would learn about Lincoln when he was

young, while another student in the group would learn about the night Lincoln was shot. To make sure that students fully understand their topic, the students who learn about, for example, how Lincoln was shot, would get together in their "expert" group to make sure they fully understand what they are to present. Then the students go back to their original group to teach the others what they have learned. In order for students to succeed, they had to learn to work together. Because the students have to rely on each other in the group to learn about each topic, instead of complaining and teasing, which is counterproductive, they learn to ask questions to get information. They are also likely to be more encouraging, which can be very helpful in learning. Being encouraged and learning to ask questions are critical parts of learning. At first, the students did not like having to work together, but after a few weeks they started to understand the process and started working together as a team. After a certain period of time, the teams would be broken up and new teams were formed. The students didn't like this at first, because they were used to the teams they had. This was important for students to realize that their success was not based on their specific team, but that they could do a good job no matter who was on their team.

17. Witmer, "Northwood's SuperCamp Eases Learning Process for Students",. *Northwest Herald.*

18. Vos-Groenendal, *An accelerated/integrative learning model program evaluation.*

19. Gladwell, *The Tipping Point,* 179.
    Research by Dunbar, highlighted in Malcolm Gladwell's book *The Tipping Point,* showed that group sizes should max out at about 150 people. When groups get larger than this, people within the group are less able to connect and there is a lack of cohesion.

20. Bureau of Justice, http://bjs.gov

21. *California Criminal Justice,* "How Much Does It Cost to Incarcerate an Inmate?".

22. American Foundation for Suicide Prevention, Facts and Figures.
23. FBI, "Violent Crime". From http://www.fbi.gov/about-us/cjis/ucr/crime-in-the-u.s/2010/crime-in-the-u.s.-2010/violent-crime
24. *FBI*. Murder.
25. *Encarta world English dictionary*.

CHAPTER 14

1. Oxford University, *New Oxford American Dictionary, 2nd edition*.
2. American Heritage Dictionary.
3. Covey, *The 7 habits of highly effective people*, 241.
4. Buscaglia, & Short, *Living, loving & learning*, 54.
5. Gottman & Silver, *The seven principles for making marriage work*.
6. Knebusch, "Urban Coyotes Never Stray".
   Also: Hennessy, Dubach & Gehrt, "Long-term pair bonding and genetic evidence for monogamy among urban coyotes".
7. Grandin & Johnson, *Animals in translation*, 88.
8. Buscaglia & Short, *Living, loving & learning*, 82.
9. Virginia Arcastle. Original source not found.
10. Buscaglia & Short, S. (1982). *Living, loving & learning*.
11. Rosenberg, "Hitler Facts: 34 facts about nazi leader Adolf Hitler".
12. Raedler, "Pol Pot's relatives recall dictator's childhood".
13. Mydans, "Pol Pot's Siblings Remember The Polite Boy and the Killer".

CHAPTER 15

1. Quinn, *Ishmael*, 54.
2. Bassler, "How Bacteria 'Talk'".
3. Chopra, "Who are you?".
4. Ibid.
5. Mills, *The sociological imagination*.

6. Original source not found but was from Dillon, 1999. Ilene L. Dillon is a Family Therapist.
7. Hoy, "Dimensions of student alienation and characteristics of public high schools." 38-52.
8. Goleman, *Emotional intelligence*, 195.
9. Covey, *The 7 habits of highly effective people*, 263.

CHAPTER 16

1. Ravven, "To get to cats, common parasite hijacks rats' arousal circuitry".
2. Eagleman, *The Secret Lives of the Brain*.
3. Grandin & Johnson, *Animals in translation*, 148.
4. Eagleman, "Incognito: what's hiding in the unconscious mind [Audio blog interview by T. Gross]".
5. Chopra, "Who are you?".
6. Parnia & Young, *Erasing* death. 127.
7. Ibid. 9-16.
8. Fromm, *The art of loving*.
9. Williamson, *A return to love*, 28.
10. Goleman, *Social intelligence*, 110.
11. Chopra, "Who are you?"
12. Interview with Pastor Billy Arnold in 2002
13. Spong, "The Theistic God is Dead".
14. http://hyperphysics.phy-astr.gsu.edu/hbase/nuclear/nucuni.html
15. Schwaller De Lubicz, Lamy, & Her-Bak. "The Living Face of Ancient".
16. Gerald Massey, Ancient Egypt the Light of the World, Volume I, page 438. http://en.wikipedia.org/wiki/Know_thyself

REFERENCES

"2011 Crime Clock Statistics." *FBI*. N.p., 20 Aug. 2012. Web. 1 Sept. 2013. <http://www.fbi.gov/about-us/cjis/ucr/crime-in-the-u.s/2011/crime-in-the-u.s.-2011/offenses-known-to-law-enforcement/standard-links/national-data>.

Alva, S. A. "Academic Invulnerability Among Mexican-American Students: The Importance of Protective Resources and Appraisals." *Hispanic Journal of Behavioral Sciences* 13.1 (1991): 18-34. Print.

The American Heritage Dictionary. New York, NY: Dell Pub., 1994. Print.

The American Heritage Stedman's Medical Dictionary. N.p.: n.p., 2002. Web. 1 Sept. 2013. <http://dictionary.reference.com/browse/alienation>.

Asch, S.E. "Effects of group pressure on the modification and distortion of judgments." H. Guetzkow (Ed.), *Groups, leadership and men.* (1951). (pp. 177–190). Pittsburgh, PA:Carnegie Press.

Asch, S. E. "Studies of independence and conformity: A minority of one against a unanimous majority". *Psychological Monographs*, (1956): 70.

Blakeslee, Sandra. "Mind games: sometimes a white coat isn't just a white coat". *The New York Times*. N.p., 02 Apr. 2012. Web 1 Sept. 2013. http://www.nytimes.com/2012/04/03/science/clothes-and-self-perception.html?_r=0

Blanchard, Kathleen. "Babies in the Womb Can Sense Mom's Emotions." *Babies in the Womb Can Sense Mom's Emotions.* N.p., 14 Nov. 2011. Web. 1 Sept. 2013. <http://www.emaxhealth.com/1020/babies-womb-can-sense-moms-emotions>.

Bland, Roger, and Helene Orn. "Family Violence and Psychiatric Disorder." *Canadian Journal of Psychiatry* 31.2 (1986): 129-37. Print.

Bocock, Robert. *Hegemony.* Chichester [West Sussex: E. Horwood, 1986. 36. Print.

Boggs, Carl. *The Two Revolutions: Antonio Gramsci and the Dilemmas of Western Marxism.* Boston, MA: South End, 1984. 159. Print.

Bower, Bruce. "Females Show Strong Capacity for Aggression." *Science News* 140.22 (1999): 359. Print.

Bridis, Ted. "Alienated Teenagers." *The Associated Press* 1999: n. pag. Print.

Buonomano, Dean. *Brain Bugs: How the Brain's Flaws Shape Our Lives.* New York: W.W. Norton, 2011. 20. Print.

Buscaglia, Leo F., and Steven Short. *Living, Loving & Learning.* Thorofare, NJ: C.B. Slack, 1982. Print.

Cain, Kevin G. "And Now for the Rest of the Story…About the McDonald's Coffee Lawsuit." *Journal of Consumer & Commercial Law.* July/August (2007): 14-19.

"California Criminal Justice FAQ: How Much Does It Cost to Incarcerate an Inmate?" *California Criminal Justice FAQ: How Much Does It Cost to Incarcerate an Inmate?* Legislative Analyst's Office, n.d. Web. 05 Oct. 2013.

"Car Accident Statistics, Stats, Auto, Fatal, Drunk Driving." *Car Accident Statistics, Stats, Auto, Fatal, Drunk Driving.* N.p., n.d. Web. 4 May 2013. <http://www.car-accidents.com/pages/stats.html>.

Cart, Julie. "Recalling the Slain and Their Slayers." *Los Angeles Times* 22 Apr. 1999: n. pag. Print.

Champion, Sandra. "The Adolescent Quest Of Meaning through Multicultural Reading: A Case Study." *Library Trends* 41.3 (1993): 462-(31). Print.

Chocyk, A., D. Dudys, A. Przyborowska, I. Majcher, M. Mackowiak, and K. Wedzony. "Maternal Separation Affects the Number, Proliferation and Apoptosis of Glia Cells in the Substantia Nigra and Ventral Tegmental Area of Juvenile Rats." *Developmental Brain Research* 133.1 (2002): 1-11. Print.

Chopra, Deepak. *Magical Beginnings, Enchanted Lives.* London: Rider, 2005. Print.

Chopra, Depak. "Who Are You?" *Who Are You?* N.p., 1993. Web. 1 Sept. 2013. <http://www.bibliotecapleyades.net/ciencia/ciencia_chopra. htm>.

Chumley, Cheryl K. "New Evidence: Starving Jamestown Settlers Resorted to Cannibalism." *The Washingtion Times.* N.p., 1 Mar. 2013. Web. 1 Sept. 2013. <http://www.washingtontimes.com/news/2013/may/1/ne w-evidence-starving-jamestown-settlers-resorted-/>.

Connelly, Matthew James. *Fatal Misconception: The Struggle to Control World Population.* Cambridge, MA: Belknap of Harvard UP, 2008. Print.

Covey, Stephen R. *The 7 Habits of Highly Effective People: Powerful Lessons in Personal Change.* New York: Fireside, 1989. Print.

Cozzarelli, C., and J. A. Karafa. "Cultural Estrangement and Terror Management Theory." *Personality and Social Psychology Bulletin* 24.3 (1998): 253-67. Print.

"Crime in the United States 2011 - Clearances." *FBI.* N.p., 29 June 2012. Web. 4 Sept. 2013. <http://www.fbi.gov/about-us/cjis/ucr/crime-in-the-u.s/2011/crime-in-the-u.s.-2011/clearances>.

Cullen, David. *Columbine.* New York: Twelve, 2009. 340. Print.

"Data Elements." *Data Elements.* N.p., n.d. Web. 5 May 2013. <http://www.transtats.bts.gov/Data_Elements.aspx?Data=1 >.

Diagnostic and Statistical Manual of Mental Disorders: DSM-IV. Washington, DC: American Psychiatric Association, 1994. 629. Print.

Durkheim, E. *Suicide.* New York: Free, 1951. Print.

Eagleman, David. *Incognito*. Rearsby: Clipper Large Print, 2012. Print.

Ellsberg, Michael. *The Power of Eye Contact: Your Secret for Success in Business, Love, and Life*. New York: HarperPaperbacks, 2010. Print.

"Emile Durkheim (1858-1917)." *Emile Durkheim*. N.p., 13 Dec. 2002. Web. 1 Sept. 2013. <http://www.emile-durkheim.com/>.

Encarta World English Dictionary. London: Bloomsbury, 1999. Print.

"Entire World - Prison Population Rates per 100,000 of the National Population." *International Centre for Prison Studies*. N.p., n.d. Web. 4 Sept. 2013. <http://www.prisonstudies.org/info/worldbrief/wpb_stats.php?area=all>.

Ezekiel, Raphael S. *The Racist Mind: Portraits of American Neo-Nazis and Klansmen*. New York: Viking, 1995. 156. Print.

"Facts and Figures." *American Foundation for Suicide Prevention*. N.p., n.d. Web. 1 Sept. 2013. <http://www.afsp.org/understanding-suicide/facts-and-figures>.

Fisher, Helen, Arthur Aron, and Lucy L. Brown. "Romantic love: an FMRI study of a neural mechanism for mate choice." *The Journal of Comparative Neurology* 493.1 (2005): 58-62. Print.

Farganis, J. (1996). *Readings in social theory: The classic tradition to postmodernism* (p. 75). New York: McGraw-Hill.

Fromm, Erich. *The Art of Loving*. New York: Perennial, 2000. Print.

Gentry, William D. "Effect Of Time-Out From Positive Reinforcement On Aggressive Behavior In Young Children." *Psychological Reports* 26.1 (1970): 283-88. Print.

Gilbert, Susan. "A CONVERSATION WITH/Elliot Aronson; No One Left to Hate: Averting Columbines." *The New York Times*. N.p., 27 Mar. 2001. Web. 13 Sept. 2013. <http://www.nytimes.com/2001/03/27/health/a-conversation-with-elliot-aronson-no-one-left-to-hate-averting-columbines.html?pagewanted=all>.

Gladwell, Malcolm. *Blink: The Power of Thinking without Thinking*. New York: Little, Brown and, 2005. Print.

Gladwell, Malcolm. *Outliers: The Story of Success*. New York: Little, Brown and, 2008. Print.

Gladwell, Malcolm. *The Tipping Point: How Little Things Can Make a Big Difference*. Boston: Back Bay, 2002. Print.

Goleman, Daniel. *Emotional Intelligence*. New York: Bantam, 1995. Print.

Goleman, Daniel. *Social Intelligence: The New Science of Human Relationships*. New York: Bantam, 2006. Print.

Gonzalez, R., and A. M. Padilla. "The Academic Resilience of Mexican American High School Students." *Hispanic Journal of Behavioral Sciences* 19.3 (1997): 301-17. Print.

Goodenow, C. "School Motivation, Engagement, and Sense of Belonging Among Urban Adolescent Students." (1992). (ERIC Document Reproduction Service No. 349-364).

Goodlatte, James. "A Mother's Emotions Affect Her Unborn Child." *The Epoch Times » The Epoch Times Is an Independent Voice in Print and on the Web. We Report News Responsibly and Truthfully so That Readers Can Improve Their Own Lives and Increase Their Understanding and Respect for Their Neighbors next Door and around the Globe*. N.p., 9 Nov. 2009. Web. 1 Sept. 2013. <http://www.theepochtimes.com/n2/life/mothers-emotions-affect-her-unborn-child-24972.html>.

Gore, Susan. "The Effect of Social Support in Moderating the Health Consequences of Unemployment." *Journal of Health and Social Behavior* 19 (1978): 157-65. Print.

Gottman, John Mordechai., and Nan Silver. *The Seven Principles for Making Marriage Work*. New York: Crown, 1999. Print.

Gottman, John M., Robert W. Levenson. "Marital processes predictive of later dissolution." *Journal of Personality and Social Psychology*. Aug (1992) Vol. 63, No. 2, 221-233. Print.

Gottschalk, Michael, and Simon Gottschalk. "Authoritarianism and Pathological Hatred: A Social Psychological Profile of the Middle Eastern Terrorist." *TERRORIST PROFILE | Simon Gottschalk - Academia.edu*. N.p., 2004. Web. 1 Sept. 2013. <http://www.academia.edu/1378183/TERRORIST_PROFILE>.

Grandin, Temple, and Catherine Johnson. *Animals in Translation: Using the Mysteries of Autism to Decode Animal Behavior.* New York: Scribner, 2005. Print.

Grant, Bernadette, and G. David Curry. "Women Murderers and Victims of Abuse in a Southern State." *American Journal of Criminal Justice* 17.2 (1993): 73-83. Print.

Guenther, Lisa. "The Living Death of Solitary Confinement." *Opinionator The Living Death of Solitary Confinement Comments.* N.p., 26 Aug. 2012. Web. 1 Sept. 2013. <http://opinionator.blogs.nytimes.com/2012/08/26/the-living-death-of-solitary-confinement/>.

Gunn, John Charles. *Violence.* New York: Praeger, 1973. Print.

Guze, S., D. W. Goodwin, and J. B. Crane. "Criminality and Psychiatric Disorders." *Archives of General Psychiatry* 20 (1969): 583-91. Print.

Haidt, Jonathan. *The Happiness Hypothesis: Finding Modern Truth in Ancient Wisdom.* New York: Basic, 2006. Print.

Hale, Matthew, Sir. *The History of the Please of the Crown.* Digital image. N.p., n.d. Web. 14 Sept. 2013. <http://books.google.com/books?id=u1FDAAAAcAAJ&printsec=frontcover&source=gbs_ge_summary_r&cad=0#v=onepage&q&f=false>.

Hamilton, Jon, "Orphans' lonely beginnings reveal how parents shape a child's brain". Audio blog post. N.p., 23 Feb. 2014. Web. 23 Feb. 2014. <http://www.npr.org/blogs/health/2014/02/20/280237833/orphans-lonely-beginnings-reveal-how-parents-shape-a-childs-brain>.

Harlow, H. F. "Total Social Isolation in Monkeys." *Proceedings of the National Academy of Sciences* 54.1 (1965): 94. Print.

Harlow, Harry F. "The Nature of Love." *American Psychologist* 13.12 (1958): 676. Print.

Hawton, Keith, Louise Harriss, Sue Simkin, Edmund Jusczcak, Louise Appleby, Ros McDonnell, Tim Amos, and Katy Kiernan. "Effect of Death of Diana, Princess of Wales on

Suicide and Deliberate Self-harm." *British Journal of Psychiatry* 177.5 (2000): 463-66. Print.

Hay, C., E. N. Fortson, D. R. Hollist, I. Altheimer, and L. M. Schaible. "The Impact of Community Disadvantage on the Relationship between the Family and Juvenile Crime." *Journal of Research in Crime and Delinquency* 43.4 (2006): 326-56. Print.

Haynie, Roena L. "Deprivation of Body Pleasure: Origins of Violent Behavior? A Survey of the Literature." *Child Welfare* 59 (1980): 287-97. Print.

Healy, M. "Back to School-surrounded by Safeguards." *Los Angeles Times* 7 Sept. 1999: n. pag. Print.

"Historic World Earthquakes." *Historic World Earthquakes*. N.p., n.d. Web. June-July 2013.
<http://earthquake.usgs.gov/earthquakes/world/historical_country.php>.

Hitler in Colour. N.d. Television.

Holt-Lunstad, Julianne, Bert N. Uchino, Timothy W. Smith, Chrisana Olson-Cerny, and Jill B. Nealey-Moore. "Social Relationships and Ambulatory Blood Pressure: Structural and Qualitative Predictors of Cardiovascular Function during Everyday Social Interactions." *Health Psychology* 22.4 (2003): 388-97. Print.

Holtzworth-Munroe, Amy, Neil S. Jacobson, Michelle DeKlyen, and Mark A. Whisman. "Relationship between Behavioral Marital Therapy Outcome and Process Variables." *Journal of Consulting and Clinical Psychology* 57.5 (1989): 658-62. Print.

Hoy, Wayne K. "Dimensions of Student Alienation and Characteristics of Public High Schools." *Interchange* 3.4 (1972): 38-52. Print.

"Innocence: List of Those Freed From Death Row." *Death Penalty Information Center*. N.p., n.d. Web. 1 Sept. 2013.
<http://www.deathpenaltyinfo.org/innocence-list-those-freed-death-row percent20 percent20>. Another websites to look at: The Innocence Project,
http://www.innocenceproject.org

Johnson, Allan G. *The Blackwell Dictionary of Sociology: A User's Guide to Sociological Language.* Cambridge, Mas. [etc.: Blakwell, 1995. 129. Print.

Kellgren, Liv. "SuperCamp: Revealing the Genius in Our Teens." *Www.supercamp.com.* N.p., July 2011. Web. 1 Sept. 2013. <http://www.supercamp.com/pdf/LifeConnectionMagazine Article.pdf>.

Richel, Matt, "Digital Overload: Your Brain on Gadgets". Audio blog post. N.p., 24 Aug. 2010. Web. 24 Aug. 2010. <http://www.wbur.org/npr/129384107/digital-overload-your-brain-on-gadgets>.

Keyes, Ken. *The Hundredth Monkey.* St. Mary, KY: Vision, 1981. Print.

Kinsey, A. C., W. R. Pomeroy, and C. E. Martin. "Sexual Behavior in the Human Male." *American Journal of Public Health* 93.6 (2003): 894-98. Print.

Knebusch, Kurt. "Urban Coyotes Never Stray: New Study Finds 100 Percent Monogamy." *ScienceDaily.* N.p., 25 Sept. 2012. Web. 1 Sept. 2013. <http://www.sciencedaily.com/releases/2012/09/12092514 2549.htm>.

Koning, Hans. "The Eleventh Edition." *The New Yorker* 2 Mar. 1981: 67-83. Print.

Kozol, Jonathan. *Amazing Grace.* New York: Crown, 1995. Print.

Krueger, Robert F., Pamela S. Schmutte, Avshalom Caspi, Terrie E. Moffitt, and Et Al. "Personality Traits Are Linked to Crime among Men and Women: Evidence from a Birth Cohort." *Journal of Abnormal Psychology* 103.2 (1994): 328-38. Print.

Latané, Bibb, and John M. Darley. *The Unresponsive Bystander: Why Doesn't He Help?* New York: Appleton-Century Crofts, 1970. Print.

Latane, Bibb, and John M. Darley. "Group Inhibition of Bystander Intervention in Emergencies." *Journal of Personality and Social Psychology* 10.3 (1968): 215-21. Print.

Lehrer, Jonah. *Imagine: How Creativity Works.* Boston: Houghton Mifflin Harcourt, 2012. Print.

Levine, S., R. M. Post, M. A. Smith, G. O. Xing, and L. X. Zhang. "Maternal Deprivation Induces Neuronal Death." (1997): n. pag. Print. This study has not been published yet. Spoke with Dr. Mark Smith on December 3, 1997.

Levinson, Wendy. "Physician-patient Communication: The Relationship with Malpractice Claims among Primary Care Physicians and Surgeons." *The Journal of the American Medical Association* 277.7 (1997): 553-59. Print.

Leyden, T. J. "Q & A and Letters about TJ." *Strhatetalk*. N.p., n.d. Web. 03 Oct. 2013.

"List of Countries by Incarceration Rate." *Wikipedia*. N.p., n.d. Web. 14 Sept. 2013. <http://en.wikipedia.org/wiki/List_of_countries_by_incarce ration_rate>. This was taken from

Loper, Ann B., and Dewey G. Cornell. "Homicide by Juvenile Girls." *Journal of Child and Family Studies* 5.3 (1996): 323-36. Print.

Luntz, Barbara K., and Cathy S. Widom. "Antisocial Personality Disorder in Abused and Neglected Children Grown up." *The American Journal of Psychiatry* 151.5 (1994): 670-80. Print.

Marshak, David. "Re-humanizing Our Children." *Education Digest* 61.4 (1995): 7-12. Print.

Massey, Gerald. *Ancient Egypt the Light of the World*. London T.Fisher Unwin Adelphi Terrace. 1907. Volume I, page 438.

Masson, J. Moussaieff. *Raising the Peaceable Kingdom: What Animals Can Teach Us about the Social Origins of Tolerance and Friendship*. New York: Ballantine, 2005. Print.

McKean, Erin. *The New Oxford American Dictionary*. New York, NY: Oxford UP, 2005. Print.

McQuarie, Donald, and R. Serge. Denisoff. *Readings in Contemporary Sociological Theory: From Modernity to Post-modernity*. Englewood Cliffs, NJ: Prentice Hall, 1995. Print.

Mills, C. Wright. *The Sociological Imagination*. New York: Oxford UP, 1959. 174. Print.

Moffett, M. W. "Tracking a 'sisterhood' of Traveling Ants." Interview by Dave Davies. Audio blog post. N.p., 17 June 2010. Web. 14 Sept. 2013.

<http://www.npr.org/2010/06/17/127238974/tracking-a-sisterhood-of-traveling-ants>.

Moffett, Mark W. *Adventures among Ants: A Global Safari with a Cast of Trillions*. Berkeley: University of California, 2010. Print.

Moncher, Frank J. "Social Isolation and Child-abuse Risk." *Families in Society* 76.7 (1985): 421-33. Print.

Montagu, Ashley. *Touching: The Human Significance of the Skin*. New York: Harper & Row, 1986. 199-201. Print.

"A Mother's Grief: The Phoebe Prince Bullying Case." *TODAY Video Player - Popup*. N.p., n.d. Web. 1 Sept. 2013. <http://www.today.com/id/26184891/vp/43682715>.

"Murder." *FBI*. N.p., 25 July 2011. Web. 1 Sept. 2013. <http://www.fbi.gov/about-us/cjis/ucr/crime-in-the-u.s/2010/crime-in-the-u.s.-2010/violent-crime/murdermain>.

Mydans, Seth. "Pol Pot's Siblings Remember The Polite Boy and the Killer." *The New York Times*. N.p., 06 Aug. 1997. Web. 1 Sept. 2013. <http://www.nytimes.com/1997/08/06/world/pol-pot-s-siblings-remember-the-polite-boy-and-the-killer.html>.

Noguchi, Yuki, "Paintballing the boss: office team-building exercises gone bad". Audio blog post. N.p., 8 July 2014. Web. 8 July 2014. <http://www.npr.org/2014/07/08/329527787/paintballing-the-boss-office-team-building-exercises-gone-bad>.

O'Neill, Ann, Brian Vitagliano, Jean Casarez, and Beth Karas. "Court Filing Reveals Taunted Teen's Anguish in Final Hours." *CNN*. N.p., 09 Apr. 2010. Web. 1 Sept. 2013. <http://www.cnn.com/2010/CRIME/04/09/massachusetts.bullying.suicide/index.html>.

Parnia, Sam, and Josh Young. *Erasing Death: The Science That Is Rewriting the Boundaries between Life and Death*. N.p.: HarperOne, n.d. 9-16. Print.

Pinker, Steven. *The Better Angels of Our Nature: Why Violence Has Declined*. New York: Viking, 2011. Print.

Prescott, James W. "Article: Body Pleasure and the Origins of Violence." *Article: Body Pleasure and the Origins of Violence*. N.p.,

n.d. Web. 1 Sept. 2013.
<http://www.violence.de/prescott/bulletin/article.html>.

Quinn, Daniel. *Ishmael*. New York: Bantam/Turner Book, 1995. 54. Print.

Rabin, Roni C. "Talk Deeply, Be Happy? - NYTimes.com." *Talk Deeply, Be Happy? - NYTimes.com*. N.p., 17 Mar. 2010. Web. 1 Sept. 2013.
<http://well.blogs.nytimes.com/2010/03/17/talk-deeply-be-happy/?pagewanted=print>.

Raedler, John. "Pol Pot's Relatives Recall Dictator's Childhood." *CNN*. N.p., 18 Aug. 1997. Web. 1 Sept. 2013.
<http://www.cnn.com/WORLD/9708/18/cambodia/>.

Ravven, Wallace. "To get to cats, common parasite hijacks rats' arousal circuitry".*The New York Times*. N.p., 17, Aug. 2011. Web 1 Sept. 2013.
http://www.nytimes.com/2011/08/23/science/23parasite.html

Redfield, James. *The Celestine Prophecy: An Adventure*. New York: Warner, 1993. Print.

Reinhardt, Liss V., and C. Stevens. "Social Housing of Previously Single-caged Macaques: What Are the Options and the Risks." *Animal Welfare* 4 (1995): 307-28. Print.

Rivera, Charles. *Violence*. Rochelle Park: Hayden Book, 1976. Print.

Rosenberg, Jennifer. "Hitler Facts: 34 Facts about Nazi Leader Adolf Hitler." *About.com 20th Century History*. N.p., n.d. Web.
<http://history1900s.about.com/od/hitleradolf/a/Hitler-Facts.htm>.

Rosenthal, Robert, and Kermit L. Fode. "The Effect of Experimenter Bias on the Performance of the Albino Rat." *Behavioral Science* 8.3 (1963): 183-89. Print.

Rosenthal, Robert, and Lenore Jacobson. *Pygmalion in the Classroom: Teacher Expectation and Pupils' Intellectual Development*. New York: Holt, Rinehart and Winston, 1968. Print.

Ryan, Jason. "Underwear Bomber Abdulmutallab: "proud to Kill in the Name of God"" *ABC News*. N.p., 16 Feb. 2012. Web. 1 Sept. 2013. <http://abcnews.go.com/Blotter/underwear-

bomber-abdulmutallab-sentenced-life-
prison/story?id=15681576>.

Schaff, Adam. *Alienation as a Social Phenomenon.* Oxford: Pergamon,
1980. Print.

Schultz, Frederick Marshall. *Annual Editions: Education.* Guilford:
McGraw-Hill, 1997. 140. Print.

"Secular Board." *Home.* N.p., 1 July 2004. Web. 1 Sept. 2013.
<http://professing.proboards.com/index.cgi?board=tempor
al>.

Seeman, Melvin. "On the Meaning of Alienation." *American Sociological
Review* 24.6 (1959): 783-91. Print.

Senunit, Mikhal, and Naʻamah Golomb. *The Soul Bird.* New York:
Hyperion, 1999. Print.

Shapiro, Svi. "Killing Kids: The New Culture of Destruction." *Tikkun*
1998: 23-25. Web.

Slater, Lauren. "True Love." *Article, Romantic Love Information, Serotonin
Level Facts.* N.p., Feb. 2006. Web. 1 Sept. 2013.
<http://science.nationalgeographic.com/science/health-and-
human-body/human-body/true-love.html>.

Snyder, Douglas K., Laurel Mangrum, Robert Wills. "Predicting
couples' response to marital therapy; A comparison of short
and long-term predictors.*" Journal of Consulting and Clinical
Psychology.* 61.1. Feb. (1993) 61-69.

Solomon, Richard L.; Lyman C Wynne. Traumatic avoidance
learning: Acquisition in normal dogs. Psychological
Monographs: General and Applied, Vol 67(4), 1953, 1-19.

Souza, Alfred D. "Happiness." *Happiness by Alfred D. Souza.* N.p., n.d.
Web. 1 Sept. 2013.
<http://www.soulonline.org/bigquest/writings/february/h
apiness.htm>.

Spielmann, Peter J. "Capital Punishment: U.S. Ranks 5th On Global
Execution Scale, Amnesty International Reports." *The
Huffington Post.* N.p., 27 Mar. 2012. Web. 1 Sept. 2013.
<http://www.huffingtonpost.com/2012/03/27/capital-
punishment_n_1381652.html>.

Spong, John S. "The Theistic God Is Dead--A Casualty of
      Terrorism." - *Beliefnet.com*. N.p., n.d. Web. 1 Sept. 2013.
      <http://www.beliefnet.com/Faiths/Christianity/Protestant/
      2001/10/The-Theistic-God-Is-Dead-A-Casualty-Of-
      Terrorism.aspx>.

Stern, Jessica. "5 Myths about Who Becomes a Terrorist." *Washington
      Post*. N.p., 10 Jan. 2010. Web. 8 Aug. 2013.
      <http://articles.washingtonpost.com/2010-01-
      10/opinions/36852738_1_terrorist-incidents-terrorist-
      organizations-terrorist-activities>.

Straus, Murray A., Richard J. Gelles, and Christine Smith. *Physical
      Violence in American Families: Risk Factors and Adaptations to
      Violence in 8,145 Families*. New Brunswick [N.J.], U.S.A.:
      Transaction, 1990. Print.

Strozier, Charles B. *Apocalypse: On the Psychology of Fundamentalism in
      America*. Boston: Beacon, 1994. 147. Print.

Szalavitz, Maia, and Bruce D. Perry. "Born for Love: Empathy, the
      Brain, and Human Connections." *Psychology Today*. N.p., 1
      Mar. 2010. Web. 1 Sept. 2013.
      <http://www.psychologytoday.com/blog/born-
      love/201003/touching-empathy>.

Taylor, David L.; Primerano, Angela; Sotack, Sue. "School Violence
      and Vandalism: A Case Study." Sociological
      Abstracts. (1980).

"Thoughts On The Business Of Life." *Virginia Arcastle: Thoughts and
      Quotes*. N.p., n.d. Web. 13 Sept. 2013.
      <http://thoughts.forbes.com/thoughts/virginia-arcastle>.

Trott, Susan. *The Holy Man*. New York: Riverhead, 1995. Print.

"Violent Crime." *FBI*. N.p., 25 July 2011. Web. 1 Sept. 2013.
      <http://www.fbi.gov/about-us/cjis/ucr/crime-in-the-
      u.s/2010/crime-in-the-u.s.-2010/violent-crime>.

Vormbrock, Julia K., and John M. Grossberg. "Cardiovascular
      Effects of Human-pet Dog Interactions." *Journal of Behavioral
      Medicine* 11.5 (1988): 509-17. Print.

Vos-Groenendal, Jeannette J. *An Accelerated/integrative Learning Model
      Program Evaluation Based on Participant Perceptions of Student*

Attitudinal and Achievement Changes. Ann Arbor, MI: UMI, [19-.
        Print.

Witmer, LaDonna. "Northwood's SuperCamp Eases Learning
        Process for Students". *Northwest Herald.* 08, May 1996.

"Why Are Micro Expressions Important?" *Paul Ekman Group LLC.*
        N.p., n.d. Web. 1 Sept. 2013.
        <http://www.paulekman.com/micro-expressions/why-are-
        micro-expressions-important/>.

Williams, Redford B., and Virginia Parrott Williams. *Anger Kills:
        Seventeen Strategies for Controlling the Hostility That Can Harm Your
        Health.* New York: Times, 1993. Print.

Williamson, Marianne. *A Return to Love: Reflections on the Principles of a
        Course in Miracles.* New York, NY: HarperCollins, 1992. Print.

Womack, William G., and Melinda S. Womack. *Speak to Me!: Public
        Speaking as Enlarged Conversation.* Dubuque, IA: Kendall/Hunt,
        1992. Print.

"World Population Balance." *World Population Balance.* N.p., n.d. Web.
        1 Sept. 2013.
        <http://www.worldpopulationbalance.org/faq>.

Wright, Robert. "The Evolution of Despair." *Time* 1995: 50-57. Print.

Zappone, Christian. "Millionaire in the Making: Daren Fike."
        CNNMoney. N.p., 31 Jan. 2007. Web. 5 May 2013.
        <http://money.cnn.com/2007/01/29/pf/millionaire/fike/i
        ndex.htm>.

Zehner, Ozzie. *Green Illusions.* N.p., n.d. Web. 1 Sept. 2013.
        <http://greenillusions.org/>.

Zimbardo, Philip G. "Stanford Prison Experiment." *The : A
        Simulation Study of the Psychology of Imprisonment.* N.p., n.d.
        Web. May-June 2013. <http://www.prisonexp.org

ACKNOWLEDGMENTS

This mission could not have even begun with out the help and encouragement of my family and my grandparents. I thank my parents for sticking with me even though their limits have been beyond tested. I also thank my friends for believing in me, even though my ideas may have seemed far-fetched and idealistic. I thank SuperCamp for helping me realize that I was intelligent all along. Without this organization, I may not have made it to college, nor would I have seen some real key evidence showing truth to some of my theories. I thank my professors and teachers who inspired me and whom I have had amazing conversations with. I thank George Lucas for creating Star Wars, which opened my mind to the reality that we live on a planet that is at the edge of an outer arm of our relatively small galaxy. As big as our global society may seem to be, in perspective, it is small, so changing our world for the better will be a relatively easy accomplishment. I also thank the musicians and DJs such as Christopher Lawrence and DJ Kristoff for providing such powerful inspiration when there was none left…keep inspiring the masses!

ABOUT THE AUTHOR

Mark Krecek devoted his entire life to making this world a better place on a revolutionary scale. He was awarded a Masters of Arts in Sociology from California State University, Fullerton upon completion of his thesis on alienation in the family and school environment. Previously, he earned his Bachelors in Sociology with a minor in Peace & Justice from Chapman University. He has also studied filmmaking extensively. All of this geared to make *The Ultimate Power*.